0/8/98

ENGLISH DRAMATISTS

Series Editor:
Bruce King

ENGLISH DRAMATISTS
Series Editor: Bruce King

Published titles

Forthcoming titles

EARLY WOMEN DRAMATISTS 1550-1800

Margarete Rubik

Associate Professor of English Literature
University of Vienna

First published in Great Britain 1998 by
MACMILLAN PRESS LTD
Houndmills, Basingstoke, Hampshire RG21 6XS and London
Companies and representatives throughout the world

A catalogue record for this book is available from the British Library.

ISBN 0–333–63025–4 hardcover
ISBN 0–333–63026–2 paperback

First published in the United States of America 1998 by
ST. MARTIN'S PRESS, INC.,
Scholarly and Reference Division,
175 Fifth Avenue, New York, N.Y. 10010

ISBN 0–312–21059–0

Library of Congress Cataloging-in-Publication Data
Rubik, Margarete, 1950–
Early women dramatists, 1550–1800 / Margarete Rubik.
p.   cm. — (English dramatists)
Includes bibliographical references and index.
ISBN 0–312–21059–0
1. English drama—Women authors—History and criticism.
2. English drama—Early modern and Elizabethan, 1500–1600—History
and criticism.   3. English drama—17th century—History and
criticism.   4. English drama—18th century—History and criticism.
5. Women in the theater—Great Britain—History.   6. Women and
literature—Great Britain—History.   I. Title.   II. Series: English
dramatists (St. Martin's Press)
PR635.W6R83 1998
822.009'9287—dc21   97–28356
                                                                            CIP

This book is printed on paper suitable for recycling and made from fully managed and
sustained forest sources.

10   9   8   7   6   5   4   3   2   1
07   06   05   04   03   02   01   00   99   98

Printed in Malaysia

Contents

Editor's Preface

Each generation needs to be introduced to the culture and great works of the past and to reinterpret them in its own ways. This series re-examines the important English dramatists of earlier centuries in the light of new information, new interests and new attitudes. The books are written for students, theatre-goers and general readers who want an up-to-date view of the plays and dramatists, with emphasis on drama as theatre and on stage, social and political history. Attention is given to what is known about performance, acting styles, changing interpretations, the stages and theatres of the time and theatre economics. The books will be relevant to those interested in or studying literature, theatre and cultural history.

BRUCE KING

Preface

This book grew out of a personal and professional interest in the theatre and enthusiasm for the Vienna productions of two plays by Aphra Behn and Susanna Centlivre, and then developed into a more comprehensive analysis of the works of the early women dramatists. It surveys more than 200 plays written by women from the Renaissance to the end of the eighteenth century. Not all these plays were actually performed on stage; some were written as closet dramas, others were rejected by the all-powerful theatre managers and then published as reading dramas by their authors. Yet among those that saw production on stage are some of the best and most successful plays written in the period, displaying a delightful vitality and theatricality largely neglected by theatre historians and scholars.

The study has been divided chronologically into three parts: the sixteenth and early seventeenth centuries, the Restoration period, and the eighteenth century. These major sections, in turn, have been subdivided into various phases of development, such as the early Restoration period and the transitional time at the turn of the century, or the early and the late eighteenth century. Each part of the book begins with a short description of the contemporary social and legal situation of women in general, and of women's involvement in the theatre and the prejudices and pressures female dramatists encountered. Separate chapters have been devoted to the major playwrights, such as Behn, Centlivre, Cowley and Inchbald, and their principal works, particularly those available in modern editions, have been given extensive analysis.

The final part of the book, 'Performance and Tradition', describes contemporary and modern stagings of some of the plays, and traces the seeds of a female dramatic tradition. Despite the great diversity of the material surveyed, and the disparities between the various playwrights in plot, style and tone, a number of similarities emerge, which set women's plays off from the male canon and point to the existence of an – albeit muted – female tradition in English theatre.

Author's Note

Some editions contain scene divisions, or at least indicate the beginning of new scenes, while others do not. References to the texts list act, scene and page numbers whenever possible. Occasionally, it seemed reasonable to refer to lines instead, to make it easier for the reader to trace the quote.

All plays reprinted in the collections *The Female Wits* (edited by Fidelis Morgan and published by Virago, London, 1981) and *Female Playwrights of the Restoration* (edited by Paddy Lyons and Fidelis Morgan and published by Dent, London, 1991) have been quoted from these editions, since they are more readily available. Aphra Behn's *The Rover* has been quoted from the Methuen edition of the play (edited by Bill Naismith, 1993). All other works by Behn have been quoted from *The Works of Aphra Behn* (edited by Janet Todd, volumes 5–7, published by Pickering, London, 1996). The plays of Centlivre, Pix and Trotter, unless published in the two collections mentioned above, have been quoted from the Garland facsimile editions (those of the first author edited by Richard C. Frushell, 1982, those of the second and third by Edna Steeves, 1982).

Margarete Rubik
July 1997

Part I
The Sixteenth and
Early Seventeenth Centuries

Women's road to acceptance in the theatrical world has been long and thorny, nor has it by any means come to an end. There has been no straightforward progress either in women's professional access to the theatre or in society's views of gender roles and of women's proper sphere, on which such access is contingent. Though the social climate from 1550 to 1800 strongly discouraged women from participating in public life, in the Restoration period there was less need for women to apologise for presuming to write than in the eighteenth century, and working women were more acceptable in the Renaissance than two centuries later.

This is not to say that women were emancipated in the Elizabethan period, or that the relationship of the sexes was conceived as anything but hierarchical, with the concept of female subservience derived from Genesis. Men were the heads of the family and women were expected to obey. The power Elizabeth I wielded as Queen of England, and the panegyrics addressed to her, should not blind us to the legally deprived status of women at her time. The example of the politically astute Queen did not alter anything in the basic misogyny of her society, though clearly one could not openly disparage the essence of women or their intellectual abilities since this would imply a criticism of the sovereign.

Our picture of the Renaissance as the heyday of humanist education for women is based on a handful of aristocratic women who
were taught alongside their brothers and who were in no way typical. As a rule, such learning would have been considered entirely
superfluous for a girl, whose education rather stressed the domestic
skills she was expected to use in her future marriage. Elizabeth's
successor, James I, is typical of this misogynist climate in having
little taste for learned women and is said to have asked, sourly, of a
female prodigy conversant in Latin, Greek and Hebrew: 'But can
she spin?'[1]

Marriage was considered a woman's proper vocation. Legally,
women were powerless and passed from the authority of the father
to that of the husband. Wives could not own property (though single
women and widows could) and they could not make wills, or testify
in court. Such indignities brought some benefits, though, for they
could not even be imprisoned for debt, since responsibility for pay-
ments was vested with the husband, who was liable for his wife's
expenses. A woman's body, her children and her money belonged to
her husband. He could separate her from her children, keep her
prisoner and beat her, and the only way she could secure any income
for herself was by way of a complicated legal procedure. The so-
called marriage settlement was an agreement made before a
marriage under which property was vested with trustees for the
benefit of the prospective wife. Because of this financial dependence,
a wife could not leave a cruel husband, unless she chose to become a
kept woman or her family was willing to shelter her. Church law did
not permit divorce unless the union itself could be shown to be illegal, in which case the marriage was declared invalid. A separation
could be agreed upon, but in this case remarriage was impossible.
Although, legally, single women and widows were slightly better off,
few women remained single by choice. Single women were often
completely dependent on the charity of male relatives unless they
had inherited money of their own.

While marriage laws were harsh, life was at times rather different,
though in this brief introduction there is little space to go beyond
generalisations. Many people, especially from the lower social orders,
were not married in church and thus not covered by the laws
mentioned. Even the law that wives were property could be used as
a way for partners to divorce by 'selling' the wife – a custom lasting
well into the nineteenth century, as readers of Hardy's *The Mayor of*

Casterbridge will remember. Besides, in other respects women in the sixteenth and seventeenth centuries were sometimes less circumscribed in their activities than in later periods.

The heavy emphasis placed on domestic duties notwithstanding, it was acceptable for women to have a job or a business. Women dominated such professions as midwifery and millinery, aided men in business, and ran enterprises after the deaths of their husbands, though less frequently in England than in the more liberal Netherlands. Even domestic duties were by no means without responsibility, since they involved the running of large households and the supervision of cottage industries. To be sure, the scope of women's possible activities had dwindled. In the Middle Ages, women could govern large territories and levy armies in the absence of their husbands, because holding a particular position involved specific functions, irrespective of sex; in the sixteenth and seventeenth centuries, however, responsibility and power increasingly shifted from any holder of a trust to those with constitutional rights, from whose number women and the unpropertied were *ipso facto* excluded.[2] In the course of the seventeenth century, women were also steadily losing ground in the workforce, partly because of the encroachment of men on typically feminine professions, such as midwifery, but also because, increasingly, working women came to be seen as ungenteel.

A woman's intellectual potential depended very much on the education she received. Illiteracy among women was naturally greater than among men, but decreased in the course of the seventeenth century, owing to the Protestant insistence on everyone being able to read the Bible. Women were, of course, barred from the universities. Men generally looked down on female education and it was a common view that women were intellectually unfit. Right to the end of the eighteenth century, women were generally very self-conscious about the shortcomings of their knowledge and their lack of formal education, though we should not take their protestations of ignorance too literally. For all their feigned humility, they were often widely read, highly cultured and interested in both science and literature.

The improvement of female education was an issue seventeenth-century feminists focused on – they did not envisage radical changes in gender roles or social norms. Indeed, the double moral standard granting men sexual freedoms but expecting women to remain chaste was universally accepted by men and women alike. In the case of women, virtue was almost synonymous with chastity, and virginity before marriage and absolute faithfulness thereafter were the pillars of a woman's reputation. There was, of course, a very practical economic reason behind this repressiveness, namely the laws on inheritance. Since it was desirable for a man that property should be bequeathed to his legitimate heirs only, female sexuality had to be checked to ensure that no bastards of the wife inherited what was not their due. A man's illegitimate issue presented no such threat.

The turmoil of the Civil War once again gave women a greater range of responsibilities and allowed them temporarily to overcome some disabilities. Royalist women tried to manage and protect their banished husbands' estates, or spied on enemy movements. On the other side, Puritan women wrote and handed in petitions to Parliament, and the Levellers even allowed women 'inspired by the Spirit' the right to speak publicly, which was normally considered unseemly. Not even the most radical sects, however, demanded legal or social equality for women. The crisis of the monarchy led to no similar crisis of the family. The King, indeed, had likened himself to a father of his people, positioned at the head of the state, as a man was at the head of his family. Now the people had risen against their absolutist monarch, had deposed and even executed him. Yet no subversive parallels were drawn with the absolute power of the husband within a marriage. The Restoration feminist prose writer Mary Astell criticised the Puritan radicals for their blinkered patriarchal view of social revolution:

> how much soever Arbitrary Power may be dislik'd on a Throne, Not *Milton* himself wou'd cry up Liberty to poor *Female Slaves*, or plead for the Lawfulness of Resisting a Private Tyranny.[3]

Not even Astell, however, was to challenge the institution of marriage itself.

The commercial theatre in the sixteenth and early seventeenth centuries was closed to women in any capacity. Acting roles were all taken by men, with women's parts being played by boys, both in the public and in the private theatres. Despite their name, the private theatres were equally accessible to the public; they merely charged higher admission prices and were therefore socially more exclusive. This was not so on the Continent. There were many actresses on the French and Italian stages, but a French troupe who had tried to introduce this custom to London in 1629 were booed and pelted off the stage. However, there were closed performances at Court and private theatricals in aristocratic country houses, where aristocratic ladies performed in masques and pastorals. Queen Anne, and especially Queen Henrietta Maria, greatly enjoyed these theatricals, encouraged their composition and even took roles themselves – a practice by no means universally approved of. Anne and her maids of honour scandalised some of the courtiers by performing in Jonson's *Masque of Blackness* in short 'barbaresque mantles' and blackened faces, 'face and neck bare', apparel which seemed too 'light and curtizanlike for such great ones'.[4] Henrietta Maria had been used to acting in Court theatricals in France, but the more staid English courtiers disapproved of her appearance on stage, especially when she played in male costume.[5] After one of Queen Henrietta Maria's performances at Court, the Puritan William Prynne in his *Historiomastrix* denounced as a whore any Christian woman who dared to speak publicly on stage in male clothing – an attack for which he had his ears cut off. On the other hand, Milton's masque *Comus* suggests that women's acting cannot have been uncommon in aristocratic Puritan circles. Whatever the public resistance of the radicals, the early-seventeenth-century private theatricals may have paved the way for the acceptance of actresses and for the emergence of high-born 'gentlemen playwrights' during the Restoration period.

1
Women Dramatists
of the Sixteenth and Early
Seventeenth Centuries

In *A Room of One's Own*, Virginia Woolf imagined how an ambitious sister of Shakespeare would have fared in Elizabethan England had she tried to copy her famous brother and write plays for the theatre herself. She would, in Virginia Woolf's imagination, have been ridiculed, exploited and made pregnant, and would ultimately have committed suicide. Indeed, the public stage in Shakespeare's time offered no place to a woman in any capacity whatever; it was to take another three-quarters of a century before actresses and professional women playwrights were to emerge. Yet there were women in the Elizabethan and Jacobean periods who did write plays – but not for public performance. All the women playwrights of this period were of the aristocracy, from the small cultural elite favourably disposed towards female education, and they wrote closet dramas for the amusement of their family and friends, or to prove their erudition, but not to make a name for themselves in the theatre. This was not only a question of gender but also of class, since aristocrats were expected to be patrons of the arts rather than writers themselves. The gentleman playwright became a prominent figure only in the Restoration period, and the nobleman in 1600 would have considered it demeaning to write for the public stage. Marketing drama in the commercial theatre was regarded as undignified for a member of the upper class, although dramatic composition in itself was perfectly legitimate and respectable, albeit less popular than poetry among the cultured class. But aristocrats wrote both verse and drama for the edification of their social equals, and circulated their work among their friends, although it could be pirated, or might be printed once the writer had achieved a literary reputation. Yet it was only in the Restoration period that publication gained respectability, and well born poets published with full attribution, though persons of quality were published anonymously well after 1700.[6]

Among the dramatic works of aristocratic women still extant we must distinguish between translations from classical models or contemporary foreign sources and original compositions. The earliest Renaissance women's plays that have survived are all translations. They testify to the linguistic competence and learning of the writers, who often received education alongside their brothers, and could boast of a thorough knowledge not only of the living languages French and Italian, but also of Latin, Greek and often Hebrew.

The earliest Renaissance play text in English by a woman that we have knowledge of is Lady Jane Lumley's translation of Euripides' *Iphigenia at Aulis*, written around 1550. It is easy to see why a woman set upon proving her skill as a translator should have been attracted to this particular story, which tells how Iphigenia is lured to the Greek camp on the pretence of marrying Achilles and then sacrificed so that the gods will end the calm preventing the Greek fleet from sailing to Troy. The translation is in prose and neither literal nor complete, yet despite the freedom this might have offered the author, the tale is told in a curiously anaemic style. Agamemnon's vacillation between his obligation as commander-in-chief and his love for his daughter, Clytemnestra's despair that her innocent daughter is to die 'for Helen's sake, which can be no lawfull cause, for it is not mete, that we sholde sleye our owne childre for a naughtie womans sake' (lines 981ff.), even Iphigenia's anguish, sound subdued, cold and unimpassioned. In the end, Iphigenia freely accepts her fate, depreciating a woman's importance and the significance of her own death: 'one noble man is better than a thousande women' (lines 1997f.). There is no sense of irony here, nor at the end, when the chorus wishes Agamemnon a

successful mission and prosperous return, which, as the reader
must know, will expose him to Clytemnestra's wrath.

The fact that the translation of plays was by no means seen as
eccentric or taboo is evinced by a famous devotee of the art: Queen
Elizabeth I herself. The Queen was conversant in French, Italian,
Spanish, Flemish and Welsh, and had received a thorough ground-
ing in Latin and Greek. Translation of poetry, prose and drama was
her lifelong avocation. The short excerpt from *Hercules Oetaeus* that
has survived is a very literal translation of the Senecan original,
with some errors, and probably represents a rough draft, intended
as confirmation of her linguistic aptitude rather than as an aesthetic
work. It slavishly follows the Latin word order and uses awkward
sentence construction.[7]

> The poor man deemeth not his happy state
> Till wealthy folk by fall it show.
> Who so, therefore, the middle way eschews,
> The wry and crooked balk's most sure to tread.
> (Lines 99 – 102)

Although the document is in the hand of a scribe, it was not meant
to be circulated, even among a tiny circle of courtiers. However, the
subject matter – the fickleness of fate, disloyalty in courts and the
middle way as against a lust to power – is indicative of the Queen's
interest in the virtue of such meditations.

Mary Sidney's translation of Garnier's *Antonie* was a much
more formidable artistic undertaking. Mary Sidney, Countess of
Pembroke, sister of Sir Philip Sidney, came from one of the leading
cultural families of the time and was an admired patroness of the
arts as well as an artist in her own right. Today she is mainly
remembered for her arrangement of *Arcadia* after her brother's
death, but her translation from the French of Robert Garnier's play,
written in 1590 and published two years later (the first play by a
woman to be published), was of considerable influence on the circle
of dramatists who enjoyed her patronage at Wilton. *Antonie* is a
pure Senecan tragedy, a genre the sophisticated literati preferred to
the English romantic drama so successful in public theatres.[8] It was
reprinted several times and inspired Kyd's translation of Garnier's
Cornelie (1594), Samuel Daniel's *Cleopatra* (1594) and *Philotas* (1604),
and several other plays written in the Senecan manner. While these

protégés of the Countess wrote for the public stage, her own play was not intended for public performance, though it may have received a private performance in the domestic circle. Private theatricals were not uncommon in aristocratic country houses and even at Court, and an amateur performance for family and friends would have provided welcome amusement, without the stigma attached to a woman's writing for the public stage. This does not mean that Mary Sidney was in any way hostile to the public theatre – indeed, she sponsored a company of actors, 'Pembroke's Men' – although she never thought of writing plays for them.

Unlike Elizabeth I's translation, Mary Sidney's work is a remarkable artistic achievement. As is typical of a Senecan play, the language is highly rhetorical and declamatory. The author rendered the French alexandrines in blank verse and heroic couplets. When the Countess is at her best, the verse lines are regular, the language elevated and impressive. The choruses are more varied in metre and rhyme scheme, and prove her ready command of different poetic forms.

> ANTONIUS: ... Die I must, and with brave end
> Conclusion make of all foregoing harms.
> Die, die I must. I must a noble death,
> A glorious death, unto my succour call.
> I must deface the shame, of time abused,
> I must adorn the wanton loves I used,
> With some courageous act; that my last day
> By mine own hand my spots may wash away....
> CHORUS: Alas, with what tormenting fire
> us martyreth this blind desire
> To stay our life from flying?
> How ceaselessly our minds doth rack,
> How heavy lies upon our back
> This dastard fear of dying?
> (*The Tragedy of Antonie*, III/lines 373–80, 387–92)

The plot covers the last hours of Mark Antony's life, after he has resolved to die heroically, but consists mainly of long monologues and contains hardly any action on stage; this is delegated to the customary chorus and messenger reports. The play ends with

Cleopatra's lament for her lover and her resolution to follow him faithfully into death.

In 1592 Mary Sidney also wrote 'Thenot and Piers in Praise of Astraea', an original composition in the form of a pastoral dialogue, though hardly a drama proper, written for the forthcoming visit of the Queen. It constituted the conventional homage that used to be paid to the monarch. Astraea is, of course, Queen Elizabeth, who is eulogised by a shepherd, while the other speaker constantly criticises his friend's panegyric – which, paradoxically, proves to be the supreme compliment, since, as he explains in the end, no praise can be adequate to express Astraea's excellence.

Mary Sidney met no opposition to her writing from her family, but Elizabeth Cary, Viscountess Falkland, seems to have been less fortunate. She was the first Englishwoman to write and publish an original play, *The Tragedy of Mariam, the Fair Queen of Jewry*, written between 1602 and 1605 and printed in 1613. Her daughters, embarrassed by a mother going public, later claimed implausibly that the manuscript had been stolen.[9] Even allowing for the fact that Elizabeth Cary was a precocious child, proficient in a number of modern and ancient languages, she achieved an extraordinary feat with this tragedy, not only because she was a mere 17 when she wrote it. Nor was it her only work, though, unfortunately, all her other plays are lost. It was one thing for a woman to translate a renowned classical work or a play by a foreign male dramatist. But moulding an entirely original drama from a historical account required a self-confidence and independence of mind unusual for a woman of the time. Indeed, Elizabeth Cary confirmed her rebellious spirit by converting to Catholicism under the influence of Queen Henrietta Maria, for which she was left in abject poverty by her husband and deprived of her children, two of whom she abducted to bring up as Catholics in France. Ironically, she started writing because her mother-in-law had forbidden her all reading, something in which she had earlier delighted.

As a source for the play, Elizabeth Cary studied Josephus Flavius' account of Mariam and Herod, and in structure she followed the Senecan model of being narrative rather than dramatic and having violence happen off stage. At the end of each act, a chorus comments on the events. The first half of the play presents the reaction of Herod's relatives to the rumour of his death – a rumour they believe all the more readily because they each in varying degrees wish him dead. His Queen, Mariam, is torn between her grief for a beloved husband and pleasure at the death of the man who had murdered her relatives and ordered that, on his death, she should be killed. Herod's first wife hopes to triumph over her hated rival and to install her own son on the throne. Herod's brother shrinks from the marriage of convenience the King has decreed for him and marries his slave. Herod's brother-in-law openly flaunts his allegiance to the King's enemies. Only Herod's sister, Salome, laments his death, since now she cannot rid herself of the husband whom she wanted to accuse of high treason in order to marry her Arab lover. When Herod safely returns in Act IV, he has his brother-in-law executed, and also sentences Mariam to death because, too sure of her power over him and unable to forget her grievances, she refuses to forgive her husband or to defend herself against false suspicions – a haughtiness criticised by the chorus, since a wife must be submissive and loyal:

> When to their husbands they themselves do bind
> Do they not wholly give themselves away?
> Or give they but their body not their mind,
> Reserving that, though best, for others, pray?…
> Then she usurps upon another's right,
> That seeks to be by public language graced;
> And though her thoughts reflect with purest light,
> Her mind if not peculiar is not chaste.
> For in a wife it is no worse to find,
> A common body, than a common mind.
>
> (III/lines 233–44)

If these reflect Elizabeth Cary's own sentiments, they are surprising in a woman who was willing to share her mind with the common multitude by having her play printed. However, she comes to view Mariam in the end as an innocent, though imprudent, victim, whose 'excellencies wrought her timeless fall' (V/line 229), as her disconsolate husband Herod realises too late. It is remarkable that this Herod, who is usually cast in the role of a blasphemous tyrant in Christian tradition, is not presented as a downright villain, but rather a man of choler, and that it is assumed that Mariam still owes full allegiance to him, even though he has murdered several members of her family.

Given this view of wifely duties, Herod's sister, Salome, is naturally seen as the villainess of the piece, a lascivious monster who has engineered the death of her first husband and is plotting the ruin of her second. It is into her mouth, however, that Cary puts the feminist protest against the unjust law of Moses which allows a husband to divorce his wife, but not vice versa.

> Why should such privilege to man be given?
> Or given to them, why barred from women then?
> Are men, than we, in greater grace in heaven?
> Or cannot women hate as well as men?
>
>   (I/lines 305–8)

Subversive as this complaint may seem, it is somewhat discredited by being uttered by an unsympathetic character, a transgressor against the divine order, whose actions threaten chaos and disruption:

> Are Hebrew women now transformed to men?
> Why do you not as well our battles fight
> And wear our armour? Suffer this, and then
> Let all the world be topsy-turveyed quite!
> Let fishes graze, beasts swim, and birds descend;
> Let fire burn downwards while the earth aspires;
> Let winter's heat and summer's cold offend;
> Let thistles grow of vines, and grapes on briars;
>
>   (I/lines 421–8)

Her husband's speech too closely resembles similar warnings about the overthrow of the natural order in other Elizabethan plays, most notably in Shakespeare's *Troilus and Cressida* and *A Midsummer Night's Dream*, to warrant an interpretation of the passage as an ironic indictment of male fear of equality between the sexes. On the contrary, this play ought to make us aware of three problems of interpretation we will do well to remember in the course of our further investigation. First, twentieth-century sympathies are an unreliable guide to the attitudes of a seventeenth- or eighteenth-century author, for contemporary evaluations may – and frequently will – be radically different from what we tend to expect. Second, it is not uncommon to find misogyny, an acceptance of double standards and a condemnation of emancipation in women's plays, even from authors who themselves laboured under these injustices and might therefore be expected to support a more subversive view of women's rights. Third, putting a feminist statement into a villainess's mouth need not imply outright condemnation of the sentiment expressed, but may constitute a safe way of expressing a dissenting view, yet of paying lip service to the mores of the culture and soothing one's own bad conscience by making an objectionable character voice the rebellious opinion.

While biography and the stance of her play seem to clash in Elizabeth Cary's case, the relationship between personal history and dramatic characters is much closer in *Love's Victory* by Mary Wroth, the first original pastoral comedy by a woman writer, meant to be read or acted in a small family circle. The author had gained some experience in private theatricals by acting at Court in Jonson's masques.[10] Mary Wroth, who also wrote a prose romance and a sonnet sequence, came from the Sidney family, was unhappily married to an uncongenial partner and after her husband's death was involved in an affair with her beloved cousin William Herbert, for which she (not he!) was banished from Court. As Ceresano and Wynne-Davies have pointed out,[11] the characters in her pastoral play correspond to real-life persons of both her own and her uncle's, Philip Sidney's, generations. She herself and her cousin are the idealised lovers, whereas her husband is cast in the unflattering part of the vulgar rustic engaged to the beautiful heroine, who, with amusing self-aggrandisement, is described as 'the star of light and beauty' (V/iii/lines 12–13), 'too rare a prize for earth' (V/v/line 16). The romantic couple, however, are not given prominence in the play, which features a number of equally important lovers, representing the types of true, flawed, chaste and comic love. Musella, whom her mother betrothed to the rich Rustic, confesses her love for Philisses, who has long languished for her, and the lovers decide to die together, but Venus turns the poison into a sleeping draught and awakens them when Rustic has renounced his claim. Lissius, who has laughed at the pangs of love, is made to adore the woman he has scorned and to suffer agonies in fear of losing her, but is similarly reunited with his beloved in the end. Silvestra has abandoned love for chastity and all her lover can gain in the end is her pity. Rustic loses his beautiful bride, but quickly consoles himself with the fickle Dalina, who is glad to catch a husband. The frame is provided by Venus, who orders Cupid to torment the shepherds so as to establish her complete sway over mortals:

> Scarce had he learned to sigh before he gained,
> Nor shed a tear ere he his hopes obtained.
> This easy winning breeds us more neglect,
> Without much pain, few do Love's joys respect;
>   (III/iii/lines 11–14)

Although Venus reigns supreme, she does not stand for sensuality, since, as is typical of the genre, wanton love is criticised, and chaste and faithful love extolled. Despite the strongly autobiographical love theme, the pastoral, written in heroic couplets and quatrains with shorter songs in varied metres, lacks the 'warmth' of female sexuality that was to inform the plays of Restoration women. On the whole, characterisation is rather superficial and the norms of female behaviour are fairly conventional: it is, for instance, considered inappropriate for a woman to woo a man ('the most unfittest, shameful'st thing to do!' (III/ii/line 188)), and a woman who has lost and loved again is less worthy of requited love than the constant one who has never looked elsewhere.

There are critics who assume that *The Pastorall of Florimene*, presented by 'the Queenes Majestie's Commandment, before the Kings Maiesty in the Hall at White-hall, on St. Thomas day the 21 of December 1635' was composed by Queen Henrietta Maria, wife of Charles I, because she is known to have taken an unusual interest in theatrical performance and to have delighted in acting. However, it is more likely that it was written by an anonymous artist – male or female – for performance at Court. The play is available only in its 'argument', that is, story line, not in the original dramatic text, nor have the songs survived. The plot again involves a group of shepherds hopelessly in love with men or women who, in turn, suffer agonies of unrequited love for others. Filene disguises himself as a woman to win Florimene – a motif Restoration playwrights used only to deride a male character – and in women's clothes elicits the admiration of Florimene's brother, although the homosexual potential of the situation is not followed up. The duped brother finally takes the woman he has hitherto disdained, who, in turn, has meanwhile been fooled into loving a girl in drag, who has pursued Filene, but in the end contents herself with an unsuccessful suitor of

Florimene's. This merry-go-round of changing amours and unrequited loves is faintly reminiscent of *A Midsummer Night's Dream*. As is the wont in the genre, the play ends in general jubilation, and there is no sense of misgiving in the lovers who are matched with second-choice partners. The acts are interrupted by allegorical representations of the four seasons, with autumn represented by Bacchus and a train of drunken satyrs and sailors as a kind of antimasque.

Lady Jane Cavendish and Lady Elizabeth Brackley,[12] the two daughters of William Cavendish, Duke of Newcastle, had been ladies-in-waiting to Queen Henrietta, but they also received keen encouragement in writing from their father, an author in his own right, who later supported his second wife's literary endeavours as well. Such support was crucial and unusual for women at the time, and deprived of it after marriage the two girls quickly gave up dramatic composition for the less controversial pastimes of private meditation and personal poetry. Indeed, the Cavendish family, like the Sidneys, belonged to the literary and cultural elite of the period. Like all aristocratic women playwrights of the time, they wrote closet drama, although *The Concealed Fancies*, written jointly by the sisters in the early 1640s, was certainly meant to be performed at home for their father. However, by the time of his return from exile in France with his second wife, Margaret Cavendish, it proved to be rather in bad taste because of its cruel attacks on their prospective stepmother, and we have no record of an actual performance. Like Mary Wroth, the Cavendish sisters strongly relied on auto-biographical material. Like the heroines of the sub-plot to *The Concealed Fancies*, during the Civil War the sisters attempted to defend Welbeck Castle and save its valuables when it was sacked by Parliamentary forces. Indeed, Jane and Elizabeth probably wrote the play while they were confined in the castle as 'prisoners'. Their brothers are cast in the roles of the heroic Cavalier lovers who (quite unhistorically) free the imprisoned girls, so despite the close correlations no direct correspondence was intended between life and art – a fact which is also indicated by the allegories implied in some of the speaking names. The two writers also mirrored themselves in the main heroines of the play, who rebel against the submissive role allotted to wives in marriage and lord it over their presumptuous suitors. Their ridicule of the exaggerated compliments of courtship and their sharp insight into men's intention to enforce obedience and submission after marriage presages the witty heroines of Restoration comedy. Quite explicitly, they refuse to accept a woman's subordinate position ('Why do you think "I take thee" shall alter me?' (I/iii/line 42); 'He is my servant, for I intend to be his mistress' (II/iii/line 113)) and demand a companionate marriage, citing even the authority of the Bible: 'How often, sister, have you read the Bible over, and have forgotten man and wife should draw equally in a yoke?' (II/iii/lines 36–8). In the end, Presumption, the high-handed suitor, turns into a loving husband, while the formerly amiable Courtley attempts to suppress his wife, who refuses to yield:

> Then he ... praised a lady, obedient fool, in town, and swore her husband was the happiest man in the world. I replied, she was a very good lady, and I accounted him happy that was her husband, that he could content himself with such a mechanical wife.... [I] admire why she will contract her family, nobleness and birth, to the servitude of her husband, as if he had bought her his slave.
>
> (Epilogue, lines 35–46)

Margaret Cavendish, whom the girls did not know at that time, is viciously caricatured as vain, greedy and ill-educated, and it is part of the fantasy that she marries a fool for money, leaving the duke (their father) free and unencumbered. Several low-life scenes are included, the servants using a vulgar and coarse language totally unexpected from the pen of an aristocratic lady, and forming an amusing contrast to the artificial diction of the courtship scenes. The structure is loose and the various strands require firm integration. Nevertheless, *The Concealed Fancies* is an interesting play, foreshadowing later Restoration comedies as well as undoubtedly exerting a powerful influence on the work of Margaret Cavendish, Duchess of Newcastle, who was hardly older than her two stepdaughters.

Part II
The Restoration and
Turn of the Century

If you were to look at the Restoration period simply through the lens of Restoration comedy, you might conclude that it was a time of profligacy and loose living, yet the records show that there were no more illegitimate children than in previous ages. The sexual freedom so often taken as typical of the time was, in fact, very much limited to Court circles, where libertinism was a conscious reaction against the Puritanism of the Commonwealth. Even this libertinism, however, was a licence very much limited to men, who indulged in promiscuity, whereas the expectation that respectable women should be chaste did not change. Indeed, terms like 'ruined' and 'undone' had distinctly different meanings for men and women, denoting bankruptcy on the one hand and premarital defloration on the other.

To be sure, in the aristocratic classes women achieved some mobility, but such liberties as visits to the theatre depended very much on the compliance of the husband, who still owned all the money his wife had brought into the marriage. There were cultured circles of literati to which women were admitted, but as a rule gentlewomen were expected to keep a low profile, and most of the names we remember today – Nell Gwyn and Lady Castlemaine, Mrs Barry, Mrs Bracegirdle and Aphra Behn – were those of royal or aristocratic mistresses, actresses or women whose doubtful reputation was earned in some other way.

Little changed in the legal status of women or gender roles on the return of Charles II. A woman still remained the property of her husband, so much so that a husband could sue the man who had cuckolded him for disturbance of property. Divorce was now possible, but only by a private Act of Parliament, unattainable for all but the wealthiest and impossible for women (since they forsook their property on marrying), unless their relatives supported them. Nor could even such a divorce by Act of Parliament be granted to a woman on the grounds of her husband's adultery, unless she could prove aggravating circumstances, such as excessive cruelty, though a wife's infidelity was sufficient ground for legal separation.

The turn of the eighteenth century saw a growing debate about women's legal status, spurred by the writings of early feminists such as Mary Astell. Yet even feminists did not question the institution of marriage, or demand social and political rights for women outside marriage – that only came a century later with Mary Wollstonecraft. Mary Astell gained a favourable hearing even among men, and her agitation for more serious female education in a women's academy aroused some attention, though her writings had, in fact, little practical impact on the eighteenth century.

While awareness of women's deprivation of rights reached a peak around 1700, paradoxically, at the same time, women were slowly edged out of traditional professions by male midwives and male milliners, as well as by a growing cult of female refinement and by prestige being attached to women of leisure rather than working women. Henceforth, women were less and less likely to run businesses on their own, their opportunities for work narrowed and the growing capitalist system, by its separation of the home and the workplace, steadily took even domestic production within the household out of their hands.

Though opportunities to work and participate in public life were being restricted for most women, the Restoration saw one great innovation: the appearance of the first English actresses. The phenomenon of allowing women on stage had been imported from France, where many Cavaliers had found refuge during the Commonwealth, but among the Puritans the old objections to this public exposure and to public speaking by women had by no means been stilled. Indeed, their presence undoubtedly led to greater sexual explicitness in drama, and a host of prologues and epilogues in which salacious reference is made to their sex. Many actresses had scandalous reputations and, indeed, many exploited their notoriety to attract rich and influential lovers. Thus, the great tragedienne Elizabeth Barry had numerous affairs and quite openly bore the Earl of Rochester a child, and the famous Nell Gwyn progressed from orange seller to actress to royal mistress of 'Charles III', the King being her third lover by the name of Charles. Nonetheless, to avoid the disreputable connotations of the designation 'Miss' (a miss was a mistress), all actresses, whether married or unmarried, were addressed as Mrs. Though some of these women achieved fame on and off stage, they were nevertheless paid less than their male colleagues and they hardly ever advanced to positions of power in theatre management.

The Elizabethan playhouses had been destroyed in the Civil War, when all public performances had been forbidden. Upon his return the King granted patents to Thomas Killigrew and William Davenant to open theatres and stage plays. The two companies, the King's Men and the Duke's Men (after the Duke of York, who later became James II), operated in two newly built playhouses, the Drury Lane Theatre and Dorset Garden Theatre, with the Lincoln's Inn Fields Theatre occasionally serving as a stopgap. After two decades of success, the political unrest during the Popish Plot and the Exclusion Crisis of 1678/79 caused audience figures to drop. In 1682 the King's Men went bankrupt owing to financial mismanagement and embezzlement, and the two companies merged, becoming the United Company, which severely limited the market for new plays. Things improved only in 1694/95, when the famous actor Thomas Betterton led an actors' revolt against the management and opened a new company at Lincoln's Inn Fields.

It is now assumed that the audiences that filled the boxes, the pits and the galleries was made up of all classes, not only of the Court coterie, though the King and the nobility certainly set the fashion and tone. The rowdiness of Restoration audiences and the presence of prostitutes in vizards is well known. Such circumstances did not improve the reputation of the theatre among its enemies. Both Charles II and James II, however, were great patrons of the theatre, and they also encouraged courtiers to write. So it was only after the Glorious Revolution and James' flight that moralists dared to attack the stage openly. William III had little interest in the theatre; Court as well as aristocratic patronage declined and audiences became more middle class.

Acting styles were highly artificial and stylised. Actors did not subordinate themselves to their roles but flaunted their own personalities, a fact that led to a confusion of on-stage and off-stage identity especially detrimental in the case of actresses and the few women playwrights. The excitement actresses generated led to a prurient interest in their private lives. Before the Restoration, the sex lives of actors like Burbage and Kempe had been of little interest to the audience, and even after 1660 the off-stage affairs of male actors did not arouse the same lecherous curiosity as those of female actors, although quite a few were 'kept' by aristocratic ladies. Lady Castlemaine, one of Charles' mistresses, saved the actor Goodman from being hanged at Tyburn for highway robbery and obtained his pardon.[13] With actresses, however, life and role were frequently blurred, and they were typecast according to their off-stage reputations, the notorious Mrs Barry taking the parts of passionate sinners and villainesses, and her virtuous colleague Mrs Bracegirdle specialising in unblemished heroines and virgins in distress. Such a confusion of life and art in the case of women set an unfortunate precedent: the same unhealthy interest was to focus on the private lives of women playwrights.

A number of Restoration dramatists were gentlemen of independent means closely associated with the Court, who wrote for pleasure, not for money. But for those men and women whose livelihood depended on their success, writing for the theatre provided a precarious income at best. Otway starved to death in the slums, Wycherley languished for years in a debtors' prison, Lee ended up in a lunatic asylum, and even Dryden had to cringe for patronage. It was not usual for theatre managers to pay playwrights for their scripts, nor was there any copyright protection; the money a dramatist made from a work depended entirely on the audience turnout every third night (or, rather, afternoon) of a performance. Every third night was for the author's benefit, and the author took the entire proceeds of the ticket sales. Friends would make a point of crowding the theatre on this occasion. However, enemy cliques could well kill a play before that by hissing, rioting or merely by spreading malicious rumours about it. A six-day run was reckoned a fair success, and a play that lasted nine days (involving three benefit nights) was a hit. Many works did not even survive for three days, which left the authors without any recompense. Selling the play text to a printer for a small sum after its stage run could bring in some additional money, as could a patron's gratuity in acknowl-edgement of a dedication, but of course authors would have to secure the proposed dedicatee's permission.

In a period when the King and the upper crust regularly crowded the theatre, the career of a playwright, of course, always carried the hope of limelight and royal patronage as well as the intoxicating possibility of lasting fame. For most contenders, how-ever, it could also be a gruelling experience, devoid of the glamour with which we tend to imbue these flamboyant Restoration figures.

2
Women Dramatists of the Early Restoration Period

Aristocratic closet drama

The Restoration period was, of course, a time of innovation as far as the involvement of women with the theatre is concerned. The first woman ever to publish her collected dramatic works in folio editions, in 1662 and 1668 – indeed, the first female playwright ever to bring out her work – was Margaret Lucas Cavendish, Duchess of Newcastle (the stepmother to Elizabeth and Jane, discussed in Chapter 1). Yet, like her aristocratic predecessors, she did not write for the public stage, less for genteel considerations than because, as she confessed in the dedication to her *Playes* (1662), she feared they would be booed. Unlike her forerunners, however, she wrote and published with the avowed hope of achieving lasting fame (Prologue of *Playes*), an ambition which echoes Aphra Behn's wistful wish for immortality. This flouted the canons of respectability of her sex and even more the decorum of her class, which regarded publication as the reward of fame, not as a means of achieving it.[14] In fact, she was more ambitious than talented as a dramatist, but by dint of her feminist outspokenness she has lately received a lot of attention from modern scholars.

Margaret Lucas had accompanied Queen Henrietta Maria as a maid of honour into exile and in Paris had married the much older,

Royalist, William Cavendish, Duke of Newcastle, who encouraged her literary activity and scientific interests, just as he had promoted his daughters' writings. Most other people, however, shook their heads in disapproval at her ambition, her eccentric dress and her unconventional behaviour, and she was known as 'Mad Madge'. She wrote widely – poetry, fiction, science, philosophy, biography (of her husband) and autobiography, besides drama. In spirit and form, her 19 plays are closely linked to the previous period, espe-cially to the play of her stepdaughters, both with regard to their allegorical action and their emancipatory concerns. They more closely resemble morality plays than Restoration dramas, with em-blematic names for the dramatis personae, who represent allegorical types and moral attitudes rather than full-blooded characters, such as Lady Bashful and Lord Loyalty (*The Presence*), Sir Thomas Father Love and Lady Innocence (*Youths Glory and Deaths Banquet*) or Am-bition, Pleasure, Faction and Virtue (*Wits Cabal* and *The Bridals*). Of course, speaking names are common in Restoration comedy as well (such as Willmore, Blunt, Sir Cautious Fullbank, Sir Patient Fancy or Lieutenant Daring in Behn's plays); however, social stereotypes such as rakes, fools and vulgar middle-class 'citizens' tend to be individualised in these comedies and do not carry the moral weight allotted to them in allegorical drama.

Margaret Cavendish's plays tend to be argumentative rather than dramatic, and they are long (many of them consist of two parts), rambling and digressive. They frequently focus on the social position of women and the prejudices, restrictions and frustrations they are subject to, and agitate for equal rights and self-determina-tion. The author often reverses sexual roles, supports endeavours to gain better education for women and ridicules double standards, for instance when a husband regards it as 'allowable and seemly' in men to flirt, but 'immodest, and unbecoming, and dishonourable' in his wife (*Loves Adventures*, IV/19). Women are shown to be as gifted as men in all walks of life, even in soldiering and scholarship. In *Loves Adventures* the disguised Lady Orphant performs miracles in battle to defend her lover; in *Bell in Campo* the heroine heads a female army which routs the enemy, and in *Youths Glory and Deaths Banquet* another female prodigy amazes the Academy of Sciences with her philosophical reasoning. Despite this feminist propaganda, however, the Duchess, like so many of her female contemporaries, remains equivocal in her attitude: there is much comment on the injustice of women's lot and on the equality of the sexes, yet the plot developments of the plays often suggest a much more traditional view of a woman's proper place. Marriage is frequently attacked in her plays. *The Matrimonial Trouble* and *The Convent of Pleasure* present a catalogue of reasons why men bring unhappiness upon women, from drunkenness and whoring to rape, the hazards of childbirth and child mortality.

> Marriage is a Curse we find
> Especially to Woman kind.
> From the Cobler's Wife we see,
> To Ladies, they unhappy be.
> (*The Convent of Pleasure*, III/x/30)

Yet the princess in *The Convent of Pleasure* quickly forgets her ambitious female academy (an idea which may have inspired Mary Astell), her vows of celibacy and her conviction that 'Men are the only troublers of Women; for they only cross and oppose their sweet delights, and peaceable life' (I/ii/7) when she falls in love with a man who entered the convent disguised as a woman. The amazon in *Loves Adventures* is only too happy to return to the conventional hearth once her lover is willing to have her, and the gifted female scholar in *Youths Glory and Deaths Banquet* is too frail for this world and has to die young.

Sexual liberties are unequivocally condemned in women, and intelligent, virtuous and chaste women are always contrasted with a crowd of fools and coquettes who seem to exemplify the common prejudices held against the fair sex. In *The Sociable Companions, or the Female Wits*, the play most resembling Restoration comedy, the heroines set out to entrap rich husbands, but there is no criticism of mercenary marriage, only admiration for their ingenuity, and the amorous old woman tricked into marrying the wrong man (who, with chilling realism, fears she 'may last longer' (V/1/84) than he might wish) is treated without sympathy or pity.

All this is surprising in a writer hailed as the first feminist playwright, and there is no way of reconciling the unresolved contradictions in her work. The plays of the Duchess of Newcastle thus illustrate the deep rift in the personality of the female dramatist between subversion and conformity, between conscious insight into gender inequalities and subconscious assimilation, between 'masculine' ambition and the doctrine of femininity, which has haunted many a woman playwright in later centuries.

If Margaret Cavendish's dramatic works look both backward and forward, the same can be said of the plays of Anne Finch, Countess of Winchilsea, writing 20 years later. She, too, placed herself within the aristocratic tradition of closet drama not intended for public presentation. Her family were staunch Jacobites and hence excluded from public preferment after the Glorious Revolution. Just as the Cavendish sisters, half a century earlier, in their confinement at Welbeck Castle had written to please themselves and their father, Finch made her beloved husband the sole arbitrator of her success (Preface to *Aristomenes*). Anne Finch is usually regarded as one of the prominent feminists of the era. Neither of her two plays, however, is in any way distinguished. *The Triumphs of Love and Innocence* (1688) is a tragi-comedy about a deposed Cypriot queen, who, after much distress and high-minded protestations, marries the victorious general who will share the throne with her. A second strand of action is concerned with a woman who has followed her seducer in male clothes, becomes the innocent cause of a political intrigue, is saved from rape and finally united with her lover. But politics constitute the mere backdrop for the love stories. In *Aristomenes, or the Royal Shepherd* (1690) the Prince of Rhodes, intent on marrying the daughter of the best man in the world, finds the object of his search in the daughter of Aristomenes. She has fled from Sparta disguised as a shepherdess and takes the Prince to be a shepherd, too. Aristomenes, the lawful king of Sparta imprisoned by a rival, is freed from prison by the latter's daughter, who loves Aristomenes' son. The princess is murdered by a villain, whereupon her lover kills himself. The desperate Aristomenes is prevented from committing suicide by his whole army threatening to fall on their swords, and he vows to free Rhodes instead. The play fails to wed a pastoral romance to a pseudo-classical tragedy plot and to establish a clear focus on one of the characters. It is characteristic that the best of men is, of course, a king and the prince's proper bride a princess in disguise, not a simple peasant girl. The appeal to the tender emotions of the audience, the savouring of virtue in distress, the wallowing in sentiment and the reliance on fate and chance rather than conflict of character are all typical of turn-of-the-century affective tragedy and eighteenth-century sentimental drama.

The first professional women playwrights

The Restoration period saw the appearance not only of the first English actresses on the public stage, but also of the first women to write specifically for the commercial theatre. These professional women dramatists all came from the middle class. The gentleman playwright was becoming a figure of fashion, but women playwrights risked their reputations in doing so. These women had no role models and they struck out in a variety of directions, working in diverse styles popular at the time. The time was not unconducive for a young would-be writer, since there were few new dramatists around at first and the market was wide open to new talents and new genres. The public, on the whole, was not against women writers in principle, but viewed them as eccentrics, whose achievement was admired by some and deplored as unnatural by others. For all the scandal attached to 'going public', women playwrights could, at least at the beginning of the Restoration period, always count on exciting curiosity, if not applause, for their very gender, much as the new actresses aroused interest. As in the case of actresses, this high exposure occasioned a prurient curiosity in their private lives and an inevitable confusion of art and life, right to the end of the eighteenth century. If actresses were confused with the roles they played, women dramatists were judged by the plays they produced, and bawdiness or immorality were attributed to immodesty of character, not to current fashions and audience tastes.

Paradoxically, the first woman dramatist to have a play performed on a commercial English stage was not of scandalous or immodest reputation, but for a century remained the epitome of chaste femininity: Katherine Philips, called 'the matchless Orinda'. Philips had won high acclaim for some very ordinary poetry, which, she asserted, had been pirated and published without her consent. She pretended to be horrified by this public exposure, indeed, made ill by it, and caused her friends to take legal action so that the book of verse had to be withdrawn. One wonders at the sincerity of these protests of feminine modesty and attempts to look genteel. In any case, her pose of amateurism and domesticity presented no threat to men, who magnanimously vouchsafed a laurel leaf to one so harmless and unpresumptuous. The situation changed quickly enough when a genuine competitor like Behn entered the arena.

Katherine Philips translated Corneille's *Pompey*, a typical choice in that she made no attempt to write an original play, but paid respect to the work of a famous male foreigner. The play was premiered in Dublin under the auspices of her aristocratic patron, the Earl of Surrey, in 1663, and, after its immediate success, transferred to London. Upon publication of her play, she continued her pose of reticence and feminine modesty: it was only to oblige her patrons that she consented to have her play printed, and had it not been for their explicit orders, 'no abuses of transcribers ... could have prevailed to send it to the Press' (Preface). No doubt the text, rendered in regular heroic couplets, proves her to be a competent translator, but the neo-classical play remains stiff, insipid and monotonous. The characters are either unbelievably noble or preposterously treacherous, wars and conquests are motivated solely by love, and conflicts are not dramatised but reproduced in long and turgid monologues. The plot describes the murder of Pompey at the hands of his treacherous Egyptian allies, for which Caesar – warned of further plots against his own life by Pompey's virtuous widow – deposes Ptolemy and crowns Cleopatra, who graciously accepts his love, since he plans to divorce his wife and marry her (no illicit love here!). The only parts of *Pompey* Philips invented herself are the songs between the acts, which were set to music and have nothing to do with the action of the play.

Spurred by the success of her first play, she began a translation of a second play by Corneille, *Horace*, but she died before she could finish it, so that the last scenes were appended by Sir John Denham. The play was performed with great splendour at Court in 1668, with Charles II's mistress, Lady Castlemaine, decked out in the crown jewels (made available for the occasion!), taking the role of Camilla. There is more action in this play and room for two tragic women's roles. Horace is married to a noblewoman, and his sister has wed her brother-in-law, who now faces Horace in combat, so that each of the women will lose either a brother or a husband in the fight. Yet one wonders why Philips should have chosen to work on a play in which the callous protagonist, as his country's champion, kills his own brother-in-law, dispatches his own sister because she resents her husband's slaying, and then receives the King's pardon for the murder because, after all, it is good Roman tradition to kill one's siblings – Romulus did so, too. The gruesome story is told with approval and admiration rather than horror. Philips' translation ends with the killing of the sister.

Philips' two plays were extremely successful, but praise was not unanimous and they called forth ridicule from some of the Royalist writers. *Pompey* was travestied in Davenant's *The Play-house To Be Let* (1663), and Pepys[15] (19 January 1669) called *Horace* a 'silly tragedy' made bearable by farcical dances between the acts – an indication that even contemporary audiences may have found it hard to stomach the Englished Corneille undiluted. The importance of Katherine Philips lies not in her work but in her immaculate personal reputation despite production on the public stage. For more than a century, 'the matchless Orinda' provided a gratefully accepted role model women dramatists could follow. By protesting their femininity and domesticity, she helped them to escape scathing personal criticism and defamation.

The first woman to have an *original* play performed on a commercial English stage was Frances Boothby, whose tragi-comedy *Marcelia, or The Treacherous Friend* was staged at Drury Lane in 1669. We know nothing of the life or character of the author, but she must have been a woman of extraordinary self-confidence to approach Thomas Killigrew, the manager of Drury Lane, with a play written under her own name. Indeed, the Prologue boldly capitalises on her sex and ironically enumerates the objections that will be levelled against a woman audacious enough to venture on playwriting. The tone is witty and self-assured and leaves no doubt that the author regards access to the stage as a woman's birthright, although she appeals to the ladies in the audience for special solidarity – a gesture which was to be imitated by most women playwrights throughout the Restoration and eighteenth century. The Epilogue asserts that the author does not seek praise unless it be her due. Later female dramatists, with the exception of Behn, were generally far less self-confident in their addresses to the public and often humbly requested special indulgence for a woman's work.

In *Marcelia*, Boothby made use of the popular pattern of the split-plot comedy Etherege had created in *Love in a Tub* (1664), combining a quasi-heroic plot along the lines of Fletcherian tragi-comedy with humorous lower-life scenes. The play has a comic sub-plot, but drags in the serious part, with its ranting love scenes and threats of Jacobean horror. A villainous courtier wants to procure the heroine for the lecherous king and plans to have her faithful lover murdered, but his machinations are discovered in time, Marcelia is reunited with her suitor and the king returns to his former mistress. The sub-plot is scarcely connected with the main action – a structural weakness – but there is humour and pace, and the Restoration stereotypes of the witty couple and of the foolish citizen turned fop and ridiculed by his own clever servant are present in embryo. Lucidore, 'a wild Lord' living by his wits, is less smooth and sophisticated than a classical Restoration rake. However, he also engages in battles of repartee with the widow he courts, and rails against marriage in humorous metaphors:

> I am not an Enemy to the Sex, but to that ceremony; I would be a Ladies servant, but not her Prentice: I love not to seal words of Complement for term of life, as that of taking a woman for better for worse.

> (II/i)

Pearson[16] has drawn attention to the play's unmasking of conventional love rhetoric, in which men call themselves a woman's servant before marriage, only to make sure of her enslavement *post festum*. The merry widow understands this hypocritical stance well enough and wryly corrects a friend who recommends the fop as a man who 'seeks to be your Servant' by answering: 'You are much deceiv'd, it is to be my Master' (IV/iii). In one of the best scenes of the play the widow rids herself of this foppish suitor by telling him of a prophecy that her second husband will be killed. He is willing to bide his time until an interloper has fulfilled this role – but when he hears that the third and fourth spouses are to be hanged, he abandons his pursuit of so dangerous a mate. Boothby never wrote a second play and disappeared from the theatrical scene, but she had created a precedent which other adventurous women could follow.

One such was Elizabeth Polwhele, whose rhymed tragedy, *The Faithful Virgins*, was performed at Lincoln's Inn Fields in 1671, but is not available in print. Her unperformed comedy, *The Frolicks, or The Lawyer Cheated*, however, has recently been edited and testifies to her remarkable dramatic talent. We do not know why the play was not performed, nor do we have reliable information about the author's background or why she stopped writing so soon. Hume and Milhous, the editors of the play, suggest that she may have been the daughter of a well known Nonconformist minister, since at that time opposition to the stage even in clerical circles had not reached the frenzy of the Collier era, who gave up her disreputable involvement with the theatre after her marriage.[17]

In the Dedication she humorously describes herself as 'an unfortunate young woman ... haunted by poetic devils'. Instead of
going in for Fletcherian tragi-comedy, as Boothby had done and
Behn was to do in her first venture, Polwhele chose to write a
realistic and bawdy sex comedy set among London low life and
consisting of three loosely integrated strands of action. The philandering Rightwit is arrested for debt by lawyer Swallow, but freed
from prison by the latter's boisterous daughter, who marries him
when he manages to trick her own father into giving him legal
advice on how to marry an heiress with impunity. Another plot
involves an unscrupulous aristocrat who seduces a country girl with
the help of a French bawd and then tricks a fellow rake into marrying her for her imaginary fortune. A third plot revolves around a
married couple, with the wife constantly attempting to cuckold her
credulous husband. In the end, the cuckold indignantly dismisses
the honest servant who all the while has tried to open his eyes – a
nice twist to an otherwise stereotypical plot. The dramatis personae
also include two foolish suitors to the heroine, who are tricked by
the hero and beaten up by their own impertinent servants. The
action moves briskly and includes various effective scenes, for instance when the heroine frees the hero from the debtors' prison, or
when, in male disguise, she joins the rakes in the tavern, where
they persuade the fops to don female clothes. Showing actresses in
male dress had become a popular plot element in the 1660s, giving
an opportunity to show female legs in tight trousers. Such a disguise is never intended to discredit the female character, but is
rather meant to show her initiative and frolicksome nature. A man
who wears a skirt, however, is always turned into a figure of contempt and ridicule in Restoration comedy, in the works of men and
women alike (which was not the case 40 years earlier in the pastoral
play *Florimene*), and in *The Frolicks* such an indignity appropriately
befalls only the two country bumpkins.

Clarabell in *The Frolicks* is a typical witty Restoration heroine, but
she is also the kind of figure who was to turn up especially in plays
by women. She is mistress of her own fate, making an active decision to catch the rake who has caught her fancy.

I fear I shall be fool enough, and madwoman together, to fall in
love with him. But I will resist it with an Amazonian courage.

> Love is but a swinish thing at best. I'll in, and study to forget
> him. If 'twill not be, I'll study how to get him.
>
> (II/81)

She saves him from ruin by rescuing him from prison and suggests
to him how he can win her from her father. Since *The Frolicks* was
never performed, it is unlikely to have inspired other writers.
Nevertheless, the similarities to the work of later female playwrights
in character conception and evaluation are striking and suggest that
it was natural for women to treat certain motifs and stereotypes
from a feminine perspective. Active, self-confident and witty
heroines can be found also in men's plays of the period, but women
playwrights were fond of allowing their female figures more independence and control over the action than was the male wont.
Polwhele's treatment of the rakish hero, too, reflects a female viewpoint: to be sure, Rightwit is manly and attractive, but he is also
discomfited for his womanising by having his bastards tied to his
back, so that he becomes the laughing stock of the two fools and the
heroine: 'How like an ass thou look'st' (IV/119). There is no
enthralled fascination here with sexual potency and elegant libertinism, as in the famous Restoration comedies by men, but a balance
between attraction and ridicule, a stance which I think is more
frequently adopted by women dramatists and used to great effect in
the best plays by Behn and Centlivre.

3
Aphra Behn

'All women ought to let flowers fall upon the tomb of Aphra Behn, for it was she who earned them the right to speak their minds,' said Virginia Woolf.[18] Indeed, Behn was the first professional woman playwright who made a regular income from writing for the theatre, 'forced to write for Bread and not ashamed to owne it,' as she says in her Address to the Reader in *Sir Patient Fancy*. Whether she was in fact able to support herself by writing is questionable, though. She may also have worked as a hack, as an amanuensis, or as a prostitute, or she may have been a kept mistress. However, as a woman who had written 19 plays and openly aspired to fame and immortality, like all her male peers, her position was utterly different from that of a Frances Boothby or Elizabeth Polwhele, or any other young woman producing the odd play, who could be regarded as a curiosity, but not as a serious rival. Behn was one of the most prolific playwrights of her time, second only to Dryden in the number of plays she wrote. If one considers that by that time very few writers, male or female, had made a regular profession of writing and that most contemporary successful male dramatists were either from the aristocracy or well connected, and had received an education at university or the Inns of Court, the pretensions of this woman must have seemed extravagant.

In spite of intensive research, we still know few facts about Aphra Behn's life, which has given rise to far-ranging speculation. Her background is obscure. She may have been the illegitimate daughter of some nobleman or noblewoman, which would account for her knowledge of French, Spanish and Italian. Or she may have been a courtesan of Creole or Jewish origin, as Germaine Greer suggests on account of her cosmopolitan culture and social and economic status.[19] In her youth she almost certainly journeyed to Surinam, then an English colony, but it is questionable whether her father, who died on board the ship, was indeed to be Lieutenant General there, as she claims in her novel *Oroonoko*. Upon her return to London she is said to have married a Dutch merchant, who may have died during the Great Plague. We know for certain that she was sent to the Netherlands to spy on the exiled regicides, some of whom she had met in Surinam, that she received no payment for these activities, and that she was thrown into debtors' prison in London. Soon afterwards, however, she surfaces among a circle of writers with good connections. In the course of her life she gained the patronage of James II and the Duke of Buckingham and among her literary friends were Dryden, Otway, Nahum Tate, Ravenscroft, Lee and Rochester, and she must also have been acquainted with all the famous actors and actresses of the time, to whose established roles she tailored many of her plays.

We know very little about her personal life. She remained unmarried after her husband's death, and difficult as it is to imagine how an unattached woman could have thrived, we have no proof of promiscuity or libertinism in her private life, although her enemies were quick to insinuate sexual licence and an immoral lifestyle on the basis of the bawdy sex comedies and passionate love poetry she wrote. Throughout her life she fervently supported the Tory cause and wrote vitriolic anti-Whig propaganda, especially during the Popish Plot and the Exclusion Crisis, a zeal that resulted in the threat of arrest in 1682 for openly criticising the Duke of Monmouth, Charles II's rebellious illegitimate son. Her unflinching royalism is somewhat surprising in a woman who was fighting for recognition in a conservative, patriarchal society which generally denied a public role to women, but both the Whig and Tory parties, at the time, were authoritarian in outlook and the question was only which privileged group would predominate. Behn always found the libertine individualism she associated with the Court more appealing than the Puritanism and commercialism of the middle classes. The choice between being a sex object or having to repress one's sexuality is itself unattractive, and in her plays Behn frequently posits women as autonomous subjects, not mere objects of barter. However, one can also see why in her political outlook Behn should have opted for the permissiveness of the Court, which still accepted women within its cultured circles, rather than for the Whig moralists and their restrictive views of female sensuality. Behn died in 1689, ill, impoverished and out of political favour, but still acknowledged for her genius, the first woman writer to be buried in Westminster Abbey.

Throughout her life fierce abuse was heaped on Behn, which feminist critics have tended to interpret as proof of the violent opposition the appearance of a female rival sparked off in her male peers. To be sure, there was plenty of nasty snickering about her supposed sexual immorality, accusations of plagiarism and cynical suggestions that her lovers, in fact, had written her plays. It is, however, one-sided to ascribe the attacks to misogyny only, nor did Behn remain without defenders, such as Dryden, who praised her wit and talent, or the poet and playwright Charles Cotton, who addressed the following lines to Behn, whose pen-name was 'Astrea':

> But when you write of *Love*, *Astrea*, then
> Love dips his Arrows, where you wet your Pen.
> Such charming Lines did never Paper grace;
> Soft as your Sex; and smooth as Beauty's Face.[20]

The age was fiercely partisan, and personal satire abounded in comedies as well as in verse and pamphlets, frequently causing scandals and violence. All writers were savaged, the satirical portrait of Dryden in Buckingham's *The Rehearsal* being the best-known example. To be included among the eminent male authors of the age in a satire on the state of contemporary art did not necessarily signify an abuse, as it was a mark of being taken seriously as an artist. Thus, Buckingham's reference to Behn in *The Rehearsal* is not ill-natured and it would indeed have been a slight to have been left out. In the 1680s, however, the acrimony of these satires increased, parallel to the bitterness of the political debate. What hurt particularly was the tendency of male satirists to pick on the physical appearance and personal lives of the women held up to ridicule – such as fading charms, crippling illness or alleged personal immorality. It is this sting that gives the unpleasant tone to some of the abuse Behn encountered.

> Doth that lewd Harlot, that Poetick Quean,
> Fam'd through White Fryars, you know who I mean,
> Mend for reproof, others set up in spight
> To flux, take glisters, vomits, purge and write.
> Long with a Sciatica she's beside lame,
> Her limbs distortur'd, Nerves shrunk up with pain,
> And therefore I'll all sharp reflections shun,
> Poverty, Poetry, Pox, are plagues enough for one.[21]

The vituperation gained in volume even after her death, because of the new century's growing hostility to sensuality, as well as for political reasons. In the course of the eighteenth and nineteenth centuries, by an absurd equation of her art and her life, Behn's name became synonymous with that of a harlot and her plays were regarded as the most infamous examples of Restoration profligacy. It is only recently that Aphra Behn has come into her own and her contribution to the theatre of her time been fully acknowledged.

We do not know how Behn actually started her dramatic career, nor who introduced her into the coterie of writers. She had had some contact with Killigrew when she was a spy in the Netherlands, but she chose to take her plays to the rival company of the Duke's Men, at that time run by a woman, Lady Davenant. Behn must have had some knowledge of stagecraft when she started her theatrical career. Before her first play was staged, she must also have acquired a reputation as a poet through verses circulated in manuscript form – so that young Otway, aspiring to become an actor, sought her out and was actually given a role to play in her first drama, in which he failed miserably. Yet she embarked on her theatrical career without the official support of a patron (whoever her *private* patrons may have been) who could have facilitated introduction to theatre managers and provided the protection from enemies and competitors so vital in those factious times. It is only later that she dedicated her plays to aristocratic patrons.

She wrote for the commercial stage, catering to the demands of the literary market, and the question of whether she still managed

to introduce a female perspective, or whether her plays are indistinguishable from those of men, has long been an issue of critical
controversy. Although I am convinced that her approach is distinct
from that of men in several aspects of character conception and
evaluation, it is certainly true that none of her plays is explicitly
feminist, and very few attempt to undermine social norms. Behn is
much more outspoken on the inequalities of the sexes and the re-
pression of women in her prefaces and prologues, in which she
vigorously defends herself against misogynist prejudices and the
double standards critics were quickly learning to use against women
playwrights. In her satirical Epistle to the 'Good, Sweet, Honey,
Sugar-candied Reader' in *The Dutch Lover*, she ridicules a fop who
denigrated the play because it was written by a woman and then
proceeds to take on the whole tribe of her male competitors by
venturing on the current literary debate as to the moral function of
literature. Plays, she claims iconoclastically, are mere entertainment,
without moral utility, and the Aristotelian rules are not needed for
effective dramatic composition; thus women, despite the lack of
classical education with which they are so frequently charged, are
as competent playwrights as any university graduate. In the Epistle
to the Reader preceding *Sir Patient Fancy* she complains bitterly that
a play's bawdiness is condemned as 'unnatural' when coming from
a woman, but is considered a venial sin in a man. In the Preface to
The Lucky Chance she claims a right of 'my masculine part, the poet
in me' to aspire to fame and 'immortality', just like any male author.

On the other hand, she also strikes poses of seductiveness and
coquettishness in her prefaces, comparing her play to a virgin offering herself up to a rake (*The Young King*), or with a new mistress
who will satisfy the libertine's quest for variety (*The Lucky Chance*),
thereby herself establishing the notorious link between the sexual
and linguistic promiscuity of a professional writer who offers her
works for public consumption. Thus even in her forewords she
assumes many roles, and plays alternately the whore, the woman
working for her bread, the literary critic, the social satirist, the
victim of unjust attacks – roles that suggest a fascinating range of
personality.

Early plays and *The Widow Ranter*
Aphra Behn wrote at least 15 plays, and four additional ones are
attributed to her tentatively, besides poetry and a number of prose

narratives, some of which were adapted for the stage by later play-wrights. In drama, she tried her hand at several genres before she found the style congenial to her. She started out with tragi-comedy in the vein of Beaumont and Fletcher, often centring on illicit love, with virtuous protagonists saved from ruin by a surprising twist in the action. All of these plays are rather superficial juvenilia, or were conceived in her youth although completed and performed later. Her first play, *The Forc'd Marriage; or The Jealous Bridegroom* (Lincoln's Inn Fields, 1670), is a variation on the *Othello* motif, featuring a virtuous woman forced to marry a jealous courtier who strangles her when the king visits her secretly. The courtier almost comes to blows with his rival when both mourn the victim at her open coffin (an echo of *Hamlet*). He is saved from the consequences of his rash deed when the revived wife, disguised as a ghost, orders him to court the princess who loves him, whereupon the two couples are happily united. All the characters are supposed to behave nobly, though neither the king's secret rendezvous with a married woman nor the murder will seem so to the spectator. The husband, in particular, who murders, mourns, fights over the coffin and then relinquishes his wife within a few hours is an entirely unconvincing character. A witty couple, the woman shying away from the bondage of marriage, the man exasperated by her independence, are more attractive, though peripheral, figures.

The *Young King, or The Mistake*, produced at Dorset Garden in 1679, was started as a sketch in Surinam and is the most baroque of all her plays, a cross between a heroic play and a pastoral idyll. One strand of action, taken from Calderon's *La Vida es Sueno*, concerns a king brought up in complete seclusion, as ignorant of mankind as Miranda in *The Tempest*. When he is brought to court for a day, he proves his prophesied cruel nature and is therefore persuaded that his short rule was but a dream. Later, however, he is reintegrated into society. The more interesting second plot line concerns the warlike Cleomena, whom love transforms into femininity. When she believes that her beloved was killed, she disguises herself and stabs the supposed murderer, who turns out to be her very lover. However, he survives and the couple are united. The portrayal of this Amazon is quite conventional: she is emasculated once the right man appears and causes mischief only when she takes vengeance into her own hands and, in male disguise, almost murders the man she loves. The play, in fact, demonstrates that Behn did not consistently deconstruct female clichés or challenge traditional gender roles, although, as will be shown, some of her comedies are more subversive of gendered norms and popular female stereotypes.

Besides tragi-comedy, Behn also wrote one full-fledged blank-verse tragedy, *Abdelazar, or The Moor's Revenge* (Dorset Garden, 1676), inspired by Jacobean sex and horror plays, in which a Machi-avellian villain induces the queen to poison her husband and disown her son as a bastard, and then murders her when he tires of her services. The very opposite of Othello, the eponymous Moorish protagonist is even willing to compromise his wife's life and honour in order to be able to kill her princely lover in flagrante, but in the end he is betrayed by his accomplices and dies basking in his mis-deeds. In its portrayal of women the play is conservative. The lustful queen is cast as a villainess who gets her comeuppance by being exploited and betrayed by the lover who feigns to adore her, but is, in fact, sick of her already. Abdelazar's wife is chaste and faithful in spite of her love for the prince, the stereotype of the tragic honest wife Behn also used in *The Forc'd Marriage*. Although the play is undistinguished, it does manage to convey lurid emotion and is noteworthy for a villain motivated by ambition and revenge rather than amorous passion – a welcome relief from the 'all for love' of so much of Restoration and eighteenth-century tragedy.

The designation of 'tragi-comedy' for *The Widow Ranter; or The History of Bacon in Virginia*, unsuccessfully and posthumously staged at Drury Lane in 1689, is actually misleading, because in this un-usual play Behn combines heroic tragedy with a boisterously comic low plot, which, in fact, constitutes the main action. In the tragic plot the brave General Bacon defends the colony against the Indians yet is denied official command by the villainous council and is considered a traitor. He kills the Indian emperor in single battle but also mortally wounds the Indian queen he loves in the course of his conquest. Thereupon he takes poison. Although Behn admires his heroic qualities, it is characteristic that the fervent royalist in her does not approve of his insubordination, even against so despicable and tyrannous a council. His followers are pardoned by the new governor, who dismisses the corrupt councillors. It is the exploits of this rabble, some of whom stem from Newgate, that provide some of the humour of the play. Their cowardice and hypocrisy are very funny and give a devastating picture of the mob ruling the American colonies, a picture that ties in with the description Behn offers in her famous story *Oroonoko*. As is already indicated by the title, the heroic plot about Bacon is placed in the background. The main character is the termagant widow, completely unfettered by social inhibitions or feminine reticence, who smokes, drinks, swears and fights like a man, and wins Lieutenant Daring by following him into battle disguised as a soldier – since she suspects that the superior male position comes from command, not courage. In fact, Daring likes her so well in breeches that he gives her 'good encouragement to wear them' (IV/iii/340) even after their marriage. Unlike the Amazon in *The Young King*, the Widow Ranter is indeed a highly novel figure, blending masculine self-confidence and independence with erotic attractiveness, and despite her unfeminine behaviour and her gleeful debunking of male presumption she retains the full sympathies of the audience and is not forced to recant or meta-morphose into a chaste and modest belle in the end. Mrs Ranter, her name reminiscent of a religious sect suspected of political and social insubordination,[22] is loud, vulgar, free-minded and splendidly vigorous and comic, the complete match of the daredevil lieutenant she woos, and as such a unique figure in the comedy of the time.

As Behn herself soon realised, her true talent was for comedy. Yet in her first plays she proceeded cautiously, by seeking to appeal to a wide audience and by combining comic action with quasi-heroic plots. So *The Amorous Prince* (Lincoln's Inn Fields, 1671) links a potentially serious plot, about a philandering prince who debauches his friend's sister and then sets out to seduce his fiancée but in the end is forced to make up to the jilted girl, with a comic second plot, concerning an absurdly jealous husband who begs his friend to feign love to his wife in order to test her virtue. The wife sees through the conspiracy; her sister takes her place and plays cat-and-mouse with the two men, until the husband is cured of his jealousy and the friend is secured in marriage for the sister. A lecherous fool who tried to bribe his way into the wife's bedroom is tricked into marrying the maid. The play is notorious for supposed bawdiness in that it shows the prince rising from Cloris' bed, having spent the night with her. But in fact this is not really a scene of extramarital sex, since the girl has received a legally valid promise of marriage; the prince chooses not to honour his vows until he realises that she is not a simple shepherdess and that her family may cause serious trouble. Then, rather suddenly, he discovers his renewed affection for his spurned bride. What has gone largely unnoticed by critics, however, is the unmistakably homosexual undertone when one of the courtiers propositions Cloris, who has followed the prince in male disguise.

The Dutch Lover (Duke's Theatre, Dorset Garden, 1673) deals with similar themes of seduction, betrayal and belated reparation, also combined with farcical low plots. It juggles four intricate strands of intrigues, which are all brought to a happy conclusion at the cost of plot credibility and character consistency. Alonzo comes to Spain to marry Hippolyta, who has been seduced by Antonio. He is accosted by Euphemia, who would rather marry this stranger than her foolish Dutch suitor, but is mistakenly led into another girl's chamber, exciting the jealousy of her betrothed, who is Hippolyta's brother. Then there is also a young man consumed with incestuous passion for his sister, who, as is the wont in tragi-comedies of the time, turns out not to be his sister after all. Hippolyta disguises herself as a man and challenges her seducer to a duel, which Alonzo and her brother join in. In the end Antonio repents and marries her, Hippolyta's brother weds his fiancée, and Alonzo Euphemia, and the boorish Dutchman is left with a maid. Antonio's turn-about from regarding Hippolyta as a mere tool for his revenge on her brother to feeling genuine affection for her is, of course, entirely unconvincing, and the threat of incest in one of the plots is a mere stereotype. Euphemia, however, is already the prototype of the active Behn heroines who take their fates into their own hands. She masterminds all the necessary intrigues and goads her rather passive lover to impersonate the foolish Dutchman. In spite of some effective farcical scenes, the play failed because of incompetent acting and sloppy staging. The costumes used were so tatty that the audience did not realise that Alonzo was meant to impersonate the Dutchman – the carelessness of which Behn bitterly complains in the Epistle to the Reader.

The Town Fop; or Sir Timothy Tawdrey (Dorset Garden, 1676) also combines a quasi-heroic main plot with low-life comedy and might, with some justice, properly be termed a tragi-comedy. The impoverished Bellmour is forced by his uncle into a bigamous union with Diana, yet nobly refuses to consummate the marriage, whereupon the bride's love turns into hatred. She tries to spur several men, as well as Bellmour's first wife in disguise, to avenge her by promising them her sexual favours. The hero, in the meantime, has turned profligate out of grief, refuses to give his siblings the heritage he owes them, and with the foppish Sir Timothy visits a brothel, where he meets the latter's mistress, Betty Flauntit, a wonderfully comic and lively figure. Sir Timothy is tricked into marrying Bellmour's sister, who has been left destitute without her portion. Bellmour gains everybody's forgiveness because of his undying love for his first wife, and Diana begs her uncle to procure a divorce. The siblings get their portions, and Sir Timothy can now dispose of enough money to maintain his mistress. The main plot, with its false heroics and ever-weeping hero offering to fall on his sword, is adapted from George Wilkins' tragedy *The Miseries of Enforced Marriage*, but Behn enlarged the role of the second wife and especially of the fop and his leeches, adding a highly effective scene in a bawdyhouse. The play vacillates between sentimentality (the bigamist is in reality eternally faithful, the hard-hearted uncle melts at just the right moment) and downright cynicism: Bellmour's sister must marry the fop because she has no money, and the less she feels, the better it is for her; no sooner has she come into her money, than Sir Timothy will use it to finance his extramarital liaison. Such a hard-boiled attitude jars with the main plot and is very rare in Behn, who as a rule castigates such loveless and mercenary marriages, but it betokens a realistic assessment of a poor woman's helplessness, which can also be found in Polwhele's *The Frolicks*, where the rake's sister must also catch a rich fool, and in the Duchess of Newcastle's *The Sociable Companions*, where the women, impoverished by their dissolute brothers, also cold-bloodedly stalk their wealthy prey.

As has become obvious from these early plays, from the outset Behn preferred the popular genre of Spanish intrigue comedy – thickly plotted and masterly timed, full of machinations, disguises, mistaken identities and farcical encounters, and sparkling with wit. She was a master of effective comic situations, eminently theatrical and stageworthy. It was not unusual for her to adapt older or foreign plays, but she usually pruned and streamlined the dialogue, rendering the scenes more dramatically effective. The charge of plagiarism, occasionally levelled against her, as against various other playwrights, both male and female, is hardly relevant in view of the wide borrowing from older plays on the part of all Restoration dramatists. Complete originality has been an artistic ideal only since the Romantic period. Reworking an old play in a striking, elegant or 'Englished' version, with only a vague acknowledgement of the source, was considered perfectly legitimate before the Romantics.

Plagiarism, of course, was a convenient stick with which to beat undesirable rivals, as was neglect of the classical unities, a charge to which women dramatists, barred from higher education, were particularly sensitive. Though these classical rules were but vaguely defined, many female playwrights were defensive about their ignorance and humbly asked the better-informed, university-educated male spectators to overlook their blunders. Few dared, like Behn in *The Dutch Lover*, to deny the utility of the Aristotelian precepts.

Modern critics have occasionally dismissed Behn's work as merely farcical and superficial, as opposed to genuine comedies of manners, but, of course, she does question social norms and, as far as women are concerned, much more profoundly than her male peers. As will be shown below, in her best comedies she subverts the view of women as property and reveals the injustices of the status quo. She paints women as desiring subjects, not merely as the objects of male lust, and clearly exposes the gendered moral norms transforming a male libertine into a model, a female libertine into a pariah. She questions the link between virginity and male desire and the suppression of female libido. She often sympathises with female sexual transgressors – character types who are generally ridiculed or turned into castrating monsters in Restoration comedy.

Major works: *The Rover, The Feigned Courtesans, The Lucky Chance*
The Rover, or The Banish'd Cavaliers is probably Behn's most famous play. Originally, a pretence was maintained in the Prologue that it had been written by a man, probably to ensure the comedy was given a fair hearing; but in fact it turned out to be an immediate success and was greeted with rapturous applause in 1677. Spurred by this success, Behn in 1681 wrote a sequel to the adventures of her hero, *The Rover, Part II*, a weaker comedy with a different plot and a new range of female characters.

The Rover features a firework of disguises, mistaken identities and intrigues, all crammed into the 24 hours required by dramatic convention. Quite appropriately, it is set in Naples during the carnival season, which gives the comedy an air of boisterous fun and playfulness, yet without depriving it of social significance. Several cavaliers exiled from England during the Commonwealth pursue their amorous adventures in the city. The play contrasts a romantic couple with a witty one and adds a low-life intrigue as a counterpoint. Belville is in love with Florinda, who is intended for a rich old suitor; Belville marries her against her brother's wishes. Willmore, the Rover, starts an affair with the famous courtesan Angelica, but jilts her for a saucy gypsy, who turns out to be an heiress in disguise. Their foolish companion Blunt, on the other hand, is fleeced by a common whore, thrown naked into a sewer, and vows to avenge himself on womankind.

Large sections of the plot were taken, often verbatim, from Killigrew's unperformed comedy *Thomaso*. Behn admitted that she had drawn inspiration from this play but pretended to have borrowed little. She added some new characters, most notably Hellena, and split up into two separate characters Killigrew's title figure, who, rather unbelievably, is both a libertine and a faithful lover. Behn contrasts the honest Belville with the rakish Willmore, thereby qualifying their characters and ironically juxtaposing them. As the title suggests, Willmore is the hero of the comedy, but Behn's attitude to this sexual predator is ambiguous. During a performance of *The Rover*, Queen Mary is reported to have said that the actor Mountfort, playing Willmore, made even vice alluring,[23] and no doubt it is possible to play him in such a way. Several modern critics as well have read *The Rover* as a celebration of Cavalier libertinism and a glorification of rakes and free-livers.[24] Indeed, the figure may well have been modelled on Behn's supposed lover, John Hoyle, or on the glamorous Earl of Rochester. The impression Willmore makes on both Hellena and Angelica, who is willing to give him free of charge what she normally sells to the highest bidder, must be taken as a gauge of his erotic magnetism. Nevertheless, the play does not endorse the libertine ideology unambiguously, but in fact presents the hero as simultaneously charismatic, foolishly meddling and destructive. His indiscriminate pursuit of every skirt, his one-track mind and drunken bluntness spoil the careful plans of his friends and expose them to constant danger. It is not without justification that he is frequently called a 'beast' in the text, even by his companions. He mistakes the virtuous Florinda for a whore and tries to rape her – a scene which, in Killigrew's original, is performed by the boorish Blunt character. In fact, Behn gives several speeches and scenes to her hero which in the original belong to the buffoon, thereby establishing links intended to ridicule the rake's insatiable lust and drunken extravagance. Behn thus debunks Willmore in a way few male dramatists ever treated their rakish heroes, yet which seemed to come naturally to female writers and can be found again and again in women's plays. Both the foolish Blunt and the over-sexed Willmore believe that they are irresistible to women and have only carnal interests. Their social attitudes are equally disruptive and potentially threatening, though, to be sure, Willmore has a charisma which the boorish knight lacks, whose upbringing and manners suggest a Puritan background and who is, therefore, fair prey for a Royalist playwright. Yet Lucetta's cruel cozening of Blunt is put in perspective by Willmore's betrayal of Angelica,[25] and can be read not only as the proper retribution to a mercenary upstart, but also as a woman's revenge on the whole tribe of predatory men.

Unlike most male playwrights, Behn does not glorify male bonding but rather exposes its potential misogyny, for instance when the English and the Spanish male characters, who come to blows at most encounters, are quite ready to join forces in pursuit of a woman of supposedly easy virtue. What is conspicuously absent in her plays – and, indeed, in the plays of all women playwrights – is the unpleasant atmosphere of male competition frequently found in Restoration comedy, which often gives the impression that the cuckolding of the husband, not the seduction of the wife, provides the ultimate gratification in an all-male power game, in which women are mere counters with which to achieve ascendancy over one's peers within the masculine hierarchy. For characters like the arch-rake Horner in Wycherley's *The Country Wife*, female lust is merely a convenient means to gain this end, and he is not really interested in the women themselves, or even in the sexual satisfaction they can afford him, but in the secret pleasure of humiliating and fooling other men. Like many later women playwrights, Behn counterpoints the male community with a female one, in which friendships, mutual help as well as rivalries are as common as in the men's world.

Characteristically, Behn devotes more space than most of her male rivals to the women characters, allowing them not only more say but also an important influence on the action. *The Rover*, in fact, starts out with an all-women scene which introduces their perspective on the events to come and firmly establishes a feminine viewpoint frequently absent in Restoration drama.[26] Both the romantic Florinda and the witty, self-assertive Hellena rebel against their father's and brother's dictates, decreeing a loveless union for the one and a convent for the other, and decide to take their fates into their own hands. In doing so, the more conventional Florinda is in constant danger of being raped and depends on her lover to save and protect her. She is pestered by the drunken Willmore, who mistakes her for a prostitute, and later falls into the hands of the misogynist Blunt, who decides to take revenge for his humiliation on the unknown woman. Hellena is much more adept at fending for herself. She is an entirely original creation of Behn's, not to be found in Killigrew, and a fitting counterpart to the Rover. In the guises first of a gypsy and then of a boy, she sets out to find herself a husband; she casts her eyes on Willmore, whose womanising she accepts as a matter of course and whom she attracts by feigning promiscuity, but also by her wit and good humour. Behn gives her erotic feelings which are as powerful as those of the hero, so that in the play both sexes become objects of desire, not just women as is commonly the case. However, in the Restoration period 'the role of the libertine could not simply be reversed to put the female into the position of sexual predator,' since 'doing the deed would be the undoing of [a woman's] power'.[27] Therefore Hellena's libertinism is verbal only. She may crave sexual fulfilment as fervently as the hero himself, but she is well aware of society's double standard and the consequences for a woman who abandons herself.

> WILLMORE: ... let's retire to my Chamber, ... I love to steal a Dish
> and a Bottle with a Friend, and hate long Graces – Come,
> let's retire and fall to.
> HELLENA: 'Tis but getting my Consent, and the Business is soon
> done; let but old Gaffer *Hymen* and his Priest say Amen to't,
> and I dare lay my Mother's Daughter by as proper a Fellow
> as your Father's Son, without fear or blushing.
> WILLMORE: Hold, hold, ... Marriage is as certain a Bane to Love,
> as lending Money is to Friendship: I'll neither ask nor give
> a Vow, tho I could be content to turn Gypsy ... to have the
> Pleasure of working that great Miracle of making a Maid a
> Mother, ... and if I miss, I'll lose my Labour.
> HELLENA: And if you do lose, what shall I get? A cradle full of
> noise and mischief, with a Pack of Repentance at my Back?
> (V/i/97f.)

She uses sexuality as a bait to attract the rake, but then restrains herself until he is so hooked that he will consent to the wedding ceremony in order to gain possession. A heroine who pretends to be sexually available in order to manipulate the man she has selected as a mate, but in fact remains scrupulously chaste, is a figure who will crop up again and again in women's drama. In *The Rover* she is contrasted with Angelica, the courtesan who falls in love with the hero and naively believes that a woman can enter into a sexual bargain with a man by granting free love in return for true love. As soon as he has gained possession, however, Willmore jilts her for a new conquest, and Angelica Bianca has to realise that a woman can never meet a man on equal terms in the sexual marketplace. A libertine may well rant at a woman's mercenary nature, he may even accept her provocative equating of a marriage of convenience with prostitution, but, quite illogically, he will nonetheless accept the doctrine of society that virginity and wealth are the prerequisites for a marriageable heroine. Behn's near-tragic treatment of the jilted whore, to whom, critics have noted, she gave her own initials, has attracted a lot of critical attention and, indeed, the portrait is highly unusual for a time in which unchaste women and ex-mistresses were treated with ridicule and contempt rather than sympathy. Behn refuses to include Angelica in the happy ending and the unsettling gaps in the text force the reader to reassess the sexual double standard and to question the status allotted by society to female sexuality.[28] Such a probing into the one-sidedness of moral norms is, as we shall see, not uncommon in women playwrights, but Behn, of all women dramatists, is most pronounced in her sympathy for sexual transgressors

The Rover, Part II (Dorset Garden, 1679) goes much further than the first play in its subversion of conventions, by making the widowed Willmore opt for the courtesan instead of the virginal heiress in a new love contest. The play is much weaker in its plot, harking back to *Thomaso* to salvage the more farcical episodes about two rich Jewish hags, a giant and a dwarf, whom Blunt and another fool intend to marry for their money, but whom the Rover, in the costume of a mountebank, helps to pass on to his friends. This plot consists mainly of farce and horseplay. It may well have been meant as a posthumous tribute to the Earl of Rochester, to whom the play is dedicated, and who is said to have disguised himself as a doctor and practised quackery. In the main action Behn again sets off a whirl of intrigues, secret meetings, mistaken identities and coincidences. Willmore, randy as ever, again rails against venial women and sings the praises of free love, and the two female rivals, the heiress Ariadne and the courtesan La Nuche, are also very similar to those in the previous play. Yet this time Behn refuses to reform the rake at the last minute and integrate into society a figure who is basically anarchic and antisocial. Indeed, the witty prostitute (appropriately played by Mrs Barry, one of Rochester's former mistresses) is a much more fitting mate for the libertine than the virgin, yet turning the whore into the true heroine and leaving the heiress to return to her despised suitor was an unheard of solution. In this extramarital relationship, concerns for property and reputation, the twin pillars of Restoration marriage contracts, are irrelevant; the couple turn their backs on social convention and, in an ending unique in Behn's oeuvre, take off to the 'open road of romance' together.[29]

The plot of *The Feigned Courtesans, or A Night's Intrigue* (Dorset Garden, 1679) is an invention of Behn's, but follows a similar pattern to *The Rover* in that two heroines, one destined for a loveless marriage and the other for a convent, flee to Rome and disguise themselves as courtesans to gain some room for manoeuvre in hooking the men they have taken a fancy to. Again, Behn introduces a romantic and a witty couple, but Marcella, unlike Florinda, is not a helpless victim; in the guise of a beautiful prostitute, she tempts the Englishman who courted her in order to test his fidelity. In the end, she does not know whether to be jealous of her alter ego or amused by her lover's bewildered vacillation. Like Hellena, Cornelia attracts the rake by feigning sexual availability, until he finally swallows the bait of marriage, but Behn again remains within social conventions by letting the women remain scrupulously chaste. Their female honour is not compromised by their disguise as courtesans, their white lies and cheating of foolish would-be customers; what would be dishonourable in a man in fact serves to preserve their female honour, that is, their virginity.[30] The misunderstandings and mistaken identities are compounded by a third woman, Laura Lucretia, who also assumes the identity of a harlot and means to entice the rake into her arms, but in the dark she mistakes the man and ends up in bed with her intended husband! Compared with Angelica Bianca, her punishment is lenient, since the fiancé she hoped to jilt, but must now marry, is portrayed as likeable, but the lesson as to the danger of female libertinism is blatant enough.

As to the men, there is a faithful romantic lover, a libertine and two fools, namely a newly knighted parvenu and his Puritan tutor, who are fleeced and beaten up by the others. As in all her comedies, the picture she paints of the Whig middle class is contemptuous and hostile, though Sir Signal Buffoon and Tickletext are drawn as fairly harmless figures of fun rather than acerbic satirical portraits. They are vain, hypocritical, boorish and constantly and comically frustrated in their amorous designs. What is more unexpected, however, is the fact that the heroes, too, are forever led by the nose by the two false courtesans, who whet the men's appetites without ever consenting to quench their desire and fool them as thoroughly as they do the two buffoons. In *The Feigned Courtesans* the women are in complete control: they initiate all the intrigues, make all the plans, determine the course of the action and fight out among themselves who is going to win the prize male. The men are reduced to following the female initiative. Their hopes of sexual gratification are always dashed at the last moment, until they have taken their vows at the altar. The fact that there is plenty of sexual innuendo in the play but no consummation is not merely a dramatic trick to avoid moral censure, but indicates that in this play it is the women who are in charge.

There is plenty of bedroom activity in *The Lucky Chance, or An Alderman's Bargain* (Drury Lane, 1686) and Behn, defending herself against charges of immorality, was certainly disingenuous in claiming in the Preface that there was no bawdiness in the play. The comedy has three intertwined strands of action. The impoverished Leticia has been tricked into marrying Sir Feeble Fainwood by false reports of the death of her fiancé Bellmour, who returns on the wedding day, gains entrance to the house under a false name and lures the groom out of the bridal chamber by telling all kinds of cock-and-bull stories and assuming different disguises, until the ageing husband relinquishes his conjugal rights to him. Sir Feeble's daughter Diana, contracted to a boor, secretly marries her lover while her foolish suitor is being beaten up by 'devils' he has 'conjured up'. Farcical scenes involving fear of the supernatural were popular in Restoration comedy, but here, as we shall see, demons also have a metaphorical function. In the third plot, Lady Julia Fulbank and Gayman start an adulterous affair, at first on her secret instigation, then actually with the connivance of her miserly husband, who loses his wife to Gayman in a game of dice – an outrage which enables Julia to enforce a separation.

On the surface, these three strands of action would seem to contradict each other. The Leticia and Diana plots hinge upon preventing the consummation of a forced marriage, while the third, the cuckolding plot, depicts how Julia and Gayman manage to amuse themselves despite her marriage to a rich alderman. In the first two cases, the assumption is clearly that defloration is a point of no return in a woman's life, beyond which the girl is irrevocably lost to her lover. For Gayman, however, Julia has not lost her attractiveness, although she must share an old man's bed and, to make things worse, must share it because of her own free decision to marry money. Julia, of course, by now bitterly regrets the step she has taken because of the disgust and erotic frustration her bed-mate inspires. As a woman, however, she cannot seek illicit sexual fulfilment openly, because this would put her into the hands of her lover, to be abused and bragged of at will.

> GAYMAN: What, I'm not discreet enough.
>> I'll babble all in my next high debauch;
>> Boast of your favours, and describe your charms
>> To every wishing fool.
> LADY FULBANK: Or make most filthy verses of me
>> Under the name of Cloris, you Philander,
>> Who, in lewd rhymes, confess the dear appointment,
>> What hour, and where, how silent was the night,
>> How full of love your eyes, and wishing mine.
>>> (II/ii/99)

So she sends her servant, disguised as a devil, with a bag of money to summon her lover to a secret tryst. Ironically, Gayman assumes that if a bag of money is to buy his favours, the lusting client must needs be old and repulsive:

> Some female devil, old and damned to ugliness,
> And past all hopes of courtship and address,
> Full of another devil called desire,
> Has seen this face, this shape, this youth,
> And thinks it's worth her hire. It must be so.
>> (II/ii/94)

Even when he embraces Julia in the dark, his delusion is so strong that he takes her for an old hag – much to her chagrin. Julia has thus managed to satisfy herself and keep her reputation intact, but at the price of anonymity and an insult to her self-respect.

In the fifth act Gayman reciprocates the favour, with the husband actually conniving in his own cuckolding to avoid having to pay money for his gambling debts. Unlike the woman, however, Gayman cannot enjoy sex incognito, for his potency gives him away at once and now puts him at Julia's mercy, who feigns outrage at this imposition to her honour. By crying scandal she manages to get rid of her husband, who has forfeited his rights by agreeing to so shameful a bargain. In the end the old man bequeaths her to Gayman after his death (a divorce by Act of Parliament would not have been granted in the circumstances), but it is to be assumed that the couple will hardly wait so long. In similar fashion many Restoration writers gloss over separation difficulties to give their plays an acceptable happy ending.

The play's two tenets – one insisting that men are attracted only to virginal brides, the other hinging upon a married woman's attractiveness – naturally clash, but what modern critics like Gallagher regard as a flaw is, in fact, an alternative vision of female sexuality and value. In the Julia plot, *honour* has nothing to do with chastity or moral worth, only with superficial reputation. Julia – as opposed to Wycherley's Lady Fidget – is not condemned by Behn for hypocrisy, but admired for her strategic talents in the unequal war of the sexes. The conventional view linking male desire and virginity is contrasted with the perception that a man may find a woman loveable beyond the desire to deflower her or lord it over her husband, and that a married woman may be a desiring subject, consummate hypocrite and 'doer of the deed'[31] and still retain the full sympathies of the audience. The play has been read as a bitter analysis of the reduction of women to the status of property, and Julia has been seen as being infuriated by the bed trick her lover and her husband have played on her.[32] However, since she herself enticed Gayman to an hour of love with a bag of gold in the second act, it must be assumed that in the fifth she merely feigns indignation at her sexual violation in order to regain the self-determination she forfeited with marriage. Degradation to the level of a piece of merchandise, symbolised by the money paid for sexual favours, applies to both men and women in this play, which, however, seems to skirt the darker implications of the theme and to assert, at least in the Julia–Gayman plot, that upon occasion you may both have your cake and eat it.

Julia is a rare example in the drama of the time of a woman who is thoroughly likeable though she is not chaste and gets all she wants. For all the amorous goings-on in Restoration comedy, an adulteress is not an attractive heroine in general, although an audience may well be on the side of an adulterous couple deceiving a jealous old husband. If, however, the focus is not on the farcical humour of the cuckolding plot, unfaithful wives tend to be portrayed as hypocrites, simpletons or whores. Behn is highly unusual in her evaluation of sexual transgressors, nor is Julia the only adulteress she treated sympathetically.

The Lucky Chance also contains effective comic scenes. Behn is at her best in the satirical portrayal of the two old aldermen foolishly doting on their young wives, and one of the best scenes in the comedy has Sir Feeble, roused from the bridal bed by reports of an uprising in the city, and Sir Cautious, who believes his friend knows of the robbery he has suffered, gape at each other and talk at cross purposes in the middle of the night.

Later Plays

In *The False Count, or A New Way to Play an Old Game* (Dorset Garden, 1682), a weaker play, the situation is very similar. The young lovers have been separated by an enforced marriage, but manage to commit adultery without losing the sympathy of the audience. Again, the jealous old husband is made to play the pander for his own wife, persuading her to yield to the disguised 'Turks' by whom they have been captured to save his own skin. In the end, the husband is informed but yields his wife to her young lover. For all the similarities, however, the focus in this comedy is on the men and their ingenious intrigues, not on the woman's feelings. Inspired by Molière's *Précieuses Ridicules*, Behn added to the cuckolding plot the comedy of a chimney sweep impersonating a count and teaching a middle-class girl the rules of fashionable behaviour. If in *The Lucky Chance* she showed that a woman's good name depends not on her intrinsic worth but rather on her public image, in *The False Count* she suggests, in similar vein, that neither money nor rank make a man, only the eyes of the world.

Surprisingly lenient judgement is passed upon the unfaithful wife also in *Sir Patient Fancy*, attacked for its immorality when it was first performed, at Dorset Garden in 1678. She cuckolds her hypochondriac husband and thereby sparks off a zany merry-go-round of hair-raising excuses, mistaken identities, narrow escapes and hilarious bedroom farce. In the dark, the daughter's suitor finds himself in bed with Lady Fancy, while the latter's lover is swearing ardent vows to the daughter. When surprised by her husband, the artful woman passes her own love letter off as her stepdaughter's, and when her lover's alarm clock goes off under the bed, she faints on him to hide him under her skirts. In the end, of course, the young couples outwit the guardians who have forbidden their marriage, and the hypochondriac is enlightened as to the true character of his wife. However, she escapes unscathed since the estate he foolishly settled on her was not conditional upon fidelity. The comedy draws on several Molière plays, not only for the figure of the *malade imaginaire*, but also for the learned Lady Knowell, who constantly shows off her knowledge of Latin and Greek. The vain female scholar is a popular stereotype in Restoration and eighteenth-century drama – though, to be sure, pedants of either sex were likely to be ridiculed. Behn does little to mitigate the usual hostile portrait of this ageing scholar, too stupid to see that the young man she fancies is devoting his attention to her daughter. She may come off better than the hypochondriac old alderman, but only, one suspects, because Behn has lost interest in her. The play illustrates how Behn, within one and the same play, maintained a traditionally misogynic view yet, on the other hand, presented a much kinder and sympathetic portrait of an adulteress than is the wont.

   Sir Patient Fancy has also been read as a political satire, with hypochondria as a metaphor for the political sickness of the Whigs.[33] Attacks on the political opponent, indeed, occur in many of her plays, most pronouncedly, of course, in her two political comedies, *The Roundheads* and *The City Heiress*, both performed at the Duke's Theatre in 1682. Both represent overt pieces of agit-prop, painting the Whigs and Puritans as greedy, treasonous hypocrites. *The Roundheads, or The Good Old Cause* is set in the times of the Commonwealth, though aimed at Shaftesbury and his Popish Plot, and tries to discredit the regicides by retelling various authentic and apocryphal tales. It shows how the hypocritical Puritan wives start amorous affairs with two Cavaliers while their supposedly republican husbands are quarrelling over who is to become the new king. One of these women is a royalist at heart and supposedly admirable for refusing to commit adultery. But the sang-froid with which she confesses that she married her husband only to restore his estate to her lover and is eagerly awaiting his death renders her an unpleasant character. The other, Lady Lambert, Cromwell's ex-mistress, already gives herself the airs of a queen, but is converted into believing that the Cavaliers are angels and the king a saint. It is hard to see what the royalist courtier sees in her; it would have taken a Horner or a Rover to make his purely sensual appetite convincing.

The City Heiress, or Sir Timothy Treat-All introduces the Whig leader Shaftesbury in the guise of Sir Timothy, who constantly intrigues against the monarchy but negotiates with Polish ambassadors for the crown. Several of the scandalous details ascribed to Sir Timothy are historical facts, but the charges of treason are hardly dramatised in the text. All that can really be levelled against Sir Timothy is that he disinherits his rakish nephew Wilding for his Tory sympathies. In the course of the action Wilding foists his old mistress on his Whig uncle, breaks into the latter's house to steal money and treasonous papers, sleeps with a merry widow, whom another suitor then bullies into marriage, and in the end weds an heiress. However, it is not this heiress who is the centre of female interest, but the widow, whose complete defeat the spectator cannot but regret. Indeed, the comedy turns decidedly ugly in the end. Unlike Willmore, Wilding is not a figure of fun, but cold-blooded and calculating, a libertine who unscrupulously boasts of his conquest of the widow, confirming Julia's fear in *The Lucky Chance* that an indiscretion will put a woman into her lover's power. The play is indeed very explicit as to the favour she has granted him:

> WILDING: I saw how at her length she lay!
> I saw her rising Bosome bare! ...
> Her loose thin Robes, through which appear
> A Shape design'd for Love and Play!
> (V/i/61)

In the end Wilding takes the heiress for her money only, with no pretence at self-reform. The widow's marriage to another man shortly after her night with Wilding could have represented a deserved debunking of the rake, but is actually turned into the misogynist coercion of an unwilling bride into a loveless union. In fact, the ending contains the seeds of future distrust, deception and marital strife.

The Younger Brother, or The Amorous Jilt, staged, after Behn's death, at Drury Lane in 1696, was also conceived as a political comedy, but the political references were omitted by the editor as they were no longer topical. What is left is a rather weak play about a faithless beauty who jilts the hero and casts her eyes on a prince. By her craftiness she manages to fool her lovers for a while, until they realise her true character and give her up in disgust. The hero is supposed to marry an old dragon, but weds her granddaughter instead, whom his father had earmarked for himself. Deprived of political satire, the drunken mumblings of the buffoons, namely the cuckolded husband and the hero's elder brother, are merely trite and vulgar, and the geriatric would-be lovers are completely stereotypical.

The Emperor of the Moon (Dorset Garden, 1687) leaves the world of intrigue comedy for sumptuous operatic spectacle, mixed with farcical low-life scenes from the commedia dell'arte. In this pleasant masque cum farce a foolish doctor, who is convinced that there are inhabitants on the moon and keeps his daughter and niece hidden from mortals to preserve them for lunar suitors, is duped by the girls' lovers, who, with the help of their servants, Scaramouch and Harlequin, gain entrance to the house under various pretences and finally make off with the girls, disguised as the Emperor of the Moon and Prince Thunderland. The play makes use of elaborate sets and stage machinery and was one of Behn's most successful works, popular way into the eighteenth century.

What, then, is distinctive about Behn's style? Critics have frequently pointed out that the theme of forced marriages dominates her work. A young couple in love outwitting parents or guardians is, of course, a stereotypical comic motif, but the fact that 11 of her plays are more or less prominently concerned with an enforced marriage (*The Forc'd Marriage; The Dutch Lover; The Town Fop; Abdelazar; The Rover I* and *II; The Feigned Courtesans; The Lucky Chance; The False Count; Sir Patient Fancy; The City Heiress*) suggests a personal interest in the issue. Also characteristic seems to be her creation of strong, independent-minded active heroines, who are given a degree of control of the action far beyond the usual influence exerted by a witty Restoration female protagonist, and are allowed to shape their own fates instead of merely responding to male manoeuvres. Euphemia in *The Dutch Lover*, Hellena in *The Rover I*, and La Nuche in *The Rover II*, Cornelia in *The Feigned Courtesans*, Julia in *The Lucky Chance*, the amorous jilt in the play of this title, and the Widow Ranter manipulate the men who, for all their courage and amorous intrigues, seem content to follow the girls' suggestions. It is this predilection for dominant, self-determined women characters that was to prove specifically attractive to Behn's female successors. This is not to say, however, that every Behn play features a dominant woman, or that every active heroine can, in fact, successfully take her life into her own hands (see, for instance, *The City Heiress*, *Abdelazar*, *The Young King*).

Most of Behn's witty heroines conform to the sexual norms of their time and merely pretend to be promiscuous, carefully guarding their virginity until they have obtained the legal security of marriage. Although Behn shows that women who are not so circumspect and cautious are likely to suffer on the marriage market, she is unusually sympathetic to sexual sinners, occasionally letting them escape unscathed and in a few instances even turning them into likeable heroines.

Like many women dramatists, Behn generally allowed her female characters more space to establish their view of events, and although she did not concentrate on female friendships as markedly as Centlivre was to do a few decades later, her women help and tease one another and occasionally jealously intrigue against one another just as her men do. The misogynist glee in putting down women and the reduction of love to a power game in an all-male hierarchy are conspicuously absent from her work. Dryden admired that she 'so well cou'd love's kind Passion paint'.[34] She could appreciate and portray convincingly the erotic appeal of a libertine, yet her rakish heroes are often presented with a mixture of accolade and ridicule, as glamorous sexual predators and buffoons at the same time, as both appealing and destructive. In all cases, however, she is on the side of the Cavaliers when it comes to exploiting, humiliating and punishing the Whiggish, Puritan middle class. A bourgeois in her play is always old and semi-senile, stupid and often miserly, vain of his political privileges and potentially treasonous, and regarded as fair game for cuckoldry.

In view of these characteristics, the four anonymous plays frequently ascribed to Behn seem at best collaborative efforts to which she may have contributed some scenes or characters. The boisterous girl who escapes from a forced marriage in male disguise in *The*

Woman Turn'd Bully (Dorset Garden, 1675) is more reminiscent of Polwhele's *The Frolicks* than of Behn's witty heroines, though the hard-drinking and smoking, eccentric mother vaguely links up with the Widow Ranter in her posthumous play of the same name. The ridicule heaped on the indiscriminate drunken exploits of the libertine in *The Debauchee; or, the Credulous Cuckold* (Dorset Garden, 1677), an adaptation of Brome's *Mad Couple Well Match'd*, corresponds to the ambiguous portrayal of the Rover and similar rakes, though the title figure is more vulgar than the usual Behn hero. The virtuous wife, who forgives her husband his infidelity and even cheats the whore out of the money he gave her, is a character worthy of Behn, but the figure of the credulous cuckold is again more related to *The Frolicks*, since Behn does not usually suggest that an unchaste wife ought to be suppressed to prevent her from deceiving her husband. *The Counterfeit Bridegroom, or the Defeated Widow* (Duke's Theatre, 1677) is least typical of Behn, both in the figure of the boorish rake who bears the (albeit false) charge of incest with surprising equanimity and in that of the woman who tricks a widow into marriage and substitutes her brother for the groom on the wedding night. The glee and brutality with which this widow is treated by both the woman and her brother would be surprising in a Behn play. *The Revenge, or a Match in Newgate* characteristically refuses to demonise the figure of the whore who tries to avenge herself on double-dealing males, but contains scenes in Newgate alien to Behn's style.

When Behn died in 1689, she had blazed a trail into a territory hitherto considered an all-male province. Nobody could doubt any longer that it could be done – that a woman could be as successful in writing for the stage as any man. Henceforth, women playwrights could go alternative ways, with some of them following Behn in boldly emulating male styles, while others resorted to Orinda's strategy of appeasing critics by domesticity, moral earnest and feminine sensibility. Yet the role model Behn provided also proved a heavy burden, because for centuries it linked the name of a female dramatist with that of a whore, and warned disciples what kind of personal abuse they had to expect if they embarked on 'unfeminine' subjects or expressions. In the following centuries, the reputation of the racy Restoration women playwrights discouraged respectable women from associating themselves with the theatre, and rendered those who did morally suspect.

4
Women Dramatists at the Turn of the Century

The 1680s and early 1690s were a difficult time for dramatists. Political unrest, from the Popish Plot to the Glorious Revolution in 1688, caused a sharp drop in theatre attendance, about which Behn complained in her Prologue to *The Feigned Courtesans*. William III showed no interest in the stage and had no intention of renewing the patronage of his predecessors. The King's Company collapsed in 1682 owing to financial mismanagement and merged with the Duke's Company to become the United Company, leaving the market for new plays extremely limited. Behn herself had been forced to find other sources of income and had started to write novels. After her death in 1689, it took six years before a play by a new woman dramatist was performed on a London stage. The situation improved only when the United Company split up in 1695, and Betterton led a group of star actors to Lincoln's Inn Field. The sudden new competition between the two playhouses revived the flagging market and also led to a spectacular upsurge in women dramatists in the 11 years between 1695 and 1706.

Playwrights at the turn of the century, however, found themselves in a different climate and were forced to cater to changed fashions and audience tastes. Criticism and theatrical reception often centred more on issues of morality than on literary merit. Already in the 1680s the immorality of Restoration comedy had been sharply attacked. Indeed, Wycherley's *The Country Wife* had been booed as early as 1675, and Behn had to defend herself against audience protests for her sex comedies *The Lucky Chance* and *Sir Patient Fancy*. She put these attacks down to the ubiquitous double sexual standard, which censured in women what it tolerated in men. But in fact the immorality of the English stage in general was increasingly criticised in these decades, long before Jeremy Collier published his notorious pamphlet. There is some indication that the ladies in the audience themselves increasingly objected to bawdy plays.[35] On the other hand, female delicacy may also have been used by moralists as a pretext to crack down on the stage. By the middle of the 1690s, the voices calling for moral reform could no longer be disregarded, and dramatists had begun to 'purify' their plays in response to the new demands. The fashion for sex comedies and cuckolding plots came to an abrupt end, and dramatists now tended to emphasise character reform and innate good-naturedness. Forewords and addresses to the audience brim over with assurances that the new play will not offend chaste ears and will provide harmless entertainment which nobody need blush about.

Female playwrights were particularly anxious to exonerate themselves from the charge of immorality, since such attacks inevitably had repercussions on their personal reputations, which were inextricably linked to the kind of fictitious material they presented on stage. Hostility against women dramatists continued unabated, and defamations were as commonplace as in Behn's time. In this situation it is, perhaps, understandable that so many women should have opted for tragedy, which was a genre generally believed to be more fitted for women dramatists on moral grounds. Besides, Betterton's company of star actors specialised in tragedy, whereas Drury Lane produced more comedies, and since many of the new women dramatists took their plays to the rebel company and wrote their plays with particular famous actors, especially actresses, in mind, it is only natural that they should have produced what was in demand there. In hindsight, their choice was unfortunate. Most of them misjudged their own talents, which were not for tragedy – very few good tragedies were written between 1660 and 1800 – and they could have created lively enough comedies instead of the turgid moralising dramas they tended to crank out.

The first woman playwright to surface after the long silence was the anonymous 'Ariadne' with *She Ventures and He Wins*, a 'reformed' comedy chosen for the opening of Betterton's new theatre at Lincoln's Inn Fields in 1695. It turned out a failure, and its diffident, unknown author, who in the Preface had depreciated her play as 'the error of a weak woman's pen', with an 'infinite number of faults', seems to have disappeared from the theatrical world. Structurally, the play is weak, combining a main plot full of refined sensibilities with a slapstick sub-plot about a lewd squire subjected to all kinds of farcical punishments by the vintner's wife he tries to seduce. What is of interest, however, is the figure of the rich heiress, who, like Behn's adventuresses, sets out to find herself a husband in the disguise of a woman of questionable morals. Unlike Behn's Hellena or Cornelia, however, she is interested in moral uprightness, in goodness of heart, rather than animal magnetism. Indeed, the play reverses the traditional pattern in that the hero is tested for *his* (sexual) virtue, and the heroine makes her acceptance contingent on how he acquits himself in these ordeals. The disguise of a loose woman is not used to entice a randy rake, but to test the suitor's devotion and find out whether he loves her for herself or for her money. The male paragon ignores the amorous advances of other women and continues to be enamoured of his beautiful incognita, although he suspects she is a whore. The reader may wonder at Ariadne's unconscious motivations for subjecting her male protagonist to such cruel generic humiliations before rewarding his constancy with a rich and devoted wife. In any case, this reversal of gender roles, which allots to women the position of arbiters subjecting their suitors to all kinds of tests, turned out to be extremely popular with female dramatists and was imitated and varied throughout the eighteenth century.

The Female Wits
Delarivier Manley
The term 'Female Wits' was originally used in a derogatory sense in an anonymous satire of this title on the three prominent women dramatists of the time, Delarivier Manley, Catherine Trotter and Mary Pix. Since Fidelis Morgan used the name as a title for her anthology of female playwrights, however, the term has come to be more widely and positively used. As opposed to 'Ariadne's' short-lived theatrical career, these three dramatists enjoyed more enduring success (which was probably the reason why they were

singled out as satirical targets) and explicitly aspired to fill the
female laureateship vacant after Behn's death. Of the three, Delarivier
Manley modelled herself most closely on Behn's image, writing as
'scandalously' and sexually explicitly as her great predecessor. She
was the precocious daughter of a Cavalier, who had been tricked
into a bigamous marriage by her cousin and left to bear the consequences. For a time she attracted the attention of the notorious
Duchess of Cleveland, in whose house she may have heard much of
the sexual gossip that later stood her in good stead in her writing.
Her reputation having been ruined beyond repair, she openly flaunted
her amours and made a commercial success of *romans à clef* about
the love lives of the Whig upper crust. Her narrative *New Atlantis*
was so notorious that Pope in his *Rape of the Lock* used it as a
yardstick for eternity: 'as long as *Atalantis* will be read'. Indeed, 250
years later, Winston Churchill was still smarting from the scandal
heaped by Mrs Manley on his Whig ancestor, Marlborough, and
wished he could toss her 'back to the cesspool from which she
crawled'.[36] Manley was also a successful journalist, a Tory pam-
phleteer and a much feared political satirist, both appreciated and
deplored by famous contemporaries such as Steele, Swift and Pope.

Her dramatic output is small – only four plays have survived,
while two have been lost – and regarded by most critics as irremedi-
ably bad. From a feminist point of view, however, at least two of her
tragedies merit closer analysis, as they endow women characters
with a political power, control over language and sexual dynamism
usually denied them in the plays of the time. Her only comedy, *The
Lost Lover, or The Jealous Husband* (Drury Lane, 1696), however, sometimes praised for its sympathetic treatment of a cast-off mistress, is,
in fact, quite misogynist and tends to endorse the male outlook. Although some justified complaints are put into the mouth of the jilted
woman, she is finally dismissed as impure and lecherous ('Thy liking
was foul Lust, not Love', III/27). The faithless rake, on the other
hand, is turned into a man of honour who will not expose an 'ill
Woman, tho' to make [him]self happy in a good' (V/37) and who can
afford a few sentimental remarks of contrition on her fate when he
has secured his aim of marrying the heiress. In the second plot, another libertine fails to seduce an honest woman and decides to chase
new game, namely a foolish poetess significantly called Orinda – a
hint at what Mrs Manley thought of the other available, more staid,
role model.

The Royal Mischief (withdrawn by the author from Drury Lane after a quarrel with the actors and successfully performed by Betterton's company at Lincoln's Inn Fields in 1696) deserves closer attention: it is one of the very rare plays in which female sexual desire is expressed in a candid, completely unabashed way and in which an author actually feels sympathy with a sexually aggressive woman, usually portrayed as a ridiculous or threatening figure in the tragedy of the time. Locked up in a castle by her jealous old husband, the Prince of Libardian, the lascivious Princess Homais falls in love with a picture of her husband's nephew, Levan Dadian, who has just concluded a political marriage with the virtuous princess Bassima. Homais lures Levan to the castle to seduce him. At the same time the Vizier Osman vainly entreats Bassima to yield to his passion. Notwithstanding, Levan sentences his innocent wife and her supposed lover to death, while Homais, to make sure her enemies are eliminated, plans to have Bassima poisoned and her own husband murdered by a former lover. Her husband, however, arrests her, but allows her time to repent before executing her. She uses this reprieve to join forces with Levan and rid herself of the hated Bassima and Osman. At Homais' moment of triumph, her husband reappears and runs her through with a sword. Like a Jacobean villain, she dies glorying in the carnage she has caused, and Levan falls on his sword.

Of course, the tragedy lends itself to ridicule for some of its excesses and absurdities of plot, though exaggerated passions and rant are the bane of many tragedies of the time. To be sure, the structuring is laborious: Manley needs almost two acts to set up the exposition and explain the various amorous involvements of the dramatis personae, and then hurries over the conflict in a ridiculously swift manner. Levan, for all his renowned virtue, offers no significant resistance to seduction, but falls prostrate at Homais' feet on first seeing her. The timing of the Vizier's sexual advances towards the virtuous Bassima is outrageous: he urges her to sleep with him when she is already writhing with the effects of poison and her enemies are breaking down the door – 'rather a necrophiliac touch'.[37] Thereupon he is used as a human cannon ball, his wife lovingly gathering up the smoking remains – a grotesque method of execution which, one suspects, was meant to top all previous stage deaths but which was actually authentic and taken from the source *The Travels of Sir John Chardin into Persia and the East-Indies.*

And yet, for all its excesses and bungled blank verse, the play is highly theatrical and indeed enjoyed a good six days' run when it came out. It is not surprising, however, that at a time when the immorality of the English stage was the target of increased censure, a play so sensual and outspoken on sexual issues should also have provoked controversy. Mrs Manley tells us in the Preface to the printed edition that the 'ladies' in the audience took issue with the 'warmth' of its language – opposition which she, like Behn before her, put down to the double standards in morality. In her Preface Manley cites Dryden's *Aureng-Zebe* and *The Double Distress* and Southerne's *Oroonoko* as evidence that descriptions of the joys of physical love were quite acceptable, provided they were written by a man. Yet none of these writers comes near being so explicit in his presentation of the female libido. What is remarkable in *The Royal Mischief* is not only the fiery description of a woman's sexual desire itself, but the ambiguous attitude the author takes to her lustful queen. Restoration playwrights generally expend little sympathy on lusting women who nourish illicit, and even incestuous, desires and take the initiative in propositioning a man. Homais' unabashed sensuality, however, places her at the pinnacle of manipulative power and does not expose her to the exploitation and humiliation at the hands of her lovers which is a common fate even for royal villainesses – compare, for instance, Behn's *Abdelazar*. It seems to be one of the problems of *The Royal Mischief* that it transgresses the boundaries between the genres and, despite its murder plot, draws the old Prince of Libardian as the comic stereotype of a jealous old husband with a lusty young wife – with all the attendant manipulation of sympathy in the latter's favour – before it unexpectedly shifts to reinstate him as the regal voice of authority.

Throughout the play Manley reverses gender roles: Homais is the sexual predator and Levan becomes the object of her desire. Like an impatient Restoration rake, she will 'push the bold adventure on, / And either die or conquer' (I/214); her flame can only 'with possession be abased' (I/215). Neither the term *conquer* nor the term *possession* for the sexual act were generally used by women, since they imply a power relationship between active and passive, subject and object in which women are traditionally cast as conquests, not as sexual conquerors. Homais assumes the male role and male diction, while Levan, in contrast, is presented in imagery traditionally reserved for women, as 'a soil so barren' (I/213). By borrowing behaviour, values and language from the Restoration rake, Homais stakes out a claim to equality which profoundly undermines the Puritan ideology of self-denial, the masculinising of desire, the creation of woman as *other* and as object, and the belief in the indivisibility of chastity and feminine identity.[38] In opposition, the virtuous Bassima has internalised sexual discipline: chastity and an immaculate reputation are second nature to her, indeed dearer than life itself, so she refuses to yield to the man she loves illicitly.

Instead of her lovers losing interest and abandoning their royal mistress after intercourse, it is Homais who contemptuously sends them packing. Here is the remarkable scene in which she tells her ex-lover, Ismael, who reminds her of the ecstasies they have shared, with unruffled candour that his services are no longer in demand:

> ISMAEL: ... Methinks you should not, sure, so far forget
>   Those moments, sacred to our love and me,
>   When close you grasped me – at your new found joys
>   An unbeliever till you proved the wonder,
>   And felt the mighty ecstasy approach –
>   Then swore, whatever royal lover should
>   Succeed, you never would forget the first
>   Discoverer.
> HOMAIS: ... Oh, did you know the difference
>   Between a new-born passion, and a former!
>   Nothing remains but memory and wonder,
>   Not the least warmth of kind desire or joy.
>   Nay, scarce can we believe, or make that faith
>   A miracle, how we could dote, as they reproach we did,
>   How love so much, that which at present seems unlovely.
>   (IV/240f.)

Again, the speakers' roles are completely reversed: the man takes the part of the forsaken, pleading paramour, the traditional role of innumerable betrayed virgins and cast-off mistresses. Homais, in turn, uses the very arguments which the Restoration libertines employed to shed their conquests. What is amazing in the play is the graphic explicitness and candour with which the female libido is described.

HOMAIS: What? To conceal desire when every
    Atom of me trembles with it! I'll strip
    My passion naked of such guile, lay it
    Undressed and panting at his feet, then try
    If all his temper can resist it.

                        (III/231)

Although this speech might suggest the traditional female postures of humility, self-sacrifice and the female body as a gift, Homais' active part in the seduction subverts any idea of female submissiveness and supine acquiescence and transforms these passive female roles into active instruments of seduction. Indeed, when he has kissed her, Levan sinks to *her* feet.

Although Manley presents the villainous heroine as charismatically attractive and largely refrains from moral comment, she is willing to appease the audience with a conventional ending and, in the Preface, justifies the four and a half acts of indulgence towards Homais by the punishment meted out to her in the last scene – a punishment not found in the historical source. No doubt it would have been unwise for female playwrights, who were frequently censured for their ignorance of the classical rules, to take issue with such entrenched norms as poetic justice; besides, Manley is much more subversive even in this ending than is obvious at first sight. Homais remains unrepentant till the very end, with her dying breath disdaining her 'effeminate' (V/259) accomplices and trying to strangle Levan so that they can continue their orgy in hell. In his moralising conclusion the Prince of Libardian exonerates his nephew, who committed incest with Homais and shed innocent blood, from all guilt – 'thy faults ... were fate's, not yours' (V/260) – and the dying Levan views himself as a victim of 'Beauty ... by whose enchantments all my glories fade / And innocence, unwary, is betrayed' (V/261). Responsibility for all the horror is heaped solely on women, the temptresses – a vision which ties in with the tenor of pathetic tragedy, viewing unchaste women as harbingers of death and dissension and as scapegoats.[39] But here this is an entirely inappropriate moral conclusion, which highlights the hypocritical strategy of demonising female sexuality. Instead of bringing the moral issues of the play into sharp focus, the sententious verse lines once more expose the double standard Manley has attacked throughout the play[40] and from which she herself suffered all her life.

After the attack on her in *The Female Wits*, occasioned by *The Royal Mischief*, Manley withdrew from the theatre for a long time, made a name for herself in journalism and fiction, and returned to the stage only in 1706 with *Almyna, or The Arabian Vow* (Haymarket), one of the first plays in English to be based on the *Arabian Nights*. After her previous experiences she was wary of having a play performed under her own name. The Epilogue pretends that the author is a man, and it was only in the printed version that she acknowledged authorship. *Almyna* reflects Manley's persistent faults: too slow in build-up, wordy, ranting and digressive. What is remarkable, however, is again the character of Almyna, the heroine, who, by her argumentative power and unflinching courage, convinces the sultan that women do have souls and makes him forswear his cruel vow to forestall cuckoldom by killing each new wife on the morning after the wedding. In intellect, Almyna easily matches the sultan, who has hitherto regarded women as 'Born to no other end, but propagation' (I/i/13) and sneered at women's education as 'a contradiction, to [their] very Nature' (I/i/10). In order to convince him of the opposite, Almyna adopts the real-life feminists' strategy of enumerating examples of famous women like Semiramis, Judith and Cleopatra. Impressed by the fortitude with which she prepares to meet death, while her father rants and weeps, the sultan pardons her and gives up his cruel practice. Almyna is strong and self-sufficient; she does not need the help of the sultan's brother, who is enamoured of her and dies trying to save her, together with the bride he has forsaken – a tragic conclusion which had to be changed into a happy ending for performance. Although the play champions women's equal mental capacities and rights to education, Almyna is seen as a glorious exception, the product of careful education by her father, rather than the norm. She is willing to sacrifice her own life to cure her beloved sovereign of his distrust and hatred of women. In the anonymous play *The Faithful General*, performed in the same year, a similarly intellectual woman character disdains to rush into the arms of a man capable of such misogyny, no matter how physically attractive she finds him. *Almyna* may show that Manley 'could have written at a respectable level for the theater had she chosen to',[41] but is less exciting and subversive than the notorious *The Royal Mischief*.

Manley's tendency towards sentimentality takes over completely in her last, very weak play, *Lucius, the First Christian King of Britain*

(Drury Lane, 1717). The political situation in this pseudo-historical tragedy, with its complicated intrigues and disguises, is confusing and unclear. Of course, the actions of all the characters are invariably motivated by love – a Restoration and eighteenth-century cliché, though no more convincing for that. It is the most conservative of Manley's plays in that it allows women no active influence on events and casts them solely in the roles of virtue in distress – significantly, the heroine is a captive queen – jealous rivals or disappointed maidens suffering the pangs of unrequited love. Unlike *The Royal Mischief*, action is exclusively initiated by the men contending for the queen, beauty personified, who is in constant danger of being abducted, raped or slandered, and is finally rescued at the point of death by the hero, who was stupid enough to be fooled by forged evidence of her faithlessness for half the play. The ups and downs of he who is in possession of the precious captive are as confusing as they are illogical and afford plenty of space for ranting heroics as well as succulent perversions. Thus the villainous king means to disguise himself as an executioner to have the pleasure of ravishing and torturing the object of his affections:

> Let Nations wonder at the horrid Deed;
> Let all the Monarchs of the World unite,
> To pour down Vengeance on our guilty Head,
> We'll meet the Torrent, when we've quench'd our Flame!
> Yes, Rosalind! thy Beauties are devoted,
> Thro' Laws we wade, to reach thy cruel Arms,
> Thro' thy own Blood to taste thy boasted Charms.
>
> (V/49)

In the best – or rather, worst – tragi-comic fashion, the hero kills his own scoundrel father disguised as the executioner, only to learn on the very last page that this tyrant was not his parent after all, but his father's murderer, and instead of committing the sin of patricide he has done a very commendable deed and can, now he has killed all his rivals, live happily ever after with the rescued queen. *Lucius* shows not only Manley's dramatic powers to be burnt out, but also her will to make a feminist stand.

The Court Legacy (1733), a ballad opera purporting to have been written 'By the Author of the *New Atlantis*', merely cashes in on the notoriety of her erotic novel. Ballad opera was a genre unknown during Manley's lifetime, and the play also refers to political events happening after her death in 1724.

It is easy to criticise Manley's drama for its many faults – the laborious structuring, irregular versification, histrionic speeches and predilection for weird perversions and overwrought emotions. Yet *The Royal Mischief* and *Almyna* make effective theatre, and are highly unusual from a feminist point of view. Quite generally, Manley was the most outspokenly feminist of the Female Wits, but like Behn she was inconsistent, vacillating in her prefaces and prologues between self-confidence and timidity, between acceptance that 'Writing for the Stage is no way proper for a Woman, to whom all Advantages by meer Nature are refused' (Preface to *The Lost Lover*) and the furious assertion that her gender was the sole reason for the unkind reception of a play (Preface to *The Royal Mischief*). She was as fickle in her friendships as in her literary poses. She wrote laudatory verses for Trotter's *Agnes de Castro*, but in her novel sniggered at her former friend's love affairs, yet Trotter still contributed to a collection of poems that Manley edited. Like so many female playwrights of the time, Manley is contradictory and inconsistent in her stance, hence impossible to pigeonhole.

Catherine Trotter

Catherine Trotter is much less ambiguous in her attitudes. She came from an impoverished but genteel family, taught herself French and Latin, and seems to have prided herself on her intellect, for which she was lampooned in *The Female Wits*. After her marriage to a clergyman, unsurprisingly, she gave up writing for the stage, but throughout her life she remained in contact with literary celebrities, from her mentor Congreve, to John Locke, whose *Essay Concerning Human Understanding* she defended in a treatise, to Leibnitz, with whom she corresponded. Her moralistic and didactic concerns are obvious in her plays, which formed part of the contemporary campaign against vice in the theatre. Since her aim was moral edification, she thought tragedy most appropriate for her purpose.

Her first play, *Agnes de Castro*, was staged anonymously in 1695 at Drury Lane, when Trotter was only 16 years old. As a novice, she was probably saddled with a prologue and epilogue written by one of her mentors, which coyly played the feminine card and capitalised on the sex appeal of the unknown 'young lady', poses entirely alien to Trotter. The tragedy draws on one of Behn's novellas for its plot, which, possibly, accounts for its brisk pace and lively character drawing. It deals with a prince's adulterous love for Agnes, which gives rise to a spurt of jealousies resulting in the killing of the princess, whom a jealous rival, Elvira, mistakes for Agnes, and the death of the heroine herself in a melée between the prince and his Macchiavellian antagonist. There is a whiff of Jacobean horror tragedy in the villain's plan to rape Agnes in order to quench his love–hate relationship and in the murderess going mad after committing the deed. However, the play also predates the eighteenth-century fashion of 'she-tragedies' in focusing on the undeserved tragic fate of two virtuous heroines, Agnes and the princess, who remain close friends despite competing for the prince's love.[42] What is also remarkable in so young a writer is the unsentimental note at the end, which leaves the desperate prince not in the throes of a heroic death but with the need to face life soberly.

> KING: Hop'd you to live in Luxury and Ease,
>   Courted by Joys, and Pleasures without end?
>   Did you ne'r hear of Pains, and Cares, in Life? …
>   Were Nature constant she'd destroy herself,
>   So strong her Motions they'd overthrow her,
>   But fiercest Transports, soonest moderate grow,
>   Thus to our Frailty, we our Safety owe.
>
>   (V/i/47)

The Fatal Friendship, performed at Lincoln's Inn Fields in 1698, in the same month as Collier's *Short View* came out, again went to Behn for inspiration, this time extracting the melodramatic plot from her play *The Town Fop*, while leaving out the comic sub-plot with its amusing brothel scenes. Although this was Trotter's most successful play, which moved the audience to tears, it is, in fact, a weak piece, a showcase of all the hazards affective tragedy, according to Laura Brown, is likely to run into.[43] Since it sets out to present virtue in distress and the sufferings of innocence rather than villainies or tragic faults, all the dramatis personae have to be basically good at heart, which leaves no possibility for dramatic conflict, unless it be based on chance, fate or character inconsistency – all of which are employed to excess.

The impoverished Gramont, secretly married to Felicia and bound to Castalio by friendship and gratitude, feels constrained to marry, bigamously, the rich widow Lamira in order to aid his family and friend. Everything seems to conspire against the hero: his baby child has been kidnapped by pirates, his friend is languishing in prison and his father refuses to provide money. This unlikely succession of horrible strokes of fate, together with the conviction that nothing will thaw the cold hearts of the couple's relatives and the code of honour requiring him to save his friend, force him to take so desperate a step. Thus Trotter, in fact, tries to sell us bigamy as a disinterested, high-minded act. The weak hero merely bemoans his fate without taking the initiative to change the course of events and actually believes he can get away with marrying a second wife without ever sleeping with her. Indeed, he claims that he sinned only out of excessive love for his first wife. If he did, he had a strange way of showing it, for it almost breaks her heart when she learns of his apparent infidelity. The passionate second wife, on the other hand, cannot forgive the scruples which kept him from consummating the marriage and from ruining her completely, which she takes as disdain for her female desirability and seductiveness and finds much more wounding than the deceitful marriage. So she turns villainess and tries to avenge herself by estranging the legitimate couple from one another. In its picture of women, the play incorporates the typical antitheses of affective tragedy, contrasting the long-suffering wife, ever faithful and forgiving, to the sexually voracious and vindictive woman. Not surprisingly, the hero prefers the submissive figure to the aggressive one. As the genre, however, generally endows all dramatic figures with a basic goodness of heart, the villainess must in the end show pity and renounce the world, just as the indomitable relatives, once Gramont has committed suicide, turn out to be the most tender-hearted and compassionate of men, when a minute before they appeared so tyrannical and unforgiving. The very bloodshed that leads to the deaths of the two men whose fatal friendship the title refers to is the result of chance. Castalio has actually forgiven Gramont for his betrayal of Lamira, whom he secretly loved himself, but when trying to prevent his brother-in-law from attacking his friend, the hero accidentally wounds the latter, a tragic accident which renders him an innocent murderer just as he was an innocent bigamist. Such absurd coincidences, however, deprive the play of all moral significance and turn it into an illustration of the malice of fate. Indeed, *fate, fatal, fateful* and so on are by far the most frequently used words in the whole play. Friendship, marriage, love, quarrels, secrets are all equally fated.

Trotter's object, quite clearly, is to elicit a tearful response from the audience. The otherwise colourless language teems with pathetic stereotypes, evocations of abject misery, destitute children and lovers starving in hovels, and is replete with repetitions, exclamations and sighs.

> GRAMONT: ... Where should I fly? To poor Felicia's arms,
> She's kind, and will be fond to share my misery.
>   ... Cruel thought!
> Must I behold that tender part of me,
> Exposed to all th' extremities of want,
> My helpless infant asking food in vain?
> Oh fate! Oh Heaven! you cannot mean it.
> They're innocent: how, how have we deserved your anger?
>   (II/i/161)

> GRAMONT: ... But can I take thee hence, to see thee perish
> Under the extremities of griping wants
> Thou hast not felt, and can'st not apprehend?
> The smallest of those hardships, to which thou would'st
>   expose
> Thy tender body, does far surpass thy strength.
> FELICIA: Love will supply my strength, and as I can,
> I'll labour for our food, or beg an alms,
> And we shall find some friendly barn to shelter us
> At night, whilst we repose our weary limbs....
> Sometimes perhaps your sleep may be disturbed
> By a poor hungry infant's cries....
>   (V/i/195f.)

In an attempt to wrest moral significance from the plot, Trotter gratuitously makes a messenger bring the king's pardon for the two friends the very moment Gramont has stabbed himself to expiate his unintentional crimes, as an awful warning that, had the hero only waited patiently, divine providence would have solved all problems for him. One only wonders why providence was so tardy in the first place.

Still more preposterous, even by Restoration standards generally complacent about the logic of didactic endings, is the moralising conclusion to *The Unhappy Penitent* (Drury Lane, 1701). The pseudo-historical tragedy centres on Margarite of Flanders, betrothed to the French king but in love with another man, while the king, who has also ceased to desire her, perversely feels honour bound to wed her the moment she asks to be free. He is supported in this unreasonable attitude by his new love, Anne of Brittany, a woman we are supposed to admire as high minded but whose sanctimonious masochism is bent on making herself and others unhappy. Nonetheless, Margarite secretly marries her lover, who, of course, immediately believes the false accusations brought against her by a traitor, who hopes to wed her himself, but who in the end confesses the fraud. By that time, however, the heroine has vowed she will enter a convent should her honour be restored, and she must now tear herself away from her husband as a punishment for her rashness and sensuality. The moral conclusions are all false and haphazard: the lovers are not unhappy because they have followed their passions, but because they have let themselves be duped by a villain. Again, Trotter tries to make us believe that providence would have intervened had they only patiently postponed their marriage, but then one must assume that the traitor would never have confessed his treason as long as he could hope to blackmail Margarite into becoming his wife. Besides, the smug self-satisfaction of the king, who has constantly wavered in his affection but now feels rewarded by heaven, seems more offensive than the courage and honest passion of the heroine.

The Revolution in Sweden (Haymarket, 1706) again has an unequivocal didactic purpose, but is a more interesting play because of its political subject matter at a time when tragedies were becoming increasingly domesticated. Quite unusually, matters of state are not subordinated to love interests, but, on the contrary, take precedence over them. In the play the heroic Swedes, rising up to free their country, are very virtuous, while the Danish occupiers and, appropriately for a Whig writer, the Catholic clergy are very wicked. Trotter's mentor, Congreve, in a letter tactfully tried to alert her to structural weaknesses, though she seems largely to have disregarded his suggestions.[44] Some of the incidents, such as the noble Arwide's signing of an agreement he is too trustful to read through, are indeed preposterous, though Congreve's advice does not mention this particular scene. However, the fact that Arwide's wife, when informed of the infamous treaty, puts patriotism above love and accuses him of treason is a very unusual action for a female figure and allows her a share in political life greater than the custom of the time, even in the times of Queen Anne. There is also a second woman who is a fervent supporter of the revolution and, disregarding her villainous husband's commands, joins the rebel forces in male disguise. The foremost thoughts of these two women are for the freedom of their country, and they are meant to serve as patriotic ideals, even in the eyes of the husband accused by his own wife:

> ARWIDE: Yes, my Constantia, thy exalted Vertue
> Constrain'd my Admiration, tho' a Sufferer by it.
> Oh wou'd Men emulate thy great Example.
>   (V/71)

Trotter wrote only one comedy, *Love at a Loss, or Most Votes Carry It*, performed unsuccessfully at Drury Lane in 1700 and dismissed by modern critics, but which, for all her disclaimers in the Dedication that she has no talent for the genre, is actually more effective than her moralising tragedies. The play reverses the standard situation of Restoration comedy by making the women inconstant and flirtatious, deceiving the men, while all the time the male characters are priding themselves on their circumspection. Lucilia has flirted with a fop, but she manages to fool her betrothed into believing that the love letters were written by her maid and that he has wronged her by his distrust. The rake Beaumine thinks that his betrothed Lesbia, whom he has seduced, is a mere puppet on a string, while in fact she has another iron in the fire. The witty Miranda, whom he tries to play off against Lesbia, refuses to engage in female rivalry and instead helps her friend, hiding her in the closet, even at the danger of losing her own faithful admirer – a motif Susanna Centlivre took up in *The Wonder! A Woman Keeps a Secret*. In the end, Lesbia cannot decide whether to marry the reformed Beaumine or her other suitor, so her friends decide for her by vote. They opt for Beaumine, since the premature consummation of the union evidently left no other solution in Trotter's eyes. However, Trotter qualifies the rake's facile reform and, in the Epilogue, reveals the happy ending to be mere wishful thinking: in true life, she warns, a ruined woman would never win a Beaumine:

Lest therefore, the mistaken Sex should plead
Custom from me to venture and succeed,
And without Hymen's leave, too rashly prove
the Dangers that attend unlawful Love....
And tho' ten thousand LESBIAS may be seen
Where is that Man alive would act BEAUMINE?

This didacticism should not blind us to the play's merits: the comedy is lively, witty and introduces some new motifs and characters Susanna Centlivre was to borrow, such as the heroine who will risk a quarrel with a lover to keep a promise to a girl friend, or the figure of the meddling busybody who tries to be helpful but in fact causes nothing but confusion. In contrast, many of Trotter's tragedies lack colour and genuine dramatic conflict, and their didacticism is tagged on incongruously rather than emerging logically from the action.

Mary Pix
Mary Pix, the third of the Female Wits, was a merchant's wife who started to write in her thirties, after the death of her child – quite unusually, since most female playwrights were unmarried. She disappeared from the London theatre scene as suddenly and unexpectedly as she had appeared. She came from a different class than Manley or Trotter, and in her prefaces and prologues showed herself humbly aware of her lack of education, yet her comedies, successful on the contemporary stage, are lively and theatrically effective, though she, too, fails when she ventures into tragedy.

Ibrahim, the Thirteenth Emperour of the Turks (Drury Lane, 1696) (she apologises in the Preface that Ibrahim ought to have been the twelfth) is a heroic tragedy based on historical events and written in highly irregular blank verse, with missing beats and supernumerary syllables. The play's primary appeal is to the emotions of the audience. The scene in which the beautiful Morena is raped by the villainous sultan despite her desperate resistance – she slashes her arm and is carried off bleeding profusely, which seems to arouse the villain all the more – was sure to draw tears from the audience. Virtue in distress was a favourite sight for turn-of-the-century audiences: the more passive and innocent the suffering woman, the more thrilling the play. The tragedy ends in general carnage: the sultan and his henchmen are slain, though not by the hero himself, regicide being incompatible with heroic status. Morena, unable to survive her dishonour, poisons herself, though her betrothed is willing to marry her despite the rape: 'thy Virgin Mind was pure!' (V/40). Raped women are hardly ever allowed to survive in Restoration or eighteenth-century tragedies. In fact, they have so internalised the equation of female virtue and chastity that they cannot look themselves in the face after losing their virginity. Bereft of his beloved, the hero prefers suicide to mounting the throne and the sultan's villainous favourite, whose influential position at court gave her a chance to provoke the sultan to his misdeeds, stabs herself. Although in the Prologue the play is advertised as 'harmless [and] modest', it called forth Steele's moral indignation for the scene in which the sultan drops a handkerchief and withdraws with the lady of his choice, just as Behn's *The Rover* was censured by him for the supposedly coarse scene in which Blunt appears in his 'Holland drawers'.[45] Nowadays, the titillation with rape (not unusual in the pathetic tragedy of the time) and the misogynist view that privileges merely tempt a woman to mischief seem much more objectionable.

The comedy *The Spanish Wives*, performed at Dorset Garden the same year, ostensibly illustrates the very opposite – namely that freedom and liberal treatment will prevent a wife from going astray, whereas tyranny and incarceration will only induce infidelity. The play juxtaposes two old men: a jolly governor of Barcelona, who allows his wife a freedom unusual in Spain, and a sour marquis, who jealously locks up his wife but is, of course, tricked by a pimp and loses her to her true lover, since the marriage turns out to be illegal and, conveniently, has not been consummated. Pix is not one to challenge conventional notions of bridal virginity. The liberal governor's wife fancies an English colonel, yet Pix gives a twist to the usual cuckolding formula by having the old husband outwit the young wife by assuming the guise of her would-be lover and catching her out. However, he forgives her and she is overwhelmed by his generosity and promises to remain true – a promise in line with the taste for sentimental comedy but of questionable sincerity, since the wife had few scruples about cuckolding her kind husband before. Despite its attractive pleas for liberalism, which feminist critics have made much of,[46] the play, in fact, seems to prove that:

Lock up a Woman, or let her alone;
Keep her in private, or let her be known:
'Tis all one, 'tis e'en all one.

(III/ii/31)

The action proceeds with a good deal of crude physical humour, especially as far as the profane Friar Andrews is concerned, who makes a point of keeping none of the vows of his order. Such anti-Catholicism is typical of Whig playwrights, but can already be found in the French novel by Gabriel de Brémond, *The Pilgrim*, which Pix adapted and which the Tory John Dryden also used as a source for *The Spanish Friar*.

Most of Pix's comedies, however, are not so farcical, but follow the Spanish comedy-of-intrigue pattern, and are overcrowded with diverse plot lines and a confusing host of characters, relying on a whirlwind of intrigues and comical situations rather than verbal wit. *The Innocent Mistress* (successfully produced at Lincoln's Inn Fields in 1697) mixes Restoration comedy with the new fashion for senti-ment. It is set in London and actually mentions various fashionable places, such as Lockett's restaurant and Mrs Bantum's coffee house. The plot features several strands of action, ranging from tragi-comedy to low farce. The romantic protagonist, Sir Charles Beauclair, has been forced to marry an old termagant but is involved in a platonic relationship with the title figure Bellinda, who has developed an impossibly idealised idea of love from her excessive reading: 'Too studious for her sex, she fell upon the seducers of the women: plays and romances' (I/i/269). Attacks on novel-reading, which was claimed to turn the heads of girls, increased during the eighteenth century, as do jibes at women's hopes of establishing platonic relationships with the other sex. After much agonising about hopeless love, the situation is solved by the unexpected resur-rection of the termagant's first husband, long thought dead, which enables the hero (who, yet again, has never consummated the marriage!) to wed his innocent mistress. Conventionally, the witty couple comprises a rake who reforms in the end and an energetic girl who spoils his intrigues in male disguise by making his conquest fall in love with her. She treats this woman with surprising indul-gence, though, and protects her from abuse. A third couple and their difficulties in overcoming the girl's greedy guardians, namely the awful Lady Beauclair and her brother, merely serve as an excuse for some horseplay with the drunken squire, who, by a profusion of spilled red ink, is made to believe that he has murdered his ward and will be hanged. In the sub-plot Lady Beauclair's fat and tippling daughter is tricked into marrying a fraud, who, in turn, is deprived of the expected dowry when her real father returns.

The marriage of Sir Charles Beauclair reverses the stock situation of contemporary marital conflict plays in turning the wife into the brute, the husband into one who is virtuous and wronged.[47] Such a reversal is in line with the predilection of female playwrights for novel perspectives on gender roles, but misfires in this case. A chaste husband who has never even touched his wife may ease separation and remarriage, but inadvertently evokes the kind of absurdity Fielding so consummately exploited in the abortive seduction of Joseph Andrews. In the complicated melée of plots, the romantic couple, however, rarely occupies centre stage. The play abounds in intrigues and farcical situations, some of which are very funny, though the plot is too complicated. The true butts of humour are the two vulgar middle-class women, the loud and aggressive virago and her uneducated daughter, who are cozened by the crooks, with whom the audience tends to sympathise because of their dexterity and wit, while their female victims have absolutely nothing to be said for them. Even the foolish squire, Cheatall, guilty of locking up the heiress to get at her money, is a figure of fun rather than contempt and is given some witty repartee:

> ARABELLA: I take Heaven and Earth to witness, I believe you design to murder me.
> CHEATALL: There's no such design. Besides, your witnesses are not valid. I never heard their evidence go in any trial in all my life.
>
> (II/2/281)

He ends the play with a cynical warning that marital bliss is not likely to last, which the romantic Sir Charles, 'raised to unexpected worlds of bliss' (V/v/328), predictably ignores. That the play is sentimental at heart and not really so sceptical about marriage as the squire's words might suggest is also indicated by the witty couple. Indeed, the formerly confident heroine offers to allow her husband every liberty and would condone a double sexual standard, if only he be kind to her. The reformed rake, however, promises to eschew such privileges, vowing everlasting love:

> MRS. BEAUCLAIR: Well, Sir, if you can give me your heart, I can allow you great liberties. But when we have played the fool and married, don't you, when you have been pleased abroad, come home surly. Let your looks be kind, your conversation easy, and, though I should know you have been with a mistress, I'd meet you with a smile.
>
> SIR FRANCIS: When I forsake such charms for senseless, mercenary creatures you shall correct me with the greatest punishment on earth, a frown.
>
> (V/iv/321)

The Deceiver Deceived (1697) involved Pix in a theatrical controversy: like Manley with her *Royal Mischief*, she had transferred her play during rehearsal from Drury Lane to Betterton's company, and George Powell, a member of the former playhouse, thereupon brought out a comedy with the same plot under the title *The Imposture Defeated*. Although neither play was a success, *The Deceiver Deceived* is probably Pix's best comedy, witty, tightly structured and original, full of effective intrigues, disguises, subterfuges and narrow escapes.

The complicated plot hinges on the feigned blindness of a Venetian senator, who thus tries to evade an unwanted appointment, but is forced to continue the deception at home, where his young wife and daughter now feel free to carry on their amours under his very eyes. They are encouraged by the brazen old Lady Temptyouth, who has marvellous impudence, all the more hilarious since the audience knows that all her aplomb is, in fact, lost on a man who can really see what is happening. The lovers are also aided by the senator's resourceful steward, who always saves them in the nick of time and terrifies his master with a false oculist and false monks, who confiscate his fortune as a punishment for the fraud. When the deceitful old man tries to save his money by settling it on his daughter he is deceived once more, because now she has become rich enough to marry her poor lover. The wife does not come off so lucky: having managed to assuage the old man's jealousy, she will not risk her life and reputation again by meeting her lover, and will have to wait till her husband is dead. The intrigues by which the members of his household try to trick the senator are ingenious and well timed, and the stereotyped characters are given original features. A woman with the name and qualities of Lady Temptyouth would normally be portrayed as an amorous old fool, but here she proves witty and good-natured. She has brought up a friend's illegitimate daughter and marries this completely materialistic but not unlikeable girl to a rich French fop, who thereby gets the consummate actress to make the impression he craves in Versailles. Even this fop is endowed with original features in his pretension to literary talent, which brings him to grief since he is stupid enough to claim authorship of a libellous satire and gets himself arrested just in time to prevent his mercenary marriage to the senator's daughter. In contrast to *The Spanish Wives*, Pix also sympathises with the unfaithful wife, but is realistic enough not to provide a facile ground for separation. Her situation is grim enough: her brothers would bloodily avenge her dishonour and her husband is planning to poison her for her infidelity. Indeed, her only safety lies in reconciliation with him and the hope that she may soon be widowed – a bleak but more realistic ending than many comedies of the time offer, where difficulties of divorce are glossed over in rather cavalier fashion.

The Beau Defeated, or The Lucky Younger Brother, performed anonymously at Lincoln's Inn Fields in 1700, and with the pretence that its author was male, is again a multi-plotted intrigue comedy, based on Dancourt's *Le Chevalier à la Mode*, from which Pix drew her first scene verbatim, satirising the social pretensions of Mrs Rich, who is shown complaining that a duchess did not make way for her coach. This nouveau riche widow vies to be accepted by the gentry, is robbed by female gamesters and courted by a fop who also makes love to her niece and turns out to be a footman in disguise. Some of the funniest scenes portray the two middle-class women's training in fashionable behaviour, for instance in the proper manner of receiving a gallant ('Seem in a cabal, then burst out a-laughing, and let fall some mysterious words that tend towards scandal' (II/i/180)) or in the appropriate affected way of speaking:

MRS. RICH: This was furiously odd....
LUCINDA: Oh la! 'Furiously' – there's a hard word! I'll learn my aunt's words that I may appear agreeable to my Lord – furiously – remember, governess!

(III/ii/199)

In the end Mrs Rich is tricked into marrying a boorish squire, the elder Clerimont. The play is not in favour of social mobility, and a rise into the coarse, fox-hunting gentry is all that Pix (a middle-class woman herself!) allows a bourgeois widow. She is contrasted with the virtuous and witty widow, Lady Landsworth, who, after an enforced marriage to an old man, now means to choose a husband herself. Unlike Mrs Rich, she is not looking for a titled suitor, but for a spouse who will love her for herself, not her money, and pretends to be a kept mistress to test the penniless younger Clerimont. He falls in love with her despite his abhorrence of her apparent immorality, yet their union is delayed by the meddling servant, who hopes to help his master by giving him the character of a libertine. While Behn's Hellena or Cornelia accepted men's philandering as a matter of course, Lady Landsworth is shocked by the (albeit false) rumour that the lover she has selected is a debauchee. Of course, in the end they are reconciled, and the younger Clerimont receives part of the estate in gratitude from the happily married squire. Lady Landsworth promises to take the education of Mrs Rich into her own hands, but the ending, far from recommending itself as an example of female solidarity, is quite disagreeable, since the 'virtuous' people, who have tricked Mrs Rich into marriage, had such overtly interested motives. Besides, even given Lady Landsworth's tutoring, a female snob can hardly be weaned from her folly by marriage to a boor in the same way as her niece can be improved by proper education. The play ends with praise of British merchants, 30 years before Lillo's *The London Merchant*, who are acknowledged as important members of the Commonwealth – as long as they are content with their place in the hierarchical order:

> The glory of the world our British nobles are,
> The ladies too renowned and chaste and fair:
> But to our City,[48] Augusta's sons,
> The conquering wealth of the Indias runs....
> (V/ii/234)

What is also interesting in the comedy is the motif of a woman testing her suitor for his true motives and the reversal of gender roles we have already encountered in Ariadne's *She Ventures and He Wins*. It is Lady Landsworth who confers status and the impecunious younger Clerimont who is raised to a position by her. Secondly,

the woman plays the whore, whereas the man is proud of his virtue. Instead of joyfully accepting the invitation of a masked woman,
as a Behn rake would have done, he shies away from vice and
moralises:

> YOUNGER CLERIMONT: But be not caught my soul! She is, what I
> would still abhor.... [Her vice] checks desire with horror ...
> me you cannot charm; there's a rustic, out-of-fashion grace,
> a modest innocence, which only takes my soul...
>
> (III/ii/192f.)

Indeed, he is invested with the chastity by which women were
generally evaluated, using the very language of virtue in distress: 'I
shall be fooled at last; believe her love; trust her, and be undone!'
(III/ii/194); 'my virtue too, the last stake that I could boast of, is
going!' (IV/i/202). Of course, Lady Landsworth is, in reality, equally
chaste herself and quite happy to confer her privileges on her
husband after the marriage ceremony. Such role reversals are not
really subversive, but what they do show is that women playwrights, much earlier than men, found a rake unacceptable as the
virtuous heroine's partner, and instead of endorsing facile fifth-act
repentances in the manner of Colley Cibber's highly successful
comedy *Love's Last Shift*, demanded the same virtue from both
partners. These plays, however, do not suggest a liberating change
in the sexual role of women, but a mere transfer of the same role to
men.

The Different Widows, or Intrigue All á La Mode (Lincoln's Inn
Fields, 1703) is more risqué in its plot and more reminiscent of Restoration comedy, although, for all the frantic seduction attempts, no
indecencies are actually committed during the play, since amours
are always interrupted just in the nick of time. Again, two widows
are contrasted. The vain and hypocritical Lady Gaylove, who hides
her son and daughter and dresses them as schoolchildren ('You conceal your Children as You do your Wrinkles, and for the same
reason', I/iii/11), is tricked into marriage by a fortune hunter. The
other widow, the virtuous but insufferably moralising Lady
Bellmont, hates the pleasures of town, preferring sober country life,
thereby anticipating much of the moralistic sentiment of eighteenth-century comedy. This paragon has a dissolute son, engaged

in amorous intrigues with all the women in the play, but finally reclaimed by a high-minded girl who whets his appetite with her supposed promiscuity, but jilts him at the last moment and has him thrown into prison for debt, where he finally repents and is restored to love and fortune. The neglected children are saved from Lady Gaylove's grip, the daughter marrying and the son turning into a fop. Other plot lines involve a doting 'cit' and his flirtatious wife, a malicious busybody trapped into marriage by the maid, a kept mistress who falls in love with a woman in disguise, and a faithless wife who wins her pardon when she can prove that her Puritanical husband is really no better than she is.

The comedy contains some effective scenes, but is, on the whole, too complicated in plot and too overcrowded with characters. Pix deals out prizes and punishments to the dramatis personae according to their merits, but although the rake's reform and the praise of country morals are features of sentimental comedy, Pix is not a sentimental writer, and in some of the minor plots is quite cynical as to a couple's married life together, who 'each knowing the others Infirmities, ... will go Home, and live like the rest of the Married World, upbraiding One another' (IV/ii/44).

At the end of her career Pix returned to a Spanish setting with *The Adventures in Madrid* (Haymarket, 1706). The play was performed anonymously, but its anti-Catholicism and patriotism tie it in with Pix's other works. The play is a conventional light-hearted intrigue comedy about two girls, one married to her own avaricious uncle but conveniently still a virgin, the other about to be forced into a mercenary marriage. They start an intrigue with two Englishmen, teasing and confusing their lovers by climbing in and out of a secret trap door connecting the two houses. The real motors of the action are the servants – a clever pimp and a maid disguised as a eunuch – who manage to dupe the suspicious old villain. In the end, the villainous uncle is reported to the Inquisition and the marriage is dissolved, so that all the lovers, including the servants, can be paired off.

Unfortunately, throughout her career Pix felt called upon to try her hand at tragedy as well, a genre for which she was much less gifted and which earned her little applause. *Queen Catherine, or The Ruines of Love* (Lincoln's Inn Fields, 1698) invites comparison with Shakespeare's histories on account of its historical subject but falls far short of its models. As in all her tragedies, there is little dramatic action and much reporting, then a spurt of bloody deeds and threatened rape, the former rather quickly dispatched, the latter savoured and painted in lurid colours. Owen Tudor, Catherine's second husband, only appears in Act III to visit his wife, and is speedily murdered by Edward IV and Richard, who have treacherously gained entrance to the castle by duping Catherine's ward, the gentle Isabella, and their own brother Clarence. Isabella is threatened with rape and stabbed when Clarence tries to save her. Catherine is left in despair, but the House of York's victory already carries the seeds of further conflict. The characters, even the majestic queen and the innocent Isabella, all remain pale and nondescript, not least because all the male characters except Richard, with his borrowed Shakespearean characteristics, are motivated exclusively by love: Clarence is driven by jealousy, Edward IV by pique at Catherine's rejection, the traitor Sir James by lecherous desire for Isabella. In view of Shakespeare's model, all this seems ridiculously reductive of the complexities of history, but is, unfortunately, typical of much of Restoration and eighteenth-century tragedy.

In the Prologue to *The False Friend, or The Fate of Disobedience* (Lincoln's Inn Fields, 1699), Pix comes down firmly on the side of reform. Yet what the supposedly 'moral' play presents is neither moral nor logical, but a confused madhouse in which all dramatis personae are exclusively motivated by love, and kill and die for no other reason, until all the main characters are laid out dead. Unknown to each other and for obscure reasons, a son and daughter of a kindly monarch – who, on hearing of their disobedience, curses them most horribly – have secretly married a sister and brother and are brought to grief through the machinations of a jealous villainess posing as a friend. The brother is killed by the prince in a duel, the sister is poisoned by the villainess, the prince commits suicide, the princess will speedily die of heartbreak, and the villainess is executed. Pix tries to pass this slaughterhouse off as a cautionary tale with a lesson:

> That Parents
> Shou'd not, beyond the hopes of Heaven
> Their Children Prize,
> *Nor Indulg'd Children dare to Disobey*
> *Lest they are punish't such a dismal way.*
> (V/ii/60)

This moralising conclusion makes no sense at all. Indeed, with more reason, it should read: never trust a friend, or never curse your children. There is no logical reason why Heaven should swiftly implement the curses to the letter and punish the lovers, but not the villains. The play is full of ranting and histrionics. The villainess, slighted by the prince, who has no idea she is even in love with him, hysterically bewails her sufferings in grotesque images:

> See
> Leprous Beggars Prisoners Ten Fathom Deep,
> In New Drain'd Wells; and Ingendring Toads
> With all their bloated Blood crawling o're 'em!...
> Parents by their Rebellious Children Torn;
> Yet all this cannot equal mine.
>
> (I/i/11)

Pix tries to wring the utmost pathos from the unfortunate lovers' fates, adding such horrible twists as the unsuspecting husband actually serving his beloved the deadly poison mixed by the villainess. The play seems to take perverse pleasure in such melodrama, yet the Epilogue praises it as being devoid of 'loose expressions' and containing only virtue and innocence.

The Double Distress (Lincoln's Inn Fields, 1701) is a tragi-comedy reminiscent of Beaumont and Fletcher's *A King and No King* and suffers from the plot absurdities endemic to the genre. It turns upon the time-worn motif of royal children, a boy and a girl, brought up abroad ignorant of their birth. This leads to the confusion of who is related to whom, and who is a legitimate lover for whom. Warned by an oracle of incest, the girl, despite the solemn warning of her father, marries the Median prince, who is, in reality, her brother, in order to escape from the temptation to commit incest with the man she takes to be her brother, but who, of course, is not. The dilemma is complicated by her friend, who, it is prophesied, will marry the Median prince, whom she dislikes, whereas her seemingly low-born suitor is the true and legitimate prince. On the wedding night the suitable lover is substituted for the brother and the truth is, at last, revealed. The pairing of the couples, however, leaves an odd man out, who, his deserving character notwithstanding, ends up empty handed and a hermit. The play seeks to prove that the gods themselves intervene to protect virtue from incest, yet their oracle, one feels, is deliberately ambiguous and timely information from their relatives would have served the young people much better than all the thunder of divine providence. Again, love is the sole motivation of all the characters and their high-strung emotions are expressed in overwrought imagery: 'Plung'd in vast Floods of flowing Joys, I drown, / My ravish'd Thoughts in heights of transports row!' (III/39). The 'double distress' of the title is the danger of the two heroines committing incest. The king is dominated completely by the unseen evil queen, but turns virtuous the very moment she dies – an insincere tribute to the power of women, who are, conversely, portrayed as passive objects of desire, likely to rush to their doom as soon as they act on their own initiative, and dependent for their wellbeing on the superior strategies of men, who have kept them ignorant in the first place.

The Czar of Muscovy (Lincoln's Inn Fields, 1701) again reduces the history of a political uprising and the overthrow of a monarch to the level of amorous intrigue. The play is not really concerned with political but with sexual tyranny, and loyalty and rebellion hinge solely on the requiting of sexual passions. Women are again put in the role of virtue in distress: noble, innocent and helpless. Neither the wife nor the new amour the usurper czar fancies is interested in political power. What upsets the villain most is not his political downfall and imminent death, but his failure to kill the one and rape the other – a gratification he intends to indulge in before dying contentedly. Of course, he is killed in the nick of time (no regicide this, since the impostor is a common man) and the two noble women sink into their lovers' arms. In political outlook the play is aristocratic, contemptuous of the cowardly common people and anti-Catholic (the villainous czar wants to introduce Papism to Moscow). Tone and attitude thus link the tragedy with Pix's other works, although it was published anonymously.

The same holds true of *The Conquest of Spain*, the first new play to be performed when Betterton's company moved into Vanbrugh's splendid Queen's Theatre in 1705, whose bad acoustics, however, were unsuitable for drama. The tragedy borrows the theme of unshakeable loyalty even in the face of outrageous tyranny from Fletcher's *The Loyal Subject*. While Jacincta's father is leading the Spanish army against the invading Moors, she is raped by the treacherous king, yet the general, her father, refuses to countenance a revolt and is horrified when the troops, led by Jacincta's fiancé, free the Moorish prisoners and raise their arms against their lawful king. Of course, the rebellion has terrible results, because the Moors use the civil unrest for their own ends, ultimately conquering Spain. Jacincta and her father are killed in the fighting and her fiancé falls on his sword. The Spanish king – excused as a noble nature led astray – flees, and the romantic hero and his wife, who has herself just been rescued from rape, are released by the victors out of respect for the noble general's dying request. The incredible loyalty of the general, who will not rebel against his monarch even when the latter breaks every sacred trust, is clearly approved by Pix. As critics like Douglas Canfield have pointed out,[49] it is typical of plays of the period to come down strongly against regicide, which always leads to dire consequences no matter how legitimate the rebels' cause might seem. Even Jacincta blames her lover for avenging the rape. As a ravished heroine, she is not allowed to survive and all that can be done for her is to give her a tearful death scene. She herself has so internalised the code of chastity that she regards herself not only as sullied, but actually sullying: 'Judge not so poorly of the lost Jacincta / To think I'll bring Pollution to thy Bed' (III/40).

With an output of 12 plays, Pix is the most prolific playwright of the Female Wits. Most of her plays were performed at Lincoln's Inn Fields. The frequency with which she juxtaposes two female characters who are given equal importance suggests that she probably wrote many of her plays with Betterton's company in mind and tailored her roles to the two leading actresses, Mrs Barry and Mrs Bracegirdle. Her true forte was multi-plot intrigue comedy; she was adroit at inventing fast-moving plots and effective comic situations, and her didacticism of contrasting sensible and moral with hypocritical and egotistic figures does not spoil the liveliness of the comedies. Her tragedies, however, are marred by incongruous moralising, on the one hand, and a penchant for lurid melodrama expressed in overwrought language, on the other. The tragedies, with their interest in incest, rape and violence, cast women exclusively in the roles of either virtue in distress or jealous villainess, and although the comedies allow women more influence on the action, Pix, like so many female dramatists, is equivocal and contradictory in her evaluation of female characters and their place in society.

The satire *The Female Wits*

The Female Wits, or The Triumvirate of Poets at Rehearsal was probably written as a revenge by Powell, an actor at Drury Lane, in 1696, after Manley had withdrawn her tragedy *The Royal Mischief* and taken it to Betterton's company, where it enjoyed a *succès de scandal*. The satire is closely modelled on Buckingham's *The Rehearsal* and also features a play within a play, in which Manley's tragedy is ridiculed, whereas the frame is devoted to fierce personal attacks on the three women dramatists, their rivalry and their pretensions. The vain and stupid Marsilia, who supervises a rehearsal of her new play, and who is supposed to represent Mrs Manley, bears the brunt of the assault and is mercilessly derided for her ugliness, promiscuity and pride. Trotter, alias Calista, though more of a background figure, fares little better because of her pretence to superior learning, whereas the fat but good-natured Mrs Wellfed, representing Pix, is let off comparatively leniently. Their grotesque literary pretensions are indicated by Marsilia's plan to adapt and improve Jonson's *Catiline his Conspiracy*, which Calista boasts 'to have turned ... into Latin' (I/i/398). The main part of the satire consists of a rehearsal of Marsilia's new work, an incongruous hybrid of heroic play, opera and ballet, which closely follows all the absurd turns the action of *The Royal Mischief* takes, only demoted to the servants' ranks and lacking the erotic fervour of the original. The Osman/Bassima couple, originally destined, as Marsilia confesses, for the kind of sensationalist deaths Manley designed for them, make a spectacular escape to the moon. By then the actors, who have constantly been protesting against their stupid roles, have so exasperated the authoress that she decides to take the play to the rival house – something which Manley indeed did.

The satire is malicious and misogynist rather than witty, and targets the 'warmth' of Manley's tragedy without being able to capture its tone or appeal, only its crude plot outline. However, it allows us an interesting glimpse at theatrical conditions, backstage customs and rehearsal procedures. As we know from *The Rehearsal* as well, playwrights were expected to supervise rehearsals of their own plays, aided by the stage manager, usually an actor, and had to flatter the actors with the roles they had to play, as well as exert authority over them to ensure that authorial intentions were scrupulously observed. This necessity of close involvement with the 'disreputable' backstage world of the actors as well as the masculine stance of authority required of them may well have been the reason why, in the course of the more squeamishly moralistic eighteenth century, so few women dramatists who had no acting experience themselves were successful in the theatre. *The Female Wits* also contains in-jokes about Betterton's and Mrs Barry's acting styles, and about the Drury Lane company, including a satirical self-portrait of the tippling Powell himself, who may have poked fun at his well known preference, or perhaps the whole satire was a collaborative effort on the part of the Drury Lane Company.

Other writers of tragedy

Next to the three successful women dramatists, three more newcomers tried their luck at the turn of the century. They wrote only one tragedy each and quickly disappeared from the theatrical scene. Tragedy was at a low ebb, but even by turn-of-the-century standards *The Unnatural Mother, The Scene in the Kingdom of Siam*, which an anonymous 'young lady' staged at Lincoln's Inn Fields in 1698, must range at the very bottom end of the scale. This incongruous mixture of horror tragedy, love romance, pastoral, farce and ghost story starts out with a potentially comic motif: a girl finds out that the husband her father has chosen for her is the very stranger she fell in love with. But the play moves on to the dirty deeds of her lascivious stepmother, who poisons the father to wed the daughter's suitor, blackens the girl's reputation, then proceeds to poison her villainous son, who tries to rape his own sister before his demise, killing her in the process. These crimes are revealed with the help of ghosts and spirits, whose aid, indeed, is required because the villains always overhear all the important soliloquies of the good characters, who, in turn, and against all reason, believe every word these villains tell them. In the end, however, the surviving lovers are united and the stepmother goes mad. Though lustful and murderous, the title figure lacks the passionate vitality of Manley's Homais and is a mere monster. The use of prose, however, points to the future, as does the choice of protagonists from the middle class.

A much better tragedy is Jane Wiseman's *Antiochus the Great, or The Fatal Relapse* (Lincoln's Inn Fields, 1701). While most women dramatists of the time came from the lower gentry or the middle class, Wiseman is said to have been a servant, or perhaps an actress, who, from her benefit money, set up a tavern in Westminster.[50] We have no knowledge of how she gained so much insight into the theatre as to be able to write such a work; perhaps she had access to a library containing collections of Restoration plays. We know that she was acquainted with Susanna Centlivre. *Antiochus* is a heroic tragedy reminiscent of Dryden's *All for Love* in its love–honour conflict of a protagonist torn between two women, in its symmetrical character grouping, and in its contrasting of two nations, the Syrians and Egyptians, each representing different values. The virtuous Egyptian princess, married to the Syrian king Antiochus for reasons of state, says a tender but firm farewell to her erstwhile fiancé, during which she is surprised by her husband, who questions her fidelity. The king, who had vowed to reject his former mistress, is now willing to reinstate her, only she is unaware of this change of heart and poisons both him and herself. With both her lover and her husband dead, the queen abdicates and departs into the wilderness with her faithful maid – female bonding which Kendal regards as unprecedented in English drama.[51] Mrs Barry excelled in the role of Leonice, the passionate mistress, who suddenly finds herself cast aside for another woman, and is given a remarkably sympathetic treatment by the author. Leonice is spared the excruciating remorse and suffering meted out by a writer like Rowe to his female sinners – remorse and suffering which eradicate the fake impression that the playwright might genuinely share the 'feminist' sentiments he puts into his heroines' mouths:

> JANE SHORE: Mark by what partial Justice we are judg'd;
>   Such is the Fate unhappy Women find,
>   And such the Curse intail'd upon our Kind,
>   That Man, the lawless Libertine, may rove,
>   Free and unquestion'd through the Wilds of Love;
>   While Woman, Sense and Nature's easy Fool,
>   If poor, weak Woman swerve from Virtue's Rule, ...
>   Ruin ensues, Reproach and endless Shame,
>   And one false Step entirely damns her Fame.
>
> *(Jane Shore*, I/ii/107)

Despite her tragic death, Leonice is *not* made to atone for her sexual licence as an unforgivable sin against the laws of patriarchy.[52] Even in the plays of male dramatists it is not unusual for the heroines to protest against the double sexual standards and discrimination against women, but Wiseman is certainly remarkably explicit in her exposure of the cruelty with which men cast off women as soon as they have gained their favours.

> LEODICE: What have I done, that you shou'd hate me thus?
> Be Just, and charge me with another Crime,
> Besides my guilty Love of false Antiochus,
> And I'll be patient, and deny I'm wrong'd.
> ANTOICHUS: What need I search for any other Faults?
> I am in Love with Vertue, yours is lost.
> LEODICE: ... If Vertue be the only thing you Love,
> And has alone the power to keep you true;
> Why does your Treacherous Sex take so much pains
> To undermine the beautiful Foundation?
> Oh! Let all fond believing Maids by me be warn'd,
> And hate as I do, base ungenerous Man; ...
> Fly from their power, laugh at their Complaint;
> Disdain their Love, and baffle their Designs;
> So you may scape my Sufferings, and my Faults.
> (III/133)

The final piece of moralising is conventional, but the sympathy for a fallen woman is not. The compulsion, almost inevitable by that time, to attach a moral conclusion to a play also spoils the ending. The guiltless queen acknowledges that she has been justly punished for breaking her secret vows to her lover so that her father, having promised her to the Syrian king, need not break his; she had no right to become engaged secretly. So Wiseman wavers between the conservative view of women as determined by men and an understanding of Leonice as a woman more sinned against than sinning.

The Faithful General (Haymarket, 1706), by an unknown young lady, is another noteworthy tragedy, although in her Dedication the author plays down these 'first fruits' of her muse as a 'trifle'. To be sure, the unflinching loyalty of the title figure towards his sovereign, even when repaid by ingratitude, treachery and murder, is an exaggerated example of the royalist propaganda popular at the time. The play treats the same theme as Pix's *The Conquest of Spain*, but the similarities in plot make the discrepancy in the portrayal of female characters all the more obvious. *The Faithful General* projects a highly unusual view of women, who refuse to be chattels of their male relatives and claim a right to pass judgement on patriarchal norms and to live by their own values. The tragedy centres on an emperor jealous of his general's fame and seeking to destroy him, yet the faithful old man will not countenance rebellion and even acquiesces in his own son's execution for disloyalty.

> Hence from my sight for ever,
> Thou scandal to my Blood, no more my Son;
> Go, by thy Death, attone thy injur'd Prince.
>
> (I/i/8)

The emperor tries to seduce the general's beautiful and learned daughter Artemisia, who indignantly rejects him. He repents, but too late. The general dies under torture, though his son is saved. Artemisia refuses to forgive the monarch and, rather than marry a man who has tried to violate her integrity, she stabs herself. The remorseful emperor becomes terminally ill and the general's son, married to the emperor's sister, ascends the throne. The emperor's vacillation between tyranny and good nature led astray is, of course, as unconvincing as the customary reform in the end, but the figure of Artemisia is fascinating. Learned women are usually butts of ridicule in seventeenth- and eighteenth-century drama, but she is seen as completely admirable and is given a mastery of language and an intellectual power which stun the royal villain, who depreciates her victory in the 'noisy War of Tongues, this Woman's Combat' (III/33) and attempts to ravish her. Although she is physically attracted to his person, she furiously rejects his dishonourable designs, and derides the maxims of her own father, who has the nerve to bid her honour the would-be rapist as her prince:

> Those Maxims are too high
> For my weak Reason, Sir, who wou'd Prophane
> My Fame, or Virtue, forfeits my Respect.
>
> (IV/45)

The action seems to be moving towards a conventional happy ending when the emperor declares himself overwhelmed by her virtue and offers her his hand and crown in marriage. Any other heroine in the drama of the period would gladly have rushed into the king's arms and even prided herself on the reform she has brought about. Manley's heroine Almyna employs her erudition for no other purpose. But *The Faithful General* is much more radical in its view of female self-determination. Although on his deathbed even her father betroths her to the emperor, Artemisia refuses to yield her self-esteem either to a sovereign or to a father. When she feels her resilience waning, she stabs herself, preferring death to submission to a love she rightly regards as debasing and merely carnal, a love that would demand the sacrifice of all her previous principles. Unlike the rape victim in *The Conquest of Spain*, who blames herself for the 'pollution' she has suffered, Artemisia understands masculine violence as a systematic attack on female integrity and despises the man despite being physically attracted to him. It is, of course, dangerous to interpret her suicide as a feminist victory, yet her stance seems to be crucially different from the Lucretia syndrome of self-contempt and death wish, from which so many violated heroines suffer, and to predate not so much Samuel Richardson's *Clarissa* and its presentation of the heroine's death as a masochistic moral victory over her ravisher, but rather novels like Kate Chopin's *Awakening* 200 years later, where the heroine's suicide also symbolises a woman's resistance to male oppression.

For women dramatists, the turn of the century was a fruitful time, and although none of the new playwrights reached Behn's eminence, the fact that seven newcomers had their works produced argues for favourable conditions despite the inevitable prejudices and jealousies against women. To be sure, three of the women chose to remain anonymous and for some reason gave up writing after their first attempts. Even Manley and Pix occasionally concealed their authorship, pretending that the writer was a man in order to be given an unbiased hearing, or perhaps for fear of becoming tedious to the audience through overproduction. But never again in the course of the eighteenth century would there be such a successful profusion of new female voices within one decade, or production conditions which gave a chance of success even to newcomers with little practical experience in the theatre.

Beyond the plays themselves, it is difficult to identify the playwrights' authentic voices, for prologues and epilogues were frequently provided as a compliment by fellow playwrights or friends and may not always have been to the taste of the women dramatists, but nevertheless difficult to refuse. This probably accounts for the surprising presence in these prologues and epilogues of misogyny and rakish double entendre, such as likening a new play to the offer of maidenhead (prologue of *She Ventures and He Wins*) and the female playwright to a literary prostitute who means to please by new tricks (prologue to *The Spanish Wives*). In their own prefatory statements, the women advertise their moral purpose, stress their support for stage reform, plead for the didactic function of the theatre and recommend their plays as being harmless and inoffensive. Even when women dramatists were being defended against prejudice, the defence often had a double edge. The quip that this anti-Sappho had better return to her housewifery, 'to keep Accounts and write Receipts at home' (Epilogue to *The Faithful General*), may deride conservative attitudes, but the jocular threat of a flood of women playwrights ready to 'talk you all to death', should this one fail (Prior's Epilogue to Manley's *Lucius*), simply adds to popular prejudice.

In their own dedications and prefaces by far the most frequent pose adopted by women playwrights of the period is one of humility and depreciation of their play as a mere trifle (*The Faithful General*), or as not even worth hissing at (*The Spanish Wives*). Some women dramatists explicitly ask the ladies in the audience for their special support. Self-assertion such as Behn's is rare at the turn of the century, though some dramatists vacillate between assertion and depreciation, and a writer like Manley took up Behn's indignant complaint that male and female writers are evaluated according to separate moral yardsticks. However, it is hard to gauge a playwright's attitudes and view of herself from dedications, addresses to the audience, let alone prologues of uncertain authorship, although Behn, occasionally, is surprisingly candid about her difficulties and aspirations. Through the haze of eulogy for the patron and the fog of excuses for their own temerity, it is hard to discern the true personalities of these women. We are left with the testimony of their plays, but even these, as I have sought to show, more often than not yield contradictory and elusive evidence of their sympathies and attitudes, their views of women's role and of their own standing within the male-dominated system.

5
Susanna Centlivre

Susanna Centlivre was a contemporary of the Female Wits and in style she is more closely related to them than to the female dramatists of the eighteenth century. She must have known Pix, Manley and Wiseman personally, since she contributed to collections they edited, or in turn received verses for her own publications. But she started to write later than most of the wits and continued after they had all long ceased. She has been the most successful English female dramatist ever, though her crowning success only came posthumously. She was one of the most frequently performed contemporaneous dramatists in the eighteenth century, and her comedies were favourite vehicles for the most celebrated actors, remaining in the repertoire for two centuries. Little, however, is known for certain about her personal life. She is said to have come from Puritan stock, and there are stories that after her parents' death she joined a troupe of strolling players, spent some months at Oxford in male disguise with a lover, married an actor, then an army officer and finally a cook in the royal household. She supported the House of Hannover at a time when the succession was not at all clear and remained a fervent Whig all her life, which earned her the enmity of Tories like Pope, who savaged her in *The Dunciad* and in *A Further Account of the most Deplorable Condition of Mr. Edmund Curll, Bookseller*.

Tragi-comedies

Like Behn, she took the poetic name of Astraea, thus firmly placing herself within the female tradition. Like Behn, she embarked on a prolific writing career with old-fashioned tragi-comedy, but soon became aware that her true talent lay in comedy; unlike Trotter or Pix, she was not seduced into using her works as instruments for moralising, although she wasted few opportunities to make her zealous political sentiments known, either in the plays themselves or in the prefatory material. Just as her plays are reminiscent of Behn's comedies, like her predecessor, in her prefaces she also takes head on the prejudices against women playwrights and the derogatory criticism they were likely to meet. Like Behn, she ridicules the fops who will admire a performance of *The Gamester* yet reject the play as soon as they become aware that it was written by a woman, or detract from her success by claiming she must have had male help in writing (Dedication of *The Platonick Lady*). Instead of meekly purging her plays of all 'loose' expressions, she defends her right to verisimilitude in character portrayal and refuses to censor the language of vicious women and unscrupulous gallants (Preface to *The Perjur'd Husband*). Like Behn, she dares to question the male canon of Aristotelian rules, and though she does not dispute their appropriateness in general, she knows that the town would rather see 'Humour lightly tost up with Wit, and drest with Modesty and Air' (Preface to *Love's Contrivance*).

Her first play, *The Perjur'd Husband, or The Adventures of Venice* (Drury Lane, 1700), incongruously yokes together a tragic plot about adultery and a comic cuckolding plot. It would be absurd to put its failure down to male prejudice. In the main part, written in blank verse, an amorous duke means to marry bigamously, but his wife disguises herself as a man and murders his mistress, and is in turn stabbed by her husband, who is then killed in a duel with the mistress's betrothed. They all forgive each other before they die. Centlivre portrays the women basically as victims, while both men act according to entirely egotistic motives, considering their own pleasure and never the women's wellbeing. The duke has not told his mistress that he is married and risks both their deaths for the sake of sexual gratification; the fiancé assumes the prerogatives of a husband even before the wedding ceremony and vows to kill his rival and her, so that 'none shall enjoy thee' (III/i/19). Sexual politics also figures in the coarse, farcical sub-plot about Lady Pizalta's

abortive attempt to cuckold her old husband with a rude and quite
unattractive Frenchman – the only lover at hand during the carnival
season. Pizalto, in turn, lusts after the maid, who, freer in this
respect than her upper-class mistress, reverses the customary
gender roles and jilts the man, guiding him into the arms of the
French gallant disguised as a woman, and making off with the 1000
pistoles Pizalto has paid her – fleecing the old man vicariously for
his whole sex:

> For did base Men within my Power fall,
> T'avenge my injur'd sex, I'd jilt 'em all.
> And would but Women follow my advice,
> They should be glad at last to pay our Price.
> (II/i/13)

Although, as is typical in an eighteenth-century play, the attempt at
cuckolding comes to nothing and the woman must remain fettered
to her old husband, the sub-plot is reminiscent of Restoration sex
comedies in language and tone, and was criticised accordingly. In
the future, Centlivre was generally to refrain from such explicitness.

For her second play she remained with the hybrid form of a
comic strand of action attached, fairly illogically, to a serious main
plot. *The Stolen Heiress, or The Salamanca Doctor Outplotted* (Lincoln's
Inn Fields, 1702) was published anonymously and refers to its
author as male. In the tragi-comic plot a miserly father spreads a
false report of his son's death in order to turn his daughter into a
fake heiress and marry her to an influential suitor. When she elopes
with her lover, he has this man and his accomplice arrested and
sentenced to death, even though the latter, through the usual *deus
ex machina*, is revealed to be the long-lost offspring of an important
courtier. The villain's supposedly dead son has, in the meantime,
returned and is hired by the suitor to assassinate the heir, that is,
himself. He exposes the plot and thereby effects a reconciliation and
a happy ending. In the sub-plot, a foolish scholar from Salamanca,
engaged to the heroine's cousin, is persuaded to play the fop,
whereas her true lover dons the scholar's clothes. When the fraud is
discovered, the girl pretends to be with child and the lover is
allowed to turn her into an 'honest' woman. As she was to do in so
many plays, Centlivre turns the male figures into possessive tyrants,
willing to kill ineligible husbands, indeed, even their own children,

if they dare to oppose their wishes. The plot of the tragi-comedy and its solution is entirely artificial, but the comic plot is effective, and was adapted by Mrs Cowley later in the century.

Late in her career Centlivre was to return to the genre of tragi-comedy once more with *The Cruel Gift, or The Royal Resentment* (Drury Lane, 1716), a weak play actually written two years earlier, which owed its success solely to party political support. Drawing a little on *Romeo and Juliet* and a lot on Boccaccio, Centlivre introduces two inimical families, whose offspring fall in love. However, the patriotic hero still refuses to allow his beloved's brother to escape from prison, where he is languishing for marrying the princess. The king orders him to be executed and the princess to be presented with her husband's heart. At this point a hermit, who has been living on the premises for 20 years but kept silent, reveals that the victim was of noble blood, which makes the cruel king rue his deed. The hero can now confess that he saved the prisoner and can reap the reward for love and loyalty, wasting few thoughts on his treacherous father, who was killed during a civil disturbance. As so often in Centlivre's plays, men regard their female relatives as mere property to be disposed of as they think fit and react with in-exorable brutality when the women fail to comply. The hero is the kind of patriotic prodigy favoured by the author, who 'know[s] no Glory, but [his] Country's Good' (I/3), and his disobedience towards his opportunistic father is approved in view of his patriotic motives.

Comedies

The Beau's Duel, or A Soldier for the Ladies (Lincoln's Inn Fields, 1702) was Centlivre's first comedy about a girl, Clarinda, who, despite tribulations, is finally allowed to marry her lover through the help of a kindly neighbour, who pretends to marry her father in the guise of a pious Quaker, then acts the reckless coquette, until, to get rid of his troublesome wife, the old man agrees to acquiesce to his daughter's wishes. The 'beau[x]' of the title are two cowardly fops, unsuccessful suitors of Clarinda's, who are persuaded that they ought to fight a duel over her and are then beaten up by the dis-guised heroine and her friend. By far the most interesting character in the whole play is the girls' friend and protectress, Mrs Plotwell, a former kept woman turned rich and honest, who now devotes her life to plaguing and ridiculing the fops and beaux she had to toady to in her former profession. She is an entirely likeable and altruistic character, a new and original presentation, and it is she who master-minds the fake marriage which humiliates the materialistic father and saves Clarinda's inheritance. To be sure, Mrs Plotwell appears, as it were, *post festum*, when she has given up her former immoral life. However, the insight that virtue has an economic basis and that a rich woman can well afford to be honest runs against convention, so Centlivre blurred it in the moralising ending, by having Mrs Plotwell, once more equating virtue and chastity, warn women not to part with 'Virtue thou shining Jewel of my Sex' (V/iii/55). Critics have pointed to several sources from which Centlivre might have drawn elements of the action, such as the trick marriage in Jonson's *Epicene*, but the characters and evaluation are Centlivre's own. The topic of the marriage into which the daughter is to be forced, the condoning of filial disobedience in the choice of marriage partner, the female figure in complete control of the intrigue and alternately employing rhetoric or keeping silent to manipulate her male an-tagonists are all features which recur frequently in Centlivre's plays.

Love's Contrivance, or Le Medecin Malgré Lui (Drury Lane, 1703) was published without a name and, as Centlivre explained later (in the Dedication to *The Platonick Lady*), with the Dedication wrongly signed RM, as a contrivance on the part of the printer to make money, since women's plays were held in low esteem. The plot again revolves round a girl about to be forced into a loveless marri-age. Lucinda, the heroine, is hard put to ward off the old suitor and, with the contrivance of the title role, reminiscent of Mrs Plotwell, feigns dumbness so that the parson cannot marry them. A drunken wife-beater is claimed by his spouse to be a doctor who can work miracles, if only he is soundly thrashed. These farcical scenes are a pastiche of three Molière plays, whose characters have been 'Englished'. Once the first trick has failed, Lucinda frightens the groom by pretending to be a woman of fashion, so that he seeks advice from two astrologers, both of whom are impersonated by Lucinda's lover. In the end the young people marry, but, as in several of Centlivre's later plays, the father and the old groom depart unreconciled and cursing. The farce concerning wife-beating is awkwardly attached to the intrigue plot and involves consider-able misogyny. Turning on a would-be rescuer, the wife claims that she likes the treatment ('May be I have a mind to be beaten, what's that to you?' (I/iii/12)) and the husband asserts, 'Look'e Wife. I love you the better for beating you, faith 'tis out of pure Love' (I/iii/14). It also contrasts with the witty exchanges between a rake and Lucinda's folicksome friend, which prove that Centlivre was well able to write sparkling dialogue:

> OCTAVIO: … In short, Madam, Women rule as they please.
> BELLIZA: But like true Englishmen, you are never pleas'd long with one Government.
> OCTAVIO: Not if they affect arbitrary Sway; Liberty of Conscience, you know, Madam.
> BELLIZA: Ay, and Men's Consciences are very large.
>
> (II/i/17)

The Gamester (Lincoln's Inn Fields, 1705), one of Centlivre's most famous plays, yet originally published anonymously for fear of prejudice against women dramatists, strikes out in a different direction, taking up the moralising strain of turn-of-the-century 'reform' comedy she generally avoids. In the Dedication she advertises the work as having been written 'without that Vicious Strain which usually attends the Comick Muse … [in order to] recommend Morality'. The plot takes up the problem of gambling, which became a national vice under Queen Anne and the first Georges, and is unusually straightforward. Valere has ruined himself by gambling and his father will pay his debts only if he marries the rich and beautiful Angelica. However, he breaks his vows of reform and even gambles away the portrait she gave him to the disguised Angelica herself. However, the girl relents and marries the repentant sinner. The reclaiming of the gamester, the intention of teaching a moral lesson by his example, and the forgiving spirit of Angelica are all typical of the new spirit of sentimental comedy. In the source, Jean-Francois Regnard's *Le Joueur*, which Centlivre otherwise followed closely, the hero fails to extricate himself from his vice and is completely ruined in the end. What made the play exciting for contemporary audiences was the realistic gambling scenes Centlivre added, in which Valere is first carried away by a run of luck, but then loses all his winnings to the disguised girl. It is characteristic of Centlivre's Whig stance that she turned the figure of the fake French marquis, who turns out to be a footman – a motif which might have been suggested by Pix's *The Beau Defeated* – into a hostile caricature. At the same time she jokes about the hypocrisy of her faction and their animosity towards the stage when she has a servant predict, on hearing of his master's losses: 'Now will [the gambler] rail as heartily against Gaming, as the Whigs against Plays' (I/6).

The success of the play obviously encouraged her to pursue the subject once more, in *The Basset Table* (Drury Lane, 1705), which starts out in very much the same way, with servants lounging around in the early morning, waiting for their gambling employers. This time the plot centres on four women and, though not overtly didactic, again aims at moral improvement. The coquettish Lady Reveller keeps a basset table, much to the chagrin of her soberminded lover, until the men conspire to frighten her by pretending to rape her, so that she is more than glad to accept her lover's protection and promises to give up gambling. The stratagem is unpleasant and it is surprising that a woman playwright should have turned rape into a joke and female vulnerability into a salutary lesson to be taught to independent-minded women. Lady Reveller's pious cousin wins the rake, though it remains a mystery why he is attracted to so sanctimonious and humourless a character. The middle-class wife, who is involved in an affair with the rake and has gambled away all her husband's money, must promise to reform and return to her husband. In a fourth strand of action Valeria, a girl more interested in dissecting animals and performing scientific experiments than in love, is finally married to the young man who adores her, since the old sea captain that her father chose for her is put off by so learned a lady.

Critical interest has centred on the portrait of the intellectual woman. Compared with the contemptuous portrayals in contemporary drama, even Behn's Lady Knowell, Valeria's exploits are viewed with humour rather than censure. The superficial Lady Reveller, who laughs at her unfeminine occupations, is hardly a reliable critic. Nonetheless, there is little doubt that Centlivre meant Valeria to be seen as a comic figure. Her preoccupation with bluebottles and tapeworms is too exaggerated to excite admiration, although when things come to a head, she does rescue her lover by hiding him in a tub and sacrificing the fish she meant to dissect. It is also remarkable that she is not required to relinquish her scientific interests on marriage, while the play forces reform upon the flighty characters, who have to eschew gambling and amours. The middle-class wife must content herself with her station, the usual fate allotted to women characters of her class affecting gentility – an indication that Centlivre, for all her Whig sentiments, had no sympathy for social climbers and a good deal of contempt for the city.

Love at a Venture (New Theatre in Bath, 1706) returns to Restoration comedy, although the women's virtue is always saved at the last moment. The well paced comic plot recounts the adventures of the rake Belair, who courts two cousins under two different names, impudently pretending to be a country gentleman to the one and a colonel to the other, appearing in both disguises (almost) simultaneously and having himself arrested by a fake magistrate so as to be able to return in new guise minutes afterwards. His friend Sir William, who is willing enough to help him, is less amused when he realises that Belair is dallying with his own bride and is trying to start an intrigue with Sir William's sister, unhappily married to an old hypochondriac, a character Centlivre must have taken from Molière and Behn. In the end Belair and one of the girls are married, Sir William's bride returns to her suitor and his sister is forced to remain with her disagreeable husband. The motif of a gallant playing a double role is not entirely new, and was stolen by Cibber in 1707 for his *Double Gallant*, but Centlivre certainly made amusing use of it. Sir William's hypocrisy is far less pleasant. He remains friends with the philandering Belair, but vents his moral indignation on his unhappy sister and advises her to be 'the Pattern of a Virtuous Wife, indulge his Age – and that way preserve your Ease, and by your Meekness and Humility, fix your Reputation' (V/55). He sanctimoniously pretends his father must have had good reason to marry her to an old fool, when he knows full well that this saved a portion and turned him into a rich man. There is no sense of irony at the unfairness of this treatment. Behn's Julia, Lady Fancy, or the heroine of *The False Count* were given outlets from marital frustration by being allowed to cuckold, but Centlivre never countenances adultery in her plays.

The Platonick Lady (Haymarket, 1707) is a weaker play whose action seems forced and illogical. The title heroine pretends to be only interested in a platonic relationship with the rake, but is, in fact, wildly jealous, thus confirming the male prejudice that such platonic relationships are impossibly romantic, very much in the same manner as Pix's *Innocent Mistress*. In the end she turns out to be the rake's own sister, which leaves him free in the end for his former love, who has pursued him throughout the play in various disguises and under hair-raising pretexts, yet whom he has somehow failed to recognise despite his assertion that he has hugged her image in his heart ever since their separation. Since he is harder and more unscrupulous than rakes generally are in eighteenth-century comedy, his metamorphosis into a true lover is all the more unbelievable. The platonic heroine marries her brother's friend, and a foolish widow is cheated out of an ill-gotten estate and tricked into marriage to a fortune hunter. This dowdy country woman is cruelly ridiculed for her homespun clothes, her ignorance and coarseness, and in one of the famous scenes of the play a whole catalogue of stays, furbelows, make-up, patches and head clothes is suggested to improve her appearance. Centlivre obviously meant to give her her deserts by marrying her to a mercenary bully – regardless of the fact that *error personae* was a legal reason to declare a marriage invalid. Restoration dramatists make little account of such legal niceties and regularly use trick marriages and mistaken identities to punish unlikeable characters or outwit watchful guardians.

The next play followed after three years, in Drury Lane in 1709, but it was a masterpiece. *The Busybody* had an inauspicious beginning when the actor who was to play the male lead (playing Sir George Airy) threw his script into the pit during rehearsals out of exasperation at his role. To make things worse, Steele failed to provide the promised Epilogue. Despite these ill omens, the comedy was ultimately to become a spectacular success and was to see 475 performances in London till the end of the century, as well as frequent revivals in Australia and America.[53]

The play is firmly structured and the whirlwind of intrigues with which two couples outwit their guardians is perfectly timed. Miranda pretends to be in love with her avaricious guardian Sir Francis Gripe in order to gain control of her estate. Sir George Airy, with whom she flirted in disguise, pays the jealous Sir Francis £100 for a one-hour interview with her, but partly to lull the old man's suspicions, partly to punish her lover for treating her like a commodity and buying her time (indeed, for a moment she suspected her guardian had sold him quite another favour!), Miranda refuses to speak a word, so that Sir George has to act both the wooer and the lady – a very funny scene. Later, when he has almost given up hope of winning the girl, a meddling but well meaning friend, Marplot, brings the message that Miranda warns Sir George to keep away from the garden lest he be shot, a message the lover correctly interprets as a clever invitation to quite a different kind of 'warm reception' (III/iv/330). However, the couple is interrupted by the guardian's untimely return and almost given away by the unlucky Marplot, who insists on seeing the supposed 'monkey' hidden behind the chimney piece. When Sir Francis hands over to his ward the deeds to her estate on his supposed wedding day, the young lovers secretly marry and then fly to the rescue of their friend Charles, in love with Isabinda, whom her father keeps locked up and means to marry to a Spaniard. Several attempts at a meeting have already misfired, owing to Marplot's meddling or the father's vigilance, though the maid has shown herself most inventive in finding excuses for her mistress. With Sir George's help Charles impersonates the Spanish suitor and marries Isabinda, though the happy ending is again almost spoiled by the uncomprehending Marplot, who blurts out the truth. However, Isabinda's father is reconciled to the trick marriage, though, typically, the unrelenting Sir Francis refuses his blessing, which, however, is not considered requisite for the couple's future happiness.

This is one of Centlivre's best plays, though critics, unwilling to credit a woman with such originality, have been anxious to find models for the plot and characterisation. Like Behn at her best, she creates a firework of mistaken identities and well timed mishaps and intrigues, but the tone of the comedy is unmistakably hers and the character of Marplot, who would 'give the world to know' what other people are doing ('Why the devil should not one know every man's concern?' (I/300)) and is rewarded for his well meant interventions with blows and curses, is highly effective. Dryden's Sir Martin Mar-All and Jonson's Pug in *The Devil is an Ass* have been suggested as sources, but neither, in fact, has much resemblance to the well intentioned but meddlesome busybody. A much more likely source is the character of the good-natured but clumsy Bonsot in Trotter's *Love at a Loss*, just as Pix's *Spanish Wives* may have suggested to Centlivre the idea that one woman sends her maid to her friend to help her concoct an intrigue.

The force of the comedy rests primarily on situation humour, such as the incomparable monkey scene, or the scene when the maid passes off Charles' love letter in cipher as a charm against toothache, yet it also gives ample proof of Centlivre's wit and verbal dexterity. Referring to the supposed monkey, Marplot asks:

MARPLOT: ... Has it got a chain?
MIRANDA: Not yet, but I design it one shall last its lifetime.

(IV/346)

On hearing that he is to marry a rich old woman, Charles protests:

CHARLES: My lady Wrinkle, sir! Why she has but one eye.
SIR FRANCIS: Then she'll see but half your extravagance, sir.

(II/311)

Indeed, language is in the foreground throughout the play. Marplot, curious and gossipy like a stereotypical woman, puts his foot in it whenever he opens his mouth. More importantly, Miranda wields power by refusing to speak, on the one hand, and masterfully manipulating language, on the other. She fools her avaricious guardian by protesting her devotion, but also ridicules Sir George's conventional love rhetoric and debunks his self-esteem. More than in any Behn play, the heroine is in control of the action and can outwit any man. While the appropriately named Sir George is airy and flighty (as a Restoration coquette might be), Miranda has a head for business, knows the importance of legal documents and is level headed even in her love affairs. Like any witty Restoration heroine, she knows that for a woman marriage is often a bad bargain.

MIRANDA: ... Now to avoid the impertinence and roguery of an old man, I have thrown myself into the extravagance of a young one; if he should despise, slight, or use me ill, there's no remedy from a husband but the grave; and that's a terrible sanctuary to one of my age and constitution.

(V/i/350)

As is typical of Centlivre's most memorable heroines, she is also altruistic and willing to help her friends. She sends her resourceful maid to aid Isabinda, and procures the documents pertaining to Charles' estate in order to give them to their rightful owner. Isabinda is more conventionally helpless, but the maid makes up for her passivity through her deviousness. The men are rather passive and often act upon the women's suggestion. Although Sir George is given a touch of the womaniser, he is, in fact, entirely different from a Restoration rake because his intentions towards Miranda are essentially honest, and he is bent upon marriage from the very beginning, as is Charles. With the financial side of the transaction satisfactorily settled, 'nothing but complaisance and good humour is requisite on either side' (V/i/350) to make the couples happy. The importance of money and the power it affords are constantly thematised, an issue which Centlivre, like Behn, took up in several plays. Isabinda's father, with his weakness for everything Spanish, is a humorous figure rather than the butt of vicious satire, but, for all her fervent Whig sentiments, she paints the city usurer as coarse, greedy and disgusting, and, characteristically, does not allow his implacability to spoil the joy and celebration in the ending.

In the sequel, *Mar-Plot, or The Second Part of the Busybody* (Drury Lane, 1710), Centlivre failed to repeat her initial success and fell far short of the original. The play is a conventional cuckolding comedy set in Lisbon, where Charles, already tired of his fawning Isabinda, and a friend have various intrigues in progress, which Marplot spoils by his inquisitiveness. Charles is saved from death for adultery by his wife, who disguises herself as the priest sent to take the confession of the adulterous couple, exchanges clothes with her husband, thus enabling him to escape, so that the wronged husband finds only two women together. There is little of the sprightliness and originality of the previous play. The two men are conventional rakes, the old husband a credulous cuckold, who, however, unlike Pix's forgiving governor in *The Spanish Wives*, turns bloodthirsty when he catches his wife in flagrante. Marplot has lost his delightful good nature and has degenerated into a dishonourable meddler, a mixture of buffoon and plotting servant. Isabinda is, of course, a model wife, but her moralising advice that a husband's vice can be overcome by indulgence, in keeping with the edifying tone of reform comedy, rings false and unconvincing, as does so much similar moralising, in view of Charles' appetite for amorous intrigue.

In between the two Marplot plays, Centlivre had written *The Man's Bewitch'd; or The Devil to Do About Her* (Haymarket, 1709), which combines three farcical plots. In the first, Captain Constant pretends his father has died, collects the year's rent from the steward and marries his daughter. When the irate father turns up, he is at first taken for a ghost, but reconciled to his son when he learns that his daughter-in-law is, in truth, an earl's offspring with a considerable income, and social decorum has been maintained. In the second strand of action, superstition also plays a role. Constant's friend rescues an heiress from the clutches of her miserly guardian by feigning bewitchment. A witty third couple, kept apart by the political enmity of their parents, also overcome this obstacle, and even the servants are neatly matched; only the villainous guardian exits cursing, as so often in Centlivre's plays. The action relies largely on horseplay and farcical scenes of witchcraft rather than on verbal humour, though the witty couple proves once more that Centlivre had a gift for lively repartee. The young man accuses women of dissimulation, but the pert heroine gives him tit for tat:

> LOVELY: ... We believe you Angels, but don't always find you so.
> MARIA: We always find you Angels, but of the fal'n kind.
>
> (I/6)

> LOVELY: You'll remember us in your Prayers, Ladies –
> MARIA: Among Jews, Turks, and Infidels –
>
> (I/8)

In connection with this play Centlivre got involved in a quarrel with the cast, who refused to perform on her benefit night, on account of an article in *The Female Tatler* complaining of changes in the play made during rehearsals. This article was ascribed to Centlivre's pen, but was probably written by Mrs Manley, to whom the author had confided her annoyance, and who printed the story, harming her colleague's credit with the actors.

The Perplexed Lovers (Drury Lane, 1712) again got Centlivre into trouble when the actors yielded to political pressure and refused to speak the 'Whiggish' Epilogue. In print, the verses seem neither particularly zealous nor offensive and hardly to merit the excitement they aroused, though they do praise Marlborough and Prince Eugene as heroes. The comedy revolves around a whirl of mistaken identities and misunderstandings when people try to steal out of their houses at night and run into the arms of tyrannical brothers or undesirable suitors; sisters are taken for lovers, servants for masters, or vice versa. The heroine is under pressure from both her father and brother, and twice in danger of being raped, before she can sink into her lover's arms. Her witty cousin marries the heroine's authoritarian brother. The scene in which this cousin hides the heroine in the closet and challenges her jealous suitor to look for the hidden person and lose her own person, or to forbear, is reminiscent of the later *The Wonder! A Woman Keeps a Secret*, but is handled with less aplomb and wit, the women generally being more passive than in the later and better play.

Centlivre dedicated *The Wonder! A Woman Keeps a Secret* (Drury Lane, 1714) to the future George I at a time when he was out of favour with the Court, and thereby secured the benevolence and patronage of the House of Hannover. She adapted Ravenscroft's *The Wrangling Lovers*, but substantially changed the character relations and incidents. *The Wonder!* is one of her best and most feminist plays, a long-time favourite with the public, performed 232 times in the eighteenth century, a play in which the great actor Garrick was to excel and which he chose for his farewell performance. The brilliant comedy of intrigue is set in Portugal, and the pompous etiquette and rigid code of honour there render all the more acute the women's dilemma, since one girl's life indeed depends on the constancy and secrecy of her friend. Isabella escapes from an enforced marriage by jumping out of a window, into the arms of a British colonel who happens to be passing by, and who carries the fainting belle to the next-best house, which is, by chance, that of Violante, who is destined for a nunnery but expects a secret visit from her banished lover Felix, Isabella's brother. Violante promises to protect and hide her friend at all costs, a motif Centlivre again may have adopted from Trotter's *Love at a Loss*, but greatly expanded. Don Felix, very much given to jealousy, is furious when he hears the colonel knocking on the window, hoping to see the girl he saved – but naturally Felix assumes he is looking for Violante. What follows is a *tour de force* of hide-and-seek, mistaken identities and last-minute escapes. Felix, the colonel, Isabella, the maid must all hide in closets and bedrooms when lovers or fathers enter the room. Felix vacillates between what seems to him justified jealousy and a bad conscience when a veiled woman emerges from a hiding place instead of the expected man. Finally, the two couples marry and the fathers are duped. They immediately quibble about money and, as is so often the case in Centlivre's comedies, remain unreconciled to the happy ending.

The play is marvellously timed, quick-paced and very witty, refuting all claims of Centlivre's detractors that she was not gifted in verbal wit. The characters, right down to the servants, engage in repartee reminiscent of sparkling Restoration comedy. Thus the mercenary maid Flora affirms that:

In my opinion, nothing charms that does not change, and
any composition of the four and twenty letters, after the
first assay, from the same hand, must be dull, except a
bank-note or a bill of exchange.

(II/i/338)

The repartee between the colonel and Isabella could well have
taken place between the Rover and his Hellena:

COLONEL: What say you, my charmer? Shall we breakfast
together? I have some of the best tea in the universe.

ISABELLA: Puh! tea! Is that the best treat you can give a lady at
your lodgings, Colonel?

COLONEL: Well hinted. No, no, no, I have other things at thy
service, child.

ISABELLA: What are those things, pray?

COLONEL: My heart, soul and body into the bargain.

ISABELLA: Has the last no encumbrance upon it? Can you make a
clear title, Colonel?

COLONEL: All freehold, child, and I'll afford thee a very good
bargain....

ISABELLA: If I take a lease it must be for life, Colonel.

COLONEL: Thou shalt have me as long or as little time as thou
wilt, my dear. Come, let's to my lodgings, and we'll sign
and seal this minute.

ISABELLA: Oh, not so fast, Colonel. There are many things to be
adjusted before the lawyer and the parson come.

COLONEL: The lawyer and parson! ... Why, this is showing a man
half famished a well-furnished larder, then clapping a pad-
lock on the door till you starve him quite.

ISABELLA: If you can find in your heart to say grace, Colonel, you
shall keep the key.

COLONEL: I love to see my meat before I give thanks, Madam.
Therefore, uncover thy face....

(III/iv/360)

The note of patriotism in praise of English liberty with which the
play starts out is soon toned down, and from then on Centlivre
makes a point of deflating high-sounding rhetoric and romantic

histrionics, from Isabella's vow that she will die rather than marry an old man, to Felix's loud-mouthed threats.

As in *The Busybody*, there are two obstructive fathers whose resistance the young couples have to overcome by superior ingenuity. The women take all the initiative, the men simply react; the women intrigue, the men are duped and manipulated. The encounters between Felix and Violante are among Centlivre's best love scenes, and Garrick excelled in the role of the jealous yet repentant Portuguese don. The point of the play is that for Violante her promise to her friend weighs more heavily than a quarrel with her lover Felix. She is even willing to break with him, not only out of female solidarity to protect Isabella, but also out of self-preservation, because his behaviour tells her that he cannot trust and love her, so she had better give him up. Whereas Felix believes that no woman can keep a secret, Violante lives by a masculine code of honour, insisting that for a woman honour does not merely lie in chastity but in keeping one's faith and word, like a man. Hence she proves that a woman is any man's equal and that a 'man has no advantage but the name' (V/iii/387).

A Bold Stroke for a Wife (Lincoln's Inn Fields, 1718) is the fourth of Centlivre's great successes, though the play, in fact, gained popularity only after her death, when it ran through 236 performances in eighteenth-century London and inspired at least the titles of both Mrs Gardiner's and Mrs Cowley's plays *A Bold Stroke for a Husband*, dating from 1777 and 1783, respectively. The play is really very much a one-man show in which the hero, in order to win an heiress, impersonates a fop, a collector of antiquities, a Dutch merchant and a Quaker, to wheedle consent to the marriage from the four guardians. The heroine is completely passive and very much in the background, and leaves the stage to the virtuoso performances of her suitor, who adapts his disguises perfectly to the prejudices and predilections of the old beau, the antiquarian, the materialistic merchant and the canting Quaker, who share responsibility for the girl's guardianship. The humour poked at these men is gentle rather than acerbic, and the tone of the play is pleasantly melodious and comic.

With *The Artifice* (Drury Lane, 1722) Centlivre, after four years of silence, reverted to bawdy Restoration comedy and a hard-boiled tone surprising in the eighteenth century. The artifice of the title refers to three different stratagems only loosely connected. Sir John Freeman, disinherited by his father for his Whig sympathies, wins back his bride from his rich brother by joining forces with a Dutchwoman his brother has seduced and forsaken. She pretends to poison him and herself, and in his supposed death throes the rake marries her to atone for his sins, but is reconciled to the fraud when he hears of her fortune:

> NED: ... What, Forty Thousand Pounds, and ask Forgiveness! ... no Woman can be Guilty of any Fault, that has Forty Thousand Pounds.
>
> (V/iii/102)

In the second intrigue a penniless ensign plays the servant to a stupid widow to further his suit, and having exposed a sharper posing as a lord, marries her himself in the disguise of a rich country gentleman. The author glosses over the de facto invalidity of marriage in the case of fraudulent identity.

In the third strand of action an adulterous wife uses all kinds of pretences to cuckold her jealous husband, until he is forced to give her more freedom. This 'Spanish' plot does not really fit into the English context. As opposed to the basically good-natured rakes of reform comedy, both Ned and the ensign are totally mercenary and cynical, though Centlivre, in the end, rather unconvincingly turns the one into a true Whig and the other into a kind-hearted husband. In accordance with the sentimental taste of the time, atonement is done to the deserted girl, but as so often, the author shows no pity for the cheated widow who hoped to climb the social ladder, but joins in the laughter of the men who are after her money. Some of the scenes are quite funny, for instance when the ensign, disguised as a stupid servant, mortifies the widow by taking her orders to bring everything on a plate literally and presents her with her dog and dirty shoes on a silver platter. Nor is the play devoid of verbal humour. Thus the Dutchwoman's complaint that Ned is her legal husband and that their vows are 'Register'd in Heaven' does not impress the English: 'Humph! that's a long way off, and very few Lawyers go that Circuit' (II/i/17). On the whole, however, the comedy is weaker and less original than her great successes.

Farces
In her comedies Centlivre partly relies on farcical encounters for her effects, and she also wrote three full-fledged farces between her

comedies. *A Bickerstaff's Burying; or Work for the Upholders* (Haymarket, 1710) is dedicated tongue in cheek 'To the Magnificent Company of Upholders', that is, undertakers, and in its title suggests a reference to Swift's treatment of the death of the almanac-maker Partridge and to Steele's satire on undertakers. The farce is set on an island where it is the custom that the surviving marriage partner be buried alive with the corpse. An Englishwoman married to a local emir is kept in constant panic by his frequent claims to be dying – the only method he has to make her gentle and loving towards him. But she turns the tables on him by pretending to die herself, and the officers are just about to bury the horrified man when it is discovered that the wife's coffin is empty and that she has escaped on board an English ship. The mild satire is directed against the custom of mercenary marriages, which Centlivre likens to the barbaric custom of interring the unhappy spouses alive 'from the first Day of their Marriage' (Dedication).

The Gotham Election, written in 1715 but denied a licence to be performed because of its sensitive political subject, is a more interesting work since it was quite new for a farceur to take up contemporary political issues and to set the play among lower-class provincial characters. Because of Centlivre's political zealousness, however, the play is crudely polemical and rarely funny. In the Dedication Centlivre indeed strikes a hysterical sectarian tone, complaining of the leniency of the English authorities towards Catholics and Jacobites, 'endeavouring to bury our Religion, and Liberty, under tyranny and Popish Superstition', while the French enemy is less squeamish about squashing Dissenters. The play exposes the electioneering practices of a Tory candidate who flatters and bribes tradesmen and their wives, promising them incredible posts at court, and making a fool of himself by kissing a cobbler. Significantly, he and his associates have a preference for French wine and are willing to aid the Jacobites. The daughter of one of the Tories, who is to be sent to a French nunnery, elopes with a complete stranger, if only he will spend her fortune 'in Defence of Liberty and Property against *Perkin* and the Pope' (vi/69f.). The play ends with the assertion that 'Who hates his Country, ne'er can love his Wife' (vi/72), but whether the argument can be reversed is left in doubt. The Whig bridegroom is a mere fortune hunter and not so scrupulously honest either, but Centlivre forgives him all his faults because of his party allegiance. She also shows herself to be quite misogynist

in her contemptuous portrayal of the 'petticoat government' of a
female politician canvassing for the Tory Party.

Centlivre's latent misogyny, as well as her hysterical anti-
Catholicism, is even shriller in her afterpiece *A Wife Well Manag'd*,
also written in 1715 but performed only in 1724. In it a wife in love
with her confessor is mercilessly whipped out of her appetite by her
husband, disguised in a priest's habit, who then complacently
watches how the woman beats up the unsuspecting monk in
return. The play ends with the man's smug claim that there is
'no Cure for Cuckoldom like Oyl of Rope' (iv/21) for passionate
wives.

In view of the farces in particular, it hardly seems justified to view
Centlivre as a whole-hearted feminist, though in some of her
comedies she is certainly much more sympathetic towards the plight
of women and introduces heroines evincing a female solidarity and
intellectual autonomy rare in the drama of the time. Like most
women dramatists we have encountered, her work is contradictory
and market oriented, not promotive of women's rights, although in
her unwavering support for the Whigs and Marlborough and
staunch anti-Catholicism she is less inconsistent, even when it
involved her plays in political difficulties. Her heroes are often
soldiers and ardent Whigs, whose fervent patriotism is meant to
illustrate their high moral stature. Like Behn, Centlivre excelled
mainly at Spanish intrigue comedy. Except for her first and final
comedies, however, her tone is mellower, though rarely downright
sentimental and didactic. Like Behn, she frequently presents the
baleful consequences of enforced marriages on frustrated women
fettered to old men, although her unhappy wives are not allowed to
escape and must bear their burden as best they can. Her most
remarkable heroines – Lady Plotwell, Miranda, Violante and Lucinda
in *Love's Contrivance* – are more level headed and practical minded
than Behn's women characters, and also take the action and their
lives into their own hands. Several plays draw attention to the
power language bestows on these women, who manipulate others
by speaking and holding their tongues alternately. A central motif in
many comedies is the outwitting of an obstructive guardian, who
frequently remains unreconciled even at the end, but whose curses
do not intrude on the young lovers' happiness. As Frushell points
out,[54] romantic intrigue leavened by farce, as practised by Centlivre,

was not the dominant form Augustan comedy was to take, but her vein of pleasantry was taken up by Hannah Cowley, John O'Keeffe, Goldsmith and Sheridan in some of the best comedies of the second half of the century.

Part III
The Eighteenth Century

Eighteenth-century England was said to be paradise for women, purgatory for horses and hell for servants. In reality, however, the situation for women was probably more repressive than it had been in previous centuries. Legally, there was little improvement. Lord Hardwicke's Marriage Act of 1753 turned marriage into a civil contract, but the measure had little effect on the actual status of women. A private Act of Parliament was still needed for a divorce; women were not legal entities, and were classed together with 'wards, lunatics, idiots and outlaws'.[55] They continued to be excluded from public and political life, although some women exerted an influence behind the scenes. Open 'petticoat government', however, was universally abhorred. Despite their powerlessness, some women engaged in political pamphleteering, and it was even fashionable for ladies to indicate their party allegiance by the spot on which they stuck their beauty patches. In the course of the century girls gradually gained a greater say in the choice of their spouses, affectionate marriages became the rule, and the relationship between parents and children became less formal.

As regards work, the situation undoubtedly became more difficult for independent-minded women. The spirit of enterprise in all fields of life, leading to the modernisation and rationalisation of production to increase profit, was turning Britain into a modern, capitalist economy. But the resulting split between workplace and home, and the decline in small landholdings, severed women from the production process. Many domestic goods, from candles to cloth and beer, were no longer made at home, but industrially, and women's managerial functions were no longer needed. Because of the increasing wealth of the bourgeoisie, who were intent on emulating the aristocracy, the need for middle-class female labour to supplement the family income declined. It was considered to be a sign of gentility that the wife of a rich merchant or craftsman should not have to work. Hence, bourgeois women were adjuncts to rather than working members of the family and leisure became their usual condition. From being producers, they turned into consumers. The main duties of a lady were to obey her husband and to produce an heir. Eighteenth-century women bore up to 20 children, but middle- and upper-class women had little to do with child rearing or even education. The pointlessness and artificiality of their lives are evinced by the grotesque fashions of hooped skirts which forced the wearers to go sideways through open doors, and of giant hairdos half a metre high and in danger of catching fire from the chandeliers.

In accordance with the new ideal of refined leisure, schools mainly taught female accomplishments designed to increase a girl's value on the marriage market, and though moralists like Steele and Addison protested against the frivolity and triviality of the idle lady of the age, few advocated serious intellectual training for women, and many of those who frequented the salons of famous women of letters were downright misogynist in their sneers at women who trespassed beyond their proper sphere – not least Pope and Johnson, the latter likening female preachers to dogs walking on their hind legs.

With nothing left to do, some women dedicated themselves to various humanitarian causes, from the abolition of slavery to the reclaiming of prostitutes, activities which were considered compatible with women's alleged moral superiority and tenderness of heart. This cult of sensibility was intended to compensate for women's complete lack of public function. They were talked into believing themselves endowed with the gift of feeling, which became a virtue in itself for women. The upsurge of feminist thought at the beginning of the eighteenth century was stifled by this cult of sentimentalism, which gave women an illusionary status and importance denied them in reality. Since custom now decreed separate spheres for men and women, it was but a small step to believe that men and women were different in nature, and that the weaker sex was constitutionally unfit for the more arduous tasks in the commercial world outside the home. Domesticity, sensitivity and selflessness were held to be natural female attributes. More than ever, a woman's place was the home and the family.

Men considered it requisite to protect women from all forms of 'indecency' (and indecency almost invariably meant sex), to drape togas around statues and veils over painted nudes, and to censor their language when ladies were present. To be sure, it was still considered completely natural that a man should sow his wild oats, and for upper-class males even open liaisons were not uncommon; easily available pornography and widespread prostitution were the reverse side of this growing prudishness and recoiling from sexuality.

For respectable women, this cult of sentimentalism involved a corseted self-image and restricted subject matter in both conversation and writing, since every syllable and gesture had to prove their perfect modesty, passivity, chastity and moral elevation. Wit was associated with the immorality of the Restoration period. Sexually liberated playwrights like Behn, Manley and Centlivre were castigated as 'Vice's friends, and Virtue's female foes'.[56] Thus, decorum left women writers with little linguistic ammunition to counter misogynist diatribes and assert their birthrights to a place in the literary marketplace. To be sure, female authors had ceased to be novelties and to excite immediate curiosity and hostility. But in a climate in which a woman's nature was defined as reticent, self-sacrificing and homely, publishing work and competing on the literary circuit required a woman to justify herself, with regard to both the public and herself, while writers like Behn, the Female Wits and even Centlivre, despite vicious attacks, had regarded such competition as a natural claim.

The theatre retained its dubious moral image. Actresses by now were well established, even though quite a few were notorious for their private lives, such as Eliza Haywood, Charlotte Charke or 'Perdita' Robinson, while others, like Elizabeth Inchbald, had unblemished reputations. There were also stories about the backstage sexual harassment of actresses and female playwrights. Audiences were still rowdy. Drury Lane was wrecked by riots in 1743, 1750,

1755, 1763, 1770 and 1776, and the star actor cum theatre manager
David Garrick had to apologise on his knees for performing a play
different from the one billed.[57]

After William III's ascension to the throne, Court patronage had
declined. During the reign of Queen Anne several patents were
granted to new houses, so that a number of fringe theatres opened
at the beginning of the century, of which Fielding's in the Haymarket was to become the most important. The first two Georges,
known as Dunce I and Dunce II, unable to speak English, were not
interested in the theatre. But the omnipotent Prime Minister Robert
Walpole cracked down on the political opposition which had used
plays to ridicule and attack him by introducing a Licensing Act in
1737 stipulating that every play performed had to be vetted by a
censor. This measure killed political theatre and gagged dramatists,
some of whom, like Fielding, turned to the novel instead. Even
more significant, however, was that the Licensing Act limited
legitimate drama to Drury Lane and Covent Garden, a new theatre
opened in 1732, with the Haymarket serving as a summer stage for
light entertainment. Any other commercial performance of plays in
London was prohibited, though ingenious people tried to get
around this measure by staging plays as puppet shows, or charging
entrance for musical entertainments and giving a play in between,
'free of charge'. Occasionally, new plays were also premiered at
Exeter or Bath, where fashionable society moved during the
summer months, when the legitimate theatres in London were
closed. Dublin, too, had a theatre of some importance. However,
performing in the provinces was not really a viable alternative,
since sizeable audiences were to be had in London only, which
remained the unrivalled centre of the theatrical world throughout
the eighteenth century. The provinces were toured by strolling
players. Therefore, the new regulation drastically limited the market
for new plays and eliminated competition, since the two privileged
London stages were happy enough to divide the market between
themselves. Managers preferred to put on old hits rather than new
and untried plays, and aspiring playwrights had to please not only
the town but also the managers of the two patented theatres to
make a career.

Dramatists still depended for their income on benefit nights, and
some complained that the all-powerful managers had contrived to
premier their plays late in the season, when the upper classes were

leaving London and the theatres were half empty, and had then pocketed the full profit when the play was taken up again in the next season. Only at the end of the century did celebrated dramatists begin to bargain for lump sums for their scripts. It also became usual in the eighteenth century to have special benefit nights for actors, who could choose the play they wanted performed for this occasion.

Augustan audiences could choose from a wide variety of entertainments, including such blood-thirsty spectacles as cock-fighting and bear-baiting, apart from various hybrid forms of theatre. Throughout the century dramatists complained about new audience tastes, from Italian opera to pantomimes and all kinds of circus shows. The legitimate stages catered to these vulgar tastes by adding a comic afterpiece to every performance, which would release the less sophisticated spectators from the rigours of a *King Lear* or *Venice Preserved*. Such afterpieces could be one-act farces, harlequinades, fairytale romances or potted legitimate plays distilled to a few effective scenes. Odd as the custom may seem nowadays, it provided women playwrights with some opportunity to make money by complying with this demand for superficial spectacles, as well as parodying its excesses.

6
Women Dramatists of the Early Eighteenth Century

There is general agreement among critics that drama went into a long decline in the course of the eighteenth century. In the general uncertainty as to what might humour theatre-goers, plays became more diversified from the second decade of the century onwards, with 'reformed' Restoration comedies, sentimental comedies, farces, harlequinades, romances, tragi-comedies, heroic plays, 'classical' tragedies and historical tragedies being performed. Yet fewer new plays were put on by theatres and production opportunities were less easily forthcoming, a stiffening of climate felt especially by women playwrights, who found it difficult to establish a career in the theatre. Even those newcomers who were given a chance seem to have been quickly discouraged. Except for Centlivre with her prolific output, in the period until 1750 only two women had more than two legitimate plays performed on a London stage: Eliza Haywood, with four productions, and Mrs Hoper, with three. Charlotte Charke had two plays performed, and a puppet show, and Mrs Cooper could boast of two productions. Plays that were performed were not necessarily printed and are therefore lost, such as Letitia Pilkington's comedy *The Turkish Court, or The London Prentice* (performed in Dublin in 1748), or the afterpiece *The Maggot*, which the actress Mrs Egleton wrote and performed on her own benefit night at Lincoln's Inn Fields in 1732. Productions of new plays, of course, fell off sharply after the Licensing Act, when those women who had found a home in Fielding's Haymarket Theatre found themselves on the street. So after 1737 it became more common to have an unacted play printed, a practice that had been comparatively rare except among aristocrats in earlier periods.

The beginning of the century had been more favourable to feminist thought. Mary Astell's arguments for female equality and a better education had some notable influence on drama and there was, in several plays by men as well as women, an awareness of the unfairness of marital law to women and the liabilities from which married women suffered. To be sure, few of the male writers had been genuinely liberal, but the marriage problem play had given a distinct tone and mark to the period. Now feminist thought was becoming increasingly unfashionable. Few women writers were willing to take up the standard of an Aphra Behn and Susanna Centlivre. At a time when it was difficult to persuade a theatre manager to produce a play, many aspiring women dramatists, who were writing for money rather than self-expression, felt it prudent to cater to the more prudish and mawkish tastes of the audience, no matter how they themselves felt about a subject. Even in prefatory material feminist arguments became rare and writers preferred to play the card of feigned humility and defencelessness, asking the male spectators for gentlemanly indulgence towards the weaker sex and appealing to the ladies in the audience for support.

Comedies and farces

Although, at the turn of the century, there had been a feeling that tragedy was a more appropriate genre, in fact women in the early eighteenth century wrote many more comedies and farces, which were in greater demand. Several of the burlesques written by actresses give the impression of being quickly penned rejoinders for injuries received, rather than serious attempts to win literary laurels as Manley and Trotter had tried to do. However, there were also some very good comedies written by women at the time, not only by Centlivre, but also by some of her contemporaries. Nor are comic heroines all passive and insipid; indeed, outspoken and self-assertive heroines survived long after their heyday in Restoration comedy, albeit chastened in their sexual liberty.

One of the best comic writers of the time, Mary Davys, a contemporary of Centlivre's and friend of Swift's, had her *The Northern Heiress, or The Humours of York* produced at Lincoln's Inn Fields in 1716. Born in Dublin, she was widowed young and settled in York, writing novels and plays for a living, and later opening a coffee house in Cambridge with the profits derived from *The Northern Heiress*. The Dedication to Princess Anne, depreciating the play as an unworthy 'trifle', yet free from 'Obscenity, faction and a general contempt of religion', may bode ill for its entertainment value, but the comedy is, in reality, robust, vivacious and totally unmoralising. The self-confidence and good humour with which, after her London success, she took as a hidden compliment the typical misogynist critique that the play could not possibly have been written by a woman – she was 'proud they think it deserves a better author' (Preface) – contrasts refreshingly with the false humility or complaints of harsh treatment usually found in women's forewords.

In the Prologue the author confesses her ignorance of classical rules, and also of French and Spanish, which might have enabled her to plagiarise foreign plays. The comedy is original. While most comedies of the time still feature London settings, this play takes the audience to York. We have already encountered the figure of the strong-minded heiress who subjects her suitor to a variety of tests in Ariadne's *She Ventures and He Wins* (1695) and Pix's *The Beau Defeated* (1700), and there is even an inkling of Centlivre's Violante in the northern heiress's assertion that she values female friendship more than a lover's sighs. Davys nicely undercuts the lover's high-mindedness by allowing the young man to find out prematurely that he is merely being screened and that he can therefore play the romantic lover with impunity. As the motif requires, he, of course, proves insusceptible to temptation by a masked female, but his exemplary virtue is satirised rather than extolled: 'Are you us'd to the Misfortune of Ravishment, Sir, that you are so mightily afraid of your self?' (IV/56). Even the patriotic tone is undermined when the hero's praise of England is specifically the outcome of his love of 'a plain Rump of Beef' (I/14). The play's true forte, however, is the various subordinate characters representing the 'humours' of York. It is the insight into some of the local customs that gives the comedy its freshness and originality. The upper echelons of provincial society consist of vulgar aldermen's wives, who go to market themselves, drink ale for their breakfast instead of new-fangled tea and pay for their fare if they are invited to their friends' houses. The most memorable among them is the splendidly coarse candle-maker's widow, who constantly utters malapropisms ('salivating' (I/20) instead of 'serenading'), beats up the cowardly men and has no scruples about speaking her mind. Thus she contemptuously comments on a young coxcomb and his stingy mother:

> I have known her wash her Hands in Butter-Milk, and then put it into her Servants Puddings: But what they sav'd at the Spiggot this Rake lets out at the Bung-Hole.
>
> (I/21)

As is to be expected in the second decade of the eighteenth century, *The Northern Heiress* completely dispenses with bawdiness, yet it retains the liveliness, wit and unsentimentality of the Restoration comedy of manners and should be ranked with Centlivre's works among the best plays of the period.

Mary Davys' second play, *The Self-Rival*, was to be acted at Drury Lane, but was never produced, and was published in 1725 without name, date or dedication. The comedy is, perhaps, not quite as original as her first, but still vivid and dramatically effective. It is again set in the country, this time in Middlesex, and describes how a young soldier disguises himself as his titled uncle to trick a tyrannical father into consenting to his marrying the latter's daughter. The girl sees through the mask at once, but is content to play the game since it gives her a chance to marry the man she loves (as usual, the author passes over the legal obstacle of *error personae*). Yet the heroine takes revenge for the intended fraud by mocking the would-be lover to his 'uncle's' face, and in the end gives him to understand that she has not been deceived for a minute and has merely amused herself. Touched by this proof of her consent to the marriage, the young husband offers her every freedom:

> You shall make your own Conditions after Surrender ... nay, shall command as before, so I may but have the Name of your superior Officer.
>
> (V/58)

The spirited battle of wit between the two lovers is reminiscent of Restoration comedy:

COLONEL: Nay Madam, why do you run away?
MARIA: Because, Colonel, I know 'tis an unspeakable Pleasure to
you to pursue a flying Enemy.

(I/7)

She loves 'trophies of victory' just as much as he does, and while he hangs his standards in Westminster Hall, she furnishes her chamber with 'the spoils of dead, or dying Lovers' (I/8f.).

In a second strand of action, a girl in the guise of a fortune teller tricks the same tyrannical father into consenting to her marriage to his son, if the latter will only have her. A third plot concerns two old maids, a hypocritical one who pretends to learning and a contempt for men, and a witty, good-natured one, who always speaks well of marriage, lest people believe that all old maids 'repine at [their] Condition' (II/19), and their farcical quarrel with an ill-natured cynic. The learned lady pretending to despise marriage receives the customary ridicule and is presented as a typical case of sour grapes. The likeable spinster, however, is a pleasant and very rare figure at a time when unmarried women were considered objects of mockery, though, predictably, she warns the heroine not to gamble away her chances of marriage. Another original minor character is the servant who has mastered Greek and quotes poetry, while his employer idled away the university terms in taverns. The Prologue, striking the same light-hearted yet confident tone we have already encountered in her first play, defends women dramatists' right to an unprejudiced hearing:

> When Women write, the Criticks, now-a-days,
> Are Ready, e'er they see, to damn their Plays;
> Wit, as the Men's Prerogative, they claim,
> And with one Voice, the bold Invader blame.
> Tell me the Cause, ye Gallants of the Pit,
> Did *Phoebus* e'er the *Salique* Law admit?

Ten years afterwards, Elizabeth Cooper, who was later to become one of the first collectors of early English poetry, followed suit in *The Rival Widows, or The Fair Libertine* (Covent Garden, 1735). The Preface reveals the novice's fear of the censure generally meted out to women for their ignorance of the classical rules and for any offence against modesty. But though Cooper assures the reader that she will not offend 'the Innocent and Virtuous', the play is, indeed, a return to Restoration modes, although without the bawdiness repugnant to the more prudish age. In the centre of the complicated plot, full of intrigues and misunderstandings, is a witty and independent-minded widow, Lady Bellair, who has so ruined her first husband that 'he left her scarce enough to carry her thro' the modish Varieties of a first Mourning' (I/iv/9), and who torments her numerous suitors, persuading a fop to turn Puritan, and, like Centlivre's Miranda, ridiculing the pining courtship of a sober lover, until he almost defects into the arms of her hypocritical cousin. In the course of the century, heroes were indeed becoming increasingly timid, using only exaggerated rhetoric to declare their love, until they were completely domesticated in sentimental comedy. A wry smile at their histrionics debunks their sentimental excesses:

> O! if 'tis my Face you are so fond of, you shall have Admission to my Picture every Day; and talk to it all the fine Things you can think of; I'll engage it shall not interrupt you.
>
> (II/vii/34)

In the end Lady Bellair wins him back, and her cousin has to relinquish the jointure she has embezzled. The comedy is sprightly and amusing, and the characters, although conventional, are well conceived, the men being shadowed by the two dominant women characters. The device of juxtaposing two widows of different characters was used by Pix in *The Different Widows* and *The Beau Defeated* as well as by Centlivre in *The Basset Table*. The hypocritical cousin, pretending to be shocked by sex but lusting after the hero, is predictably exposed in the end. Few heroines, however, are simultaneously so giddy and flirtatious, yet so rational and likeable, and so unflinching an advocate of female equality as Lady Bellair, who holds that 'Virtue is of neither Sex, but the same in both' (II/ii/23). Such heroines were becoming few and far between as the century wore on. Lady Bellair masterminds every intrigue, counteracts every plot and lords it over everyone. Like a Restoration heroine, she has no intention of losing the freedom her widowhood has granted her:

> Men only buy their Slaves, but Women their Masters.... There's some Joy in having the Man you doat on for your Slave, but none for your Lord.
>
> (II/ii/23)

Nor is she forced to repent and tone down her manners in the end to win her lover, like many coquettes in reform comedy. In a surprisingly unromantic ending, she forbids him all exaggerated professions of love: as long as they are sincerely devoted to each other, they will stay together, but they promise to separate if their marriage should turn sour. The railing against marriage and the ridicule heaped upon Puritan cant looks back to the Restoration period. Cooper's anti-Whig outlook is also suggested by the fact that, unlike Centlivre's patriotic figures, her heroine remains unimpressed by the approaches of a soldier, who, she cautions, 'has his Honour to serve, as well as his Wife; and two Mistresses are to the full as hard to please as two Masters' (II/v/29). She is equally contemptuous of a bishop:

> it may be against the Canon to let a Woman be the Head of the Church. – Beside, I should be loth to kneel for a Blessing to him, who should think it a Blessing to kneel to me.
>
> (II/v/29f.)

A second comedy by Mrs Cooper, *The Nobleman; or, The Family Quarrel*, was performed on three nights at the Haymarket in the following year, but, unfortunately, was not printed and has therefore not survived.

Lady Mary Wortley Montagu also wrote one play, *Simplicity*, a translation of Marivaux's *Le Jeu de l'Amour et du Hasard* probably written in the thirties after the French play had been performed in London, but, like the aristocratic ladies of earlier centuries, she sought neither production nor publication. *Simplicity* is a vivid and witty comedy about a betrothed couple assuming the identity of servants to test each other's characters, while the footman and maid play the gentlefolk. As is to be expected, the young aristocrat falls in love with the supposed maid, and she with the supposed valet, each suffering agonies of shame over this inappropriate match, while the two servants are plagued with bad consciences about courting their betters. These misunderstandings give rise to a series of comic encounters and good-natured teasing.

That Restoration comedy, even in its more bawdy variant, was not completely dead, is evinced by Penelope Aubin's *The Humours of the Masqueraders* (Haymarket, 1730), which uses the old cuckolding motif of sex comedy, albeit pretending somewhat unbelievably that nothing improper has happened during the nightly romps presented. We know little about Aubin's personal life. The didactic and religious tone of her novels forms an odd contrast to the sexual innuendo of her only comedy, in which a young wife is all too eager to cheat on her old husband with a rake, who, together with his friend, haunts the house in a devil's costume. When the suspicious old miser also dons the same disguise, he is mercilessly beaten up by the young men, who are saved from exposure by an amorous widow, who has followed the hero into the house also wearing the identical costume and pretends to have spent the night with the wife. In the end the hero marries the widow, and the usurer decides to hoard his money no longer for unlawful heirs. All the characters are stereotypes and the action is mere farce. The sentiments voiced are surprisingly licentious for the time. The disagreeable old husband, who takes medicine for wind before bedtime, is even more off-putting than the one in Behn's *The Lucky Chance*, and it is hardly surprising that his wife 'freeze[s] at his Touch, and loath[es] his Embraces' (I /iii/10). She is not censured for her immorality and, atypically, is not made to reform and repent, although she loses her lover to the widow. In contrast, the young wife in the anonymous farce *The Little French Lawyer* (Drury Lane, 1749), adapted from Beaumont and Fletcher, decides to stay faithful to her old husband and jilts the rake. Her story is loosely linked with that of a puny lawyer who, having acquired a taste for duelling, challenges even a judge and is beaten out of his bravery.

The move from more sophisticated comedy to farce is also exemplified by *The City Farce*, intended for performance in Drury Lane in 1737 but unacted. It consists of a loosely connected series of scenes ridiculing the follies and fopperies of the cowardly London militia, whose annual parade gives tradesmen an opportunity to show off their finery and ape their betters. In the Dedication the author attacks the contemporary fashion of pantomime and foreign imitation, avowing her intention to revive the spirit of old English farce. The play's focus is on slapstick, with no attempt at rounded characterisation or consistent plot. The play was published anonymously, and attributed by Allardyce Nicoll to one Mrs Weddell.[58] However, there is reason to doubt whether the writer was a woman at all. The Dedication to 'the Gentlemen of the Pit' indeed has a masculine ring to it and, like the Epilogue, is particularly contemptuous of women and explicitly neglectful of the customary appeal to the ladies in the audience. The assertion that the author does not depend on theatre managers for bread but seems to write for personal gratification is at odds with the tone of almost all other women playwrights, who turned to the stage to support themselves, and even without such incentive never confessed to being interested in self-realisation, since in view of the prevalent prejudices against women dramatists this would have added insult to injury. The suspicion that the author was, in fact, a man is reinforced by the lengthy discussion of the dramatic rules in the Preface to a second anonymous unacted play attributed to Mrs Weddell, *Incle and Yarico* (1742), as most female dramatists of the time professed to ignorance of the classical rules.

Farcical entertainments were greatly in demand, as is evinced by the increasing number of burlesques, travesties and harlequinades. Mrs Aubert's mock opera *Harlequin Hydaspes, or The Greshamite* (Lincoln's Inn Fields, 1719), a burlesque of the opera *Hydaspes* and derivative of *What D'ye Call It* in its mixture of opera, comedy, farce and heroic drama, describes the attempt of Scaramouch and Harlequin to free the two wards of a doctor, a quack who treats everyone with vomiting oil. The doctor relinquishes his ward to Harlequin, after the latter, a second Daniel, has survived the lion's den and has killed the beast with his bare hands. The superficial plot is interspersed with arias taken from various Italian operas, but the piece is too long and lacks drive, pace and genuine wit. Mrs Haywood's *The Opera of Operas; or Tom Thumb the Great* (Haymarket, 1733), set to music 'after the Italian manner', rechannels Fielding's attack on heroic drama into a satire on Italian opera, but was also influenced by Gay's *The Beggar's Opera*. Haywood borrows most of Fielding's plot and characters, including the diminutive hero, who is loved by a giantess and a princess and eaten by a cow, and retains the splendid mock-heroic tone of the original, excelling in outrageous imagery – 'for Liberty we fight, / And Liberty the mustard is of life' (III/ii/37). Thus, the king, who proclaimed general rejoicing at the news of the great victory, now orders state mourning on Tom Thumb's death:

> Shut up again the prisons – bid my treasurer
> Not give three farthings out – hang all the Culprits,
> Guilty, or not, – no matter – ravish virgins –

Go bid the school-masters whip all their boys;
Let lawyers, parsons and physicians loose
To rob, impose on, and to kil [sic] the world.
(III/ii/40)

Since the opera critic in the frame play objects to the general carnage at the end as being inappropriate to Italian opera, the corpses
are resuscitated and made to marry.

Much less enjoyable and witty is Elizabeth Boyd's unacted *Don
Sancho, or The Students Whim* (1739), a ballad opera about a student
prank to conjure up the spirits of Shakespeare and Dryden, who
indeed appear, but have nothing much to say except that fame no
longer is a concern in their blessed abodes. In Minerva's temple the
priests (mistaken by the irreverent students for strolling players)
pay obeisance to the statues of the world's greatest poets, among
whom are the predictable choices of Shakespeare, Dryden, Gay,
Congreve and Addison, with the somewhat surprising addition of
Waller, Boyle and Lansdowne. In the Prologue to the printed edition, addressed to Pope, the author, an 'untaught female' in need of
a mentor, implored the great poet to correct her 'medley-whim', but
he evidently took little interest in this farce.

Several burlesques modelled on Buckingham's *Rehearsal* were
written by actresses angry at the prevailing demand for unsophisti-
cated entertainments, or personally threatened by quarrels with
management. In Charlotte Charke's[59] *The Art of Management, or
Tragedy Expell'd* (York Buildings, 1735) the inexperienced manager,
Brainless, who 'resolv'd his players should not put him out of
Countenance, by having more Wit than himself' (1/12), dismisses
the best actors, including Mrs Tragic (Charke herself, who played
this role), and means to make money from animal shows, clownery
and prize fights. With appealing self-irony, Charke makes fun of her
own histrionic style and grand gestures. In the end the manager is
arrested for debt and Tragic reinstated in her power. The play is
dedicated, tongue in cheek, to the theatre manager Charles
Fleetwood, begging him not to encumber his 'Head with Theatric
Affairs any longer, but leave it to the Fools who are us'd to it',
wishful thinking that did not materialise in real life. Although in the
unusually self-confident Preface the author denies having based her
characters on real-life models, it is quite obvious that the play is
meant as a personal revenge on Charke's enemies in the theatre,

since she complains at great length that she has been unjustly dismissed for loose morals, and has thus been deprived

> of the means of an honest livelihood, without giving some immediate provocation; and for my private misconduct, which it seems, has been (for want of a better alledged as a reason), tho' a bad one; for while my follies only are hurtful to my self, I know no Right that any Person, unless Relations, or very good Friends, have to call me to Account. I'll allow private Virtues heighten publick Merits, but then the Want of those private Virtues wont affect an Actors Performance.

This vigorous refusal to be defined by the traditional equation of female virtue and chastity came from the pen of one of the most eccentric and flamboyant women playwrights of the whole period. The tenth child of Colley Cibber, Charlotte showed an early predilection for male clothing and role play, and indeed in later life was a transvestite frequently mistaken for a man and involved in complicated situations with women. Left by her philandering husband, she turned to the stage to support herself and her child, but was dismissed by Charles Fleetwood for unspecified 'immorality'. Though she was later reinstated in Drury Lane through the influence of her father, she soon fell out with him, too, the two remaining at loggerheads for the rest of their lives. She joined Fielding's company, which, however, was forced out of business after the Licensing Act of 1737, and henceforth supported herself in a variety of odd jobs, working as a valet, farmer, pastry cook and prompter, selling groceries and sausages, running a tavern and a puppet theatre, becoming a strolling player (under a male pseudonym) and trying to avoid the Licensing Act with various tricks, such as announcing concerts with a play 'gratis' in between, or selling tickets for a pint of ale, not for a performance. She wrote novels and a sexually explicit autobiography. However, she did not find an adequate means of support and died in poverty in 1760. Charlotte Charke continued the tradition of Behn and Manley, who had defied public prejudice by claiming sexual freedom, but what had been difficult enough in the Restoration carried an ineradicable stigma in a more restrictive age, and led to ostracism.

Mrs Hoper's farce *The Cyclopedia* (Haymarket, 1748) was not published, but her *Queen Tragedy Restor'd* (Haymarket, 1749) is inspired by a similar concern with the demise of the tragic muse. However, unlike Charke's, her burlesque is devoid of wit and self-irony, lacking both structure and coherent plot, and rendering somewhat presumptuous the author's hopes 'to be rank'd with *Sappho, Phillips, Behn,* / And prove that Women write as well as Men' (Prologue, by a friend).

The play presents some vain attempts to cure the melancholic 'tragic queen' (played by the author herself) by performing insipid tragedies and stale comedies, until she is revived by Shakespeare's ghost, who alone can make the stage flourish again. The Prologue pleads for tolerance towards a woman who, after foundering in business, has turned to the semi-legitimate source of the stage to earn some money:

> Left in Distress, what can a Woman do?
> By Nature helpless, and by Want beset:
> Is Playing meaner, than to run in Debt?
> The Stage is innocent, and brings no Shame,
> Unless the Players are themselves to blame.

Catherine Clive's *The Rehearsal, or Bays in Petticoats* (Drury Lane, 1750), performed for the actress's own benefit, is a more amusing piece, which stayed in repertoire for a decade. Its title deliberately refers to Buckingham's caricature of Dryden as the asinine playwright Bayes, but its plot is modelled more closely on *The Female Wits*. Again, the protagonist is a female playwright at a rehearsal, played by Clive herself, an actress who excelled in the roles of country girls, hoydens, viragos and chambermaids, and had survived in the theatre despite quarrels with several eminent colleagues, including Garrick himself. Like the Manley character in the older satire, the female dramatist pompously shows off her talent, abuses her maid and is ridiculed by her foppish acquaintances. Yet, unlike the earlier, more malicious satire, Clive's play does not really target female literary ambition, but the misogynist prejudices levelled against women playwrights, such as the rumour that their plays were ghost-written by men, and their ignorance of the classical rules, charges which the fictitious authoress rejects furiously:

MRS HAZARD: And so, you're hand in Glove with the classics, are you?... Consult my Male Acquaintance! I thank my Stars, thou art not one of 'em.

(II/39)

The play abounds in self-irony. When an actress called Mrs Clive does not show up for the rehearsal, the female playwright played by Clive herself takes her part, but is so frustrated by constant interruptions that she leaves, threatening to tear up her script. While theatrical in-jokes were directed at Betterton and his company in *The Female Wits*, now Garrick comes in for his share of satirical abuse. Clive's other farces and short dramatic sketches, *Every Woman in Her Humour* (Drury Lane, 1760), the translation from Marivaux, *The Island of Slaves* (Drury Lane, 1761), *The Sketch of a Fine Lady Returning from a Rout* (Drury Lane, 1763) and *The Faithful Irish Woman* (Drury Lane, 1765), were not printed.

All these farcical pieces, amusing and fascinating though they may be for their insight into contemporary backstage life, are slight and superficial entertainments, restricted to topical issues and personalities, and working with rather heavy-handed satirical humour. The eighteenth century, however, is not usually associated with farcical comedy, but with its 'sentimental' variety, aimed at inspiring pity and moral edification, cultivating sentiment and emphasising innate goodness, the reward of virtue and moral reform, instead of ridiculing foibles or satirising society. However, at least in the first half of the century, sentimental comedy was much less frequent than its satirical, 'laughing' counterpart, though most comedies include sentimental ingredients, such as abruptly obliging guardians, long-suffering suitors, or last-minute reforms. Of all the plays written by women in this period, only Eliza Haywood's *A Wife to be Lett* would qualify as a fully fledged sentimental comedy.

Eliza Haywood was a very prolific writer, but, like Delarivier Manley, she achieved notoriety rather than fame and became chiefly known for her scandalous romances and *romans à clef*. She was reticent about her lowly origins and youthful indiscretions, but it was known that she had left her husband to make a living by acting and writing. In the 1728 version of *The Dunciad*, Pope coarsely attacked her as 'Juno of majestic size, / With cow-like udders, and with ox-like eyes'.[60] Despite her unorthodox lifestyle, however, she does not advocate feminist issues in her works, but holds conventional views as to a woman's place in society. She wrote two original plays and two adaptations (among them the above-mentioned *Opera of Operas*), but drama was not really her forte. Her stage career came to an end when Fielding's Little Theatre in the Haymarket had to close because of the Licensing Act.

A Wife to be Lett (Drury Lane, 1723) makes its didactic purpose amply clear in the Prologue, by warning the female spectators: 'Learn, from the opening scene, ye blooming Fair, / Rightly to know your Worth, and match with Care' (vi). The comedy interweaves several strands of action. In the sentimental plot, the miser Graspall sells his paragon of a wife to her admirer for £2000 and is exposed to all his neighbours when she pretends to turn licentious and make love to a woman in male disguise. This is loosely linked to a conventional story about two young men who rescue the girls they love from mercenary marriages to rich and foolish suitors. The sub-plot involves the tricking of a rich old woman into marrying a footman disguised as a baronet, a motif familiar from *The Beau Defeated* and *The Gamester*, where the victims are in fact saved from so disgraceful a match in the nick of time. Here, however, the old woman is merely counselled to content herself with the union and to buy the wretch a title. The two girls of the sub-plot are pleasant enough in their good-natured intrigues and the fun poked at the hyperboles of courtship is mild:

> Do you think it reasonable, that a Woman, who believes herself in some measure agreeable, should luse the pleasure of seeing her Lover tremble at her Approach, and by his Sighs and Melancholy betray the Passion he has for her to all who know him, admire all she says, and cry up all she does, and threaten to poison, stab or drown himself to pacify her, whenever she happens to be in the humour of giving Pain.
>
> (V/58f.)

But Haywood spoils even amusing scenes by excessive moralising, and the wife of the title is really too good to be true. In fact, she likes the man she is sold to, but, of course, is much too virtuous even to consider adultery. On the contrary, she reconciles her purchaser to the bride he has forsaken, another 'Prodigy of Goodness' (IV/i/54), who has followed him in male clothes and instantaneously regains his love because of her 'unexampled Tenderness and Generosity'

(IV/i/55). Having exposed her husband in a fake love scene with this woman, the long-suffering wife meekly returns to the man who meant to prostitute her. Behn, one suspects, would never have ended a play this way and let the despicable husband off the hook with so facile a repentance. Fielding, who may have been inspired by Haywood to tackle a similar theme in *A Modern Husband* (1732), is much more relentless in his exposure of contemporary mores.

It was, evidently, not completely uncommon for an unscrupulous husband to prostitute his wife in much the same manner that Haywood and Fielding portrayed. In 1738 there was a big scandal involving Colley Cibber's son Theophilus (Mrs Charke's brother), who promoted his wife's adulterous affair, but sued for damages when she left him to live with her lover and the financial subsidies he had enjoyed hitherto dried up. This wife, Susanna Cibber, wrote an otherwise unremarkable romance, *The Oracle* (Covent Garden, 1741), about a princess falling in love with a supposed statue, but the fairy godmother's enjoining the young groom to be a '*careful, compassionate* and *complaisant* husband' (viii/46) gains an ironic touch in view of the writer's fate.

Tragedies

Tragedy, on the whole, became more difficult to market than innocuous entertainment, and the output of tragedies written by women is considerably smaller than in the preceding period of the Female Wits. In fact, only six new tragedies by women were performed on the London stages between 1710 and 1750, this figure including Centlivre's *The Cruel Gift* and Manley's *Lucius*, as well as Mrs Hoper's *The Battle of Poictier, or The English Prince* (1747), the last unpublished. Two more were printed but not acted, though, as has been argued above, Mrs Weddell probably was not a woman at all. *Incle and Yarico* (1742), attributed to her, was probably written by a man.[61] While the latter play takes up the contemporary issue of slavery, most tragedies, even in the decades to come, opt for an oriental, classicised, or medieval setting – although distance in space and time does not preclude topical political relevance.

At the request of the manager Rich, Eliza Haywood extensively revised the plot, dialogue and characters of a work by Captain Hunt, which was staged at Lincoln's Inn Fields in 1721 under the title of *The Fair Captive*. In the Dedication the author disclaims a pretence to talent, yet at the same time laments the envy with which gifted writers are pursued. However, the ill success of this weak neo-heroic drama can hardly be blamed on envious cliques. As is the wont in oriental settings, the tragedy shows a virtuous virgin in distress in a seraglio, where she is saved from being raped by the wife of the lustful vizier, who suspects her husband's infidelity and is stabbed by him. The virgin's betrothed, coming to her rescue, hurls abuse at her for her supposed unchastity, until she offers to stab herself to prove her innocence. In the end he takes her back contentedly when the vizier is killed during an uprising and with his dying breath regretfully testifies to her inviolateness. The play concludes with some moralising against unrestrained passion and power, which may be a veiled reference to the excessive authority placed in the hands of Prime Minister Walpole.[62]

Like her sentimental comedy, Haywood's heroic tragedy, too, is melodramatic and full of false emotion. Her language is heavily clichéd: bosoms heave and swell, tears flood, hearts bleed, and souls feel tender transports. The heroine is entirely passive and so helpless that all she can do to prove her chastity is to offer suicide. The hero and the villain are motivated solely by love or lust, to the exclusion of all common sense. The latter risks a rebellion and the sultan's displeasure to gratify himself; the former suspects his bride to be a whore because she disobeyed his command and went to see the vizier, regardless of the fact that she went to save his own life:

> Thy Disobedience and Self-conceit,
> That very Crime that damn'd thy Grandame Eve,
> Has ruin'd thee.
>
> (V/71f.)

There is no indication in the play that the author regards such male authoritarianism as inappropriate. Indeed, the 'noble' Turkish rebels despise the vizier for yielding to his wife's influence, just as the Epilogue, written by a male friend, sneers at 'our Petticoat Dominion' in England.

With *Frederick, Duke of Brunswick-Luneburgh* (Lincoln's Inn Fields, 1729) Haywood ventured into a medieval setting long before the romantic revival made the Middle Ages an immensely popular backdrop for drama in the second half of the century. Haywood selected the historical subject to prove her patriotism by celebrating the glory and virtue of the House of Brunswick, from which the

Hannovarians were descended. The play shows how Frederick of Brunswick, elected Emperor of Germany, is murdered by a conspiracy headed by the Bishop of 'Mentz' – a typical piece of Whig anti-Catholicism. The warning of a woman who hopelessly loves him comes too late and all that is left for him to do is to die a heroic death in the arms of his equally heroic and virtuous wife. The play ends with a prophesy that the future issue of Brunswick will equal Frederick in glory. Throughout, the action is initiated by the villains and the protagonist remains entirely passive, though right up to his demise he constantly prattles on about patriotism and philanthropy – an example of *male virtue in distress*. To Haywood's disappointment, none of the royal family honoured the play with his or her presence, and it had none of the success she had anticipated.

The Fatal Legacy by Jane Robe met with equally cold encouragement at Lincoln's Inn Fields in 1723. The play, at least in the first four acts adapted from Racine, is entirely different in tone, taking its subject matter from classical myth and for once presenting a genuine dramatic conflict. Oedipus' sons, Eteocles and Polynices, battle for the throne of Thebes they are supposed to share, each of them asserting his claim and refusing to yield. Spurred by the villainous Creon, the brothers finally kill each other in single combat, their mother Jocasta commits suicide, their sister Antigona stabs herself and Creon, who has seemed to crave nothing but the crown, disconsolately kills himself out of unrequited love. The title refers both to Oedipus' family and to the dagger which Jocasta bequeaths to her daughter. The concept that the gods will be appeased for Oedipus' sins only by the extinction of his whole family is awe inspiring enough, but Robe spoils it all in the ridiculous all-for-love appended in the fifth act, which exchanges the myth for an entirely conventional eighteenth-century finale. Even the myth, however, is not without topical significance and reference: Polynices, to whom Eteocles unlawfully refuses to cede his rights, is in fact a tyrant, whose insistence on the divine rights of kings and refusal to give 'the People Privilege to chuse, Or to reject a King, as Humour serves' (II/36) would naturally render him unlikeable to English eyes at the time.

Mary Leapor, a self-taught lower-class woman, in *The Unhappy Father* (published posthumously in 1751, but not acted) also opted for a vaguely classicised background, at least as far as the names of the dramatis personae are concerned, but in fact wrote the usual tear-jerker about love, jealousy and unmerited strokes of fate. The kindly title figure sends his two sons away from home on errands because they are rivals for the love of his ward. Then his innocent daughter is murdered by her jealous husband, who, as husbands are wont to do in tragedy, readily believes any slander told against her. One of her brothers avenges the crime, killing the husband and the villain who connived the plot, but succumbs to mortal wounds himself. When news arrives that the old man's other son has been eaten by a shark, the unhappy father dies of grief, but the ward is saved from committing suicide by the return of the son who has been reported dead. Despite its absurd plot, the tragedy is of some interest for the abused wife's feminist complaints about the lifelong subjection of women by parents and husbands, and for the father's advice to his sons to treat their inferiors with 'winning Mildness' (I/iv/147) and to relieve poverty and starvation, testifying to an awareness of social evils absent in most tragedies of the time.

The tragedies discussed are all undistinguished, but are too diverse to allow us to establish common denominators more specific than the use of virtuous and entirely passive protagonists – both male and female – a savouring of pathos and sentiment, ranting rhetoric and much wringing of hands and breaking of hearts. Unlike some of the comedies, none of them merits resurrection, and none of them, indeed, was successful in its time or made it into the repertory. Dr Johnson was right to complain about the low ebb tragedy had reached by his time:

> Then crushed by rules, and weaken'd as refin'd
> For years the pow'r of tragedy declin'd;
> From bard, to bard, the frigid caution crept,
> Till declamation roar'd, while passion slept.[63]

7
Women Dramatists of
the Late Eighteenth Century

The situation in the second half of the century was entirely different. If female dramatists had been scarce in the early decades of the eighteenth century, and few had achieved a lasting reputation, women writers flocked to the theatre in the second part, and we are faced with a flood of dramas by numerous novices, and with three playwrights who had a great number of performances to their credit: Griffith, Cowley and Inchbald, the last achieving a position of popularity and authority which would have been unthinkable for Aphra Behn one and a half centuries earlier. The reason was not really that production conditions had become more favourable for women. Performances were still limited to the two patent theatres, with a third, the Haymarket, serving as a summer stage, a situation which stifled competition and inhibited experimentation and innovation. Theatre managers were deluged with scripts, but in general were unwilling to take risks with untried new playwrights, male or female, and preferred to put on an old favourite, or a play by a dramatist who had already made a name. It was difficult for a woman to establish the necessary connections and to gain an introduction, unless she was an actress. It was also arduous for a 'respectable' woman to acquire the backstage experience essential to the successful staging of a play – practical questions of stage mechanics, scenery, effective timing – and some writers even hesitated to attend rehearsals, where they would have had to assert themselves against the manager or his deputy, and against the actors, in a milieu which still had a reputation for promiscuity and sexual harassment. To be sure, the actor and manager David Garrick made a point of lending a helping hand to a chosen few, but his patronage was idiosyncratic and condescending, and the censoring of subjects and styles this involved, though often helpful, was a mixed blessing. But Garrick's successors at Drury Lane and the rival managers at Dorset Gardens ceased promoting female writers.

The reason why so many women were still attracted to the possibility of writing for the stage was the fact that a successful play could earn as much as £500 for the author, though it was a high-risk business, since the play might close after the first night. Besides, there was a great demand for printed versions of successful plays, and booksellers were willing to pay more for a hit comedy than a novel, and financial necessity, after all, was the motive for many women to write. No wonder, then, that they should try their hand at drama, though most of them were active in several literary genres, often making a name as a novelist or journalist while failing to make an impact on the theatre. Indeed, few of those who tried could actually get their work accepted for production, and the ever increasing number of plays printed without previous staging testifies to the disappointed hopes of many female authors, who hoped to salvage what they could be get by cheaply selling the manuscript to a printer. In the period between 1660 and 1800, only seven per cent of all the plays produced on London stages were written by women.[64]

Comedy, as a genre, was more popular than tragedy, and although all critics agree that drama, in general, had reached a nadir, there were still a few amusing comedies written, while tragedies were turgid, histrionic and melodramatic.

French drama continued to be a major source of inspiration, especially for comedy, somewhat paradoxically since France, of course, was still the main Continental rival politically and anti-French sentiment ran high among the population. Political hostility, however, did not detract from admiration for French culture in fashionable circles. Besides, the construction of a dramatically effective plot proved a stumbling block for many an aspiring playwright and theatre managers, afraid to invest their money in a costly new flop, were indeed happy to suggest, especially to women dramatists, that they turn their eyes to a French model. What had been a box office success at Paris was likely to be a low-risk venture in London – as long as the story was appropriately adapted to English tastes, namely, uprooted to a London setting, populated with English stereotypes, purged of potentially offensive levity and atheism, and perked up with an elevating moral conclusion. Nor did English dramatists have any qualms about tacking on such adaptations resounding patriotic sentiments about British liberty, glory and general superiority to the rest of the world. To be sure, there were occasional complaints in prefaces and prologues about the theatre-goers' 'Frenchified' tastes, as opposed to wholesome indigenous plants, but on the whole it was perfectly acceptable for a playwright to scavenge Continental literature for effective plots to amuse an English audience. Native Jacobean and Restoration plays proved useful sources as well, though they, too, had to be 'refined' for the squeamish sensibilities of the age and laundered as to their bawdy language and more robust view of human sexuality.

Tragedy was more likely to sift classical myths and – preferably medieval – history for appropriate tales, though, again, it was considered desirable to prune the original story to fit the tastes and expectations of the prospective audience. Plays based on original stories, unfortunately, are often the weakest and most mawkish ones.

For the late eighteenth century it becomes increasingly difficult to discover a distinctive tone in women dramatists. It was inopportune for a prospective writer to align herself with such disreputable figures as Aphra Behn or even Susanna Centlivre, who was censured as coarse and immoral by none other than Elizabeth Inchbald. Although there is the occasional protest against male prejudice in a preface, female dramatists tended to ask for preferential treatment and indulgence rather than boldly to assert their rights. If a woman writing for the stage was less of a freak and anomaly at the end of the period under survey, she had bought this acceptance by keeping to her station and endorsing the standard view of women and their proper sphere. Despite the tentative acceptance of women dramatists, the double standard continued to be applied to them. By the stringent norms of what was permissible for a decent woman, they were narrowly restricted in their subject matter as well as in

their language in an age when decorum even required men scrupulously to restrain their diction in the presence of a lady. It was more
prudent, and certainly more profitable, to abide by such rules instead of antagonising the all-powerful theatre managers, alienating
the audience and jeopardising a chance of making a living as a
playwright.

The 1750s was a period of low production. The records yield only
a musical drama, *Susanna* (published in 1755 but not performed) by
Elizabeth Tollet, based on the biblical story; a lachrymose *Virginia* by
Mrs Brooke, journalist, playwright and novelist, rejected by the
London stages because there was a surfeit of Virginia tragedies at
the time,[65] and an unperformed 'dramatic pastoral', *Philander* by
Mrs Lennox, a woman of letters and friend of Dr Johnson's, about a
chaste huntress who falls in love with the suitor she has spurned
when he offers to die instead of her. Pastoral drama was going out
of fashion, though one *Occasioned by the Collection at Glocester on the
Coronation Day for Portioning Young Women of Virtuous Character*, written by a Mrs Thomas in praise of the royal couple, was performed
for the benefit of this charitable project in 1762. Hannah More, remembered today as a novelist and religious essayist, also wrote a
pastoral in the early sixties, but published *The Search After Happiness*
only in 1773 for performance at a girls' school. The play has the
pronounced didactic purpose of teaching the young female audience the vanities of fashionable life, romantic fiction and
unfeminine learning, and urging them to seek happiness in religion
and at the domestic hearth. It is disconcerting that a woman as
educated and strong minded as Hannah More should come down
so unequivocally in favour of 'these female bonds, which held my
sex in awe' (16).

> Let the proud sex possess their vaunted pow'rs,
> Be other triumphs, other glories, ours!...
> For Woman shines but in her proper sphere.
>
> (27)

The playwright must, however, have been aware of the masochistic
paradox of such doctrines because in the Epilogue, while one
speaker condemns learned ladies as 'sad Mothers, and still sadder
Wives' (33), another defends the chaste verse of a drama that means
to move the heart. In an attempt to inspire more appropriate

sentiments than the run-of-the-mill tragedies, in 1782 More published *Sacred Dramas*, with biblical settings (unperformed owing to
the outcry against blasphemy). However, she never quite reconciled
her contradictory attitudes towards play-writing and in her final,
evangelical, days rejected the theatre altogether, decrying the sin-
fulness of the stage.

On the whole, however, the public was willing to accept the phenomenon of the woman dramatist. After the inauspicious decade in
the middle of the century, theatrical life, also for women, picked up
from the 1760s onwards, with an increasing number of new publications, as well as a great diversity of genres and approaches.

Tragedies
Tragedy covered a wide range of topics, yet despite this diversity
most of the plays sound disconcertingly alike, revolving, almost
invariably, on a love conflict[66] and, for whatever market reasons,
social prudence, or genuine belief, transporting conservative images
of womanhood. Plays with a classical (or pseudo-classical) subject
often tearfully present virtue in distress, as in Mrs Brooke's above-
mentioned *Virginia* and her *The Siege of Sinope* (Covent Garden,
1781), borrowed from an Italian opera, which exploits the anguish
of the heroic queen of Pontus, whose father wages war against her
noble husband and threatens to kill her children. As is characteristic
of affective tragedy, the heroines in these plays, for all their ranting
and rhetoric, are essentially passive and suffering, placing their fates
in the hands of men. Mrs Hughes' *Constantia* (unperformed), on
the other hand, though equally unhistorical, is a villainess tragedy
about a usurping queen of Cyprus, who orders the rightful king
murdered and inspires his son with blind devotion, until a virtuous
courtier, by means of a fake death warrant, induces the villainess to
take poison and so frees the hero from the vengeance of the
gods. The play, published under the heading of *Moral Dramas*, is
somewhat confused as to the moral lesson it professes to teach,
since it seems to recommend fraud and murder to eliminate villains.
Its view of women, however, is also essentially domestic: the
queen is presented as unfit for the throne both because of her evil
character and because of her feminine weakness in general. In
this respect Mrs Cowley's *The Fate of Sparta* (Drury Lane, 1788) is
a notable exception, as the love–duty conflict in this neo-heroic
play in classical garb focuses on a woman as the centre of action

and moral decision. The play will be more fully discussed in Chapter 8.

Hannah More's neo-classical tragedy *The Inflexible Captive*, translated from Metastasio's *Regulus* and staged at Bath and Exeter in 1775, quite unusually, dispenses with a love plot in favour of patriotism and austere stoicism. The hero of the play, sent by his captors to negotiate a peace treaty, counsels Rome to reject the enemies' proposals, although this will mean torture and death for him upon his promised return to Carthage. Like Addison's Cato, More's Regulus seems cold and inhuman, a man who does not even allow his son to embrace him, forbids his daughter any attempt to save him, and censures his friends for thinking of private concerns when the public welfare is concerned. So overdrawn are the virtues of all the Romans involved that the modern reader cannot but share the derision voiced by one of the Carthaginians, though More can hardly have approved of these sentiments.

> Why – what a strange fantastic land is this!
> This love of glory's the disease of Rome;
> It makes her mad, it is a wild delirium,
> An universal and contagious frenzy;
> It preys on all, it spares nor sex nor age;
> The Consul envies Regulus his chains —
> He, no less mad, contemns his life and freedom —
> The daughter glories in the father's ruin –
> and Publius, more distracted than the rest,
> Resigns the object that his soul adores,
> For this vain phantom, for this empty glory.
> This may be virtue; but I thank the Gods,
> That Barce's soul is not a Roman soul.
>
> (V/76)

While 'classicised' tragedy had gained in popularity, oriental settings, in vogue in previous periods, were on the wane. Mrs Griffith's *Amana* (1764) was inspired by the *Arabian Nights*, and makes use of the stereotypical paraphernalia of seraglio settings. A virtuous wife is torn from the arms of her loving husband to provide a new pleasure for the jaded appetite of a villainous sultan, who means to possess her in the guise of her husband, and is thereupon stabbed as a trespasser, while the heroine takes poison to preserve her chastity, at the moment that her husband has entered the palace to free her, disguised as the sultan. This gratuitous tragic ending, meant to 'show the folly of human wishes and schemes for correcting the moral government of the world' (Preface), is explained as divine retribution for the apostasy of the heroine's father, who for obscure reasons forsook incomparable British liberty and faith for Muslim tyranny. The only other Moorish setting is used in Sophia Lee's *Almeyda* (Drury Lane, 1796), an obsolescent heroic tragedy about the queen of Granada, in love with the prince of Castile, who goes mad when she believes that her lover has been murdered by her villainous uncle, though he has, in fact, been rescued by her noble cousin, though the latter is the prince's rival in love. The catastrophe in which the heroine dies from a supposed antidote to poison administered to her is, as the author confesses, taken from Shirley's *The Cardinal.*

A new type of oriental setting was used by Mariana Starke. Her tragedy *The Widow of Malabar* (Covent Garden, 1790) and her comedy *The Sword of Peace, or A Voyage of Love* (Haymarket, 1788) are set in India, a location which was becoming increasingly important with the expansion of trade and the increase of British colonies. *The Widow of Malabar* gives an exotic appeal to the presentation of topical issues, which were rarely treated in tragedy, though Starke, of course, was not the first or only person to do so. The author had personal experience of Indian colonial life, though in this case she adapted a French model. The sensational plot centres on the practice of suttee, with the heroine rescued from her late husband's funeral pyre in the nick of time by a British officer and his troops, the embodiments of Christian virtue and heroism, who came to India not to build an empire, but 'to save and humanize Mankind' (III/45). In her view of the backwardness of the indigenous population, incited by a crafty priesthood, and her idealisation of colonialism, Starke endorses the official ideology of the time, just as she maintains the typical role division, with an entirely passive female, whose weal and woe are determined by the male characters.

In 1790 Maria Barrell, who was languishing in a debtors' prison at the time, took up another topical issue in her mawkish melodrama *The Captive* (unperformed), about a soldier starving to death in prison, with his wife unable to help, since she refuses to prostitute herself to the cruel creditor. The play works with simplistic black and white contrasts, setting a hard-hearted creditor against a benevolent one, a callous gaoler against a humane one. In the Dedication, to the Prince of Wales, the author rejoices at the destruction of the Bastille and complains that African slaves find their champions in England, but poor debtors do not. Both the tragedy itself and the reasoning in the Dedication are weak, but show that writing a play – even when there was little hope of an actual production – had become a resort a woman could fall back on if in desperate need of money or in hope of attracting the ear of a patron.

Elizabeth Inchbald treated the shocking theme of the Terror during the French Revolution in *The Massacre*, a play not intended for performance (see Chapter 8). On the whole, however, topical events were avoided in the tragedy of the eighteenth century, which preferred to give to its serious drama a fake mantle of classical dignity, or to transport it to the cloud-cuckoo-land of medieval romance. Indeed, the most frequently used backdrop in women's tragedies in the second half of the eighteenth century is a picturesque past of knights errant and villainous usurpers, with England, the Holy Land, the Italian duchies and the German Empire (under the influence of Kotzebue) as their battleground. In 1729 Eliza Haywood's patriotic propaganda piece *Frederick, Duke of Brunswick-Luneburgh* had already gone back to the Middle Ages to trace the heroic forefathers of the present dynasty, and Mrs Hoper, in her lost tragedy, had depicted *The Battle of Poictier*. Now the new romantic interest in the past found reflection in more than a dozen dramas about Edwins and Ethelbertas fighting against the infidels or in civil wars at home, but the leopard had not really changed its spots, since plots continued to focus on love conflicts, threatened rape and enforced marriage.

Dorothea Celesia, an Englishwoman who had married a Genoese patrician and was resident in Italy, adapted Voltaire's *Tancrède*, which was produced at Drury Lane under the title of *Almida* in 1771, with considerable alterations made by Garrick. Because of Mrs Barry's excellent acting and the beautiful scenery it ran successfully for 10 nights, but it is actually a weak play, especially where the author departs from the original. The heroine is sentenced to death for sending a letter to the Saracens – a letter which was, in reality, addressed to the exiled ruler of Syracuse, Tancred. The latter returns in disguise, frees the heroine, but seeks death in battle with the Moors because of her supposed unfaithfulness (as usual, the hero believes her guilty without ever questioning her). He wins a glorious victory, but is mortally wounded, and the heroine expires on his breast. Unlike Shakespeare's Coriolanus, Tancred is portrayed as a completely admirable character, and the senate that banished him is blamed for his tragic demise – an authoritarian attitude quite surprising in view of English pride in political liberty.

Medieval subjects were equally attractive to an aristocratic woman. In view of her social position, however, Mary Bowes, Countess of Strathmore, shunned public production and had only a few copies of her *Siege of Jerusalem* printed, in 1774, to be given away as presents. This was while she was still married to the earl and before she was involved in a notorious divorce suit against her second husband, who maltreated her and kept her prisoner until she was granted the divorce. Her tragedy, as usual, involves a tangle of unrequited loves, with the crusade merely as a colourful backcloth. The Syrian princess, about to be married to the sultan, is in love with a Christian war hero, who in turn loves a Turkish amazon, whom he kills in battle, before being mortally wounded himself. By the end, all the main characters are stone dead. The only figure of interest is the highly unlikely Turkish warrior maid, who leads the Muslim forces against the Christians and pines for fame instead of love.

Despite such precedents, medieval plays were still something of a novelty in the seventies, so Mrs Cowley's distress at seeing her *Albina* shelved for three years (between 1776 and 1779) and superseded by More's *The Fatal Falsehood*, with a similar subject and setting, is understandable enough, though the heated controversy on plagiarism, gleefully taken up by the press, did neither of the rivals any good. In fact, More had already used a medieval setting in her earlier tragedy *Percy* (Covent Garden, 1777). This blank-verse drama, as usual, involves an amorous triangle between a woman of exalted virtue, her noble but insipid erstwhile fiancé Percy and her jealous husband, whom she serves submissively, but whom she cannot bring herself to love. The play ends with the death of all three protagonists, the lover slain in a duel, the wife running mad and taking poison and the repentant husband committing suicide. Despite the conventional plot the play manages to evoke some psychological interest in the husband, who is pathologically possessive not only of her body, but of also her mind.

Will it content me that her person's pure?
No, if her alien heart dotes on another,
She is unchaste.

(II/198)

The heroine's dilemma is genuine. For once, she is a wife teetering on the brink of adultery, instead of the usual virgin, although her unlawful passion and her grudge against the father who forced her into a loveless marriage are never allowed to cloud the picture of angelic virtue in distress, and the play, like so many she-tragedies of the early eighteenth century, revels in descriptions of her anguish and her death wish. It is, however, remarkable that at a time when many women dramatists were trumpeting about their patriotism, the heroine, Elwina, iconoclastically questions the justification of any crusade or 'holy war':

When policy assumes religion's name,
And wears the sanctimonious garb of faith
Only to colour fraud, and license murder,
War then is tenfold guilt....
'Tis not the cosier, nor the pontiff's robe,
The saintly look, nor elevated eye,
Nor Palestine destroy'd, nor Jordan's banks
Deluged with blood of slaughter'd infidels;
No, nor the extinction of the eastern world,
Nor all the mad, pernicious, bigot rage
Of your crusades, can bribe that Power who sees
The motive with the act.

(II/201)

It is difficult to determine whether the characters, incidents and atmosphere of More's second tragedy, *The Fatal Falsehood*, were plagiarised from *Albina*, as Cowley claimed. Garrick, who had rejected Cowley's play, may inadvertently have leaked some of the plot to his protégée, but on the whole amorous triangles, gullible suitors, villains killing their own accomplices by mistake and coming to grief themselves, while the virtuous couple survives, are much too commonplace to permit speculation about plagiarism. Cowley (see Chapter 8) was certainly the better playwright and More's talent was not for the theatre, whatever her mentor Garrick may have thought. The less courteous R. B. Sheridan, who wrote the Epilogue for More's play, in fact satirised the pretensions of female scribblers by pretending to be jealous of their successes. *The Fatal Falsehood*, however, turned out to be something of a flop. The action, set in Italy, is stereotypical, though some of the characters are not uninteresting, especially the subtle villain, who plays on the heart-strings of the hot-blooded Orlando, inciting him to frenzied love for his friend's bride. The villain shows Orlando a letter in which the heroine summons her lover to a secret rendezvous (conveniently, she has written neither name nor address on her letter), where Orlando kills a man in the dark, who turns out not to be his rival, but the villain skulking in the bushes. The lovers are thus safe, but a gentle maid enamoured of Orlando goes mad and dies from un-requited love (a common affliction in tragedy), and he commits suicide, having forfeited his honour. Like many other writers of the age, More hoped to imitate Shakespeare in describing the horror of the crime, but managed only to sound pathetic.

With the performance of these plays, medieval settings were becoming all the rage. A Miss Roberts in *Malcolm* (1779, unper-formed) naively tried to reconcile the English to the Scots by reminding them that their glorious dynasty descended from Malcolm, the son of the murdered Scottish king Duncan. Malcolm is married to an English princess, and so he promises to aid his brother-in-law Edgar in the fight against the invading Normans, but is also forced to fight the Norwegians, whose leader raids the country solely to win the love of a beautiful girl. When the angelic ghost of King Edward beseeches his heir not to try to regain the English crown, since fate has decreed that King William should rule, he is immediately 'content, in private happiness and love serenely [to] pass ...[his] heirless life, proud of the issue of [his] sister's bed' (V/67). Thus the heroic Malcolm is conveniently absolved from waging a hopeless war against the Normans. The plot involves such staple tragic ingredients as a rape attempt by the villain and several love–honour conflicts. Purporting to present historical fact, the author in reality reduces history to a series of love conflicts, and, like Haywood half a century earlier, fawns to the House of Hannover by idealising its ancestors. In similar fashion Jane West, a self-taught farmer's wife who wrote to provide for her children, in her *Edmund, Surnamed Ironside* (1791) reduces the Danish conquest of Britain to a family conflict in which the noble Englishman Edmund and the equally noble Danish king face each other in single combat, but so admire each other's virtue that they decide to partition the realm, the Dane marrying the long-beloved queen dowager. Yet during the festivity Edmund is stabbed by his ambitious brother, which leaves the Dane in sole possession of the throne.

If these plays are thoroughly conventional in characterisation and political outlook, Mary Deverell's *Mary, Queen of Scotts* (1792, unperformed) evinces a remarkable change of allegiance and evaluation of historical figures. Deverell, a surprisingly self-assertive essayist, poet and playwright of plebeian origin, who scandalised the clergy by publishing her own sermons, and, despite a feigned humility, was fully conscious of the disabilities pursuant to her gender and class, did not write a feminist play, but at least shows an interest in the psychology of the two female antagonists; she presents Mary as a victim of political expediency and as a martyr to her Catholic faith. She is one of the few playwrights of her time to do justice to historical complexities by presenting political pressures and considerations of state as motives for action.

The actress Hannah Brand, on the other hand, in her tragedy *Huniades, or The Siege of Belgrade*, fell back on love as the staple motivating force for political conflicts. The play was performed by the Drury Lane company at the Opera House in the Haymarket in 1792, with Brand herself in the cast, but was soon withdrawn and produced equally unsuccessfully as *Agmunda*, with the original title hero completely removed. Indeed, the author had failed to introduce this nominal hero before the very last act, but his elimination did little to save an entirely conventional play about a princess delivered up to the sultan besieging the town, and poisoned by him when he loses the battle, just at the moment when her lover appears to free her. To justify such gratuitous appeal to the tear ducts, the author, in an unconvincing moral conclusion, attributes the princess's horrible fate to her forbidden secret marriage to the hero.

Medieval settings, of course, opened up vistas for Gothic horrors. Mrs Hughes, whom we have already met as the author of the classicised tragedy *Constantia*, is somewhat more benign in the ending of her *Cordelia* (1790), which transposes a watered-down *Romeo and Juliet* plot to Saxon times. The heroine has secretly married the rightful prince, but faced with being forced to wed another takes poison. The poison, however, turns out to be quite harmless and the virtuous lovers face a happy ending, once the wicked father has been eliminated. In her *Adela* (rejected by both main theatres) Mrs West, author of *Ironside*, preferred a more 'tragic' ending by having the hero receive his death wound when saving his beloved from rape, leaving her a disconsolate 'widow' for the rest of her life. In her Preface the author attacks the fashion for Gothic superstition, but in fact writes very much in the same vein, especially in her *The Minstrel, or The Heir of Arundel* (unperformed), which has a villainous usurper, bent on murdering his rival's daughter, providentially stab his own beloved child, who has changed clothes with her friend.

Gothic horror could, of course, be set with even more gusto in medieval Italy, where villainous aristocrats are credited with all kinds of atrocities and perversions. In *The Sicilian Lover* (1796) a villain, in the dead of night, murders the suitor he favours, instead of his daughter's lover, and is himself killed by the latter, whereupon the girl expires in a convent, where her long-lost mother happens to be a nun, and the desperate lover, wounded by a poisonous dagger, dies at her bier. The action is even more illogical than that in other plays, and characters constantly rant with overwrought emotions.

> Let the fierce tempest of a father's rage
> Dash my soul's purpose, and the foaming waves
> Waste their vain fury on the flinty shores!
>
> (I/iii/14)

There is little wonder that the author, Mary Robinson, nicknamed Perdita, an ex-mistress of the Prince of Wales and the butt of gross satires, could not get the play acted.

Harriet Lee, sister of the more famous Sophia and a dramatist in her own right, a woman who had so impressed William Godwin that he made her an offer of marriage, which she refused on religious grounds, blamed the rejection of *The Mysterious Marriage, or the Heirship of Rosalva* (1798) on the sorry situation of the stage, but in fact this play, too, is confused, lacking dramatic conflict despite its murders, threatened rapes, and pseudo-Shakespearean ghost scenes. The rightful princess is poisoned and haunts the castle, but in the end her brother, who has disguised himself, asserts his rights and wins back the throne.

The tragedies of Fanny Burney dispense which such melodramatic scenes. Nonetheless, her talent was for fiction, not for drama, and all her plays tend to be repetitive, lacking dramatic drive. None was printed during her lifetime, and only one – *Edwy and Elgiva* – ever reached the stage, where, because of incompetent acting, it met with such disastrous failure that her father had little trouble in discouraging his daughter from venturing to stage her other plays. *Edwy and Elgiva*, started during the unhappy time Burney spent at Court in attendance to Queen Charlotte, and performed at Drury Lane in 1795, is an anti-Catholic propaganda piece in which the hot-headed King Edwy and his virtuous wife are separated by a hard-hearted prelate, who declares the marriage illegal, incites a civil war, has the queen abducted and murdered but, on Edwy's death in battle, suddenly and incredibly repents. *The Siege of Pevensey*, set in the aftermath of the Norman conquest, is equally unoriginal, and includes the usual character stereotypes of an unbelievably noble knight, a virtuous heroine, a brave and loyal general, a tyrannical king and a villainous suitor. The heroine is about to enter a convent, to escape from a hateful marriage and save the lives of her father and lover, when peace is unexpectedly declared, the tyrant relents, and the virtuous couple are united. *Elberta*, a mere fragment, concerns the conflict between honour and the need to save one's children from starvation, and makes much of the agony of the unhappy parents. *Hubert De Vere* revives the genre of pastoral drama in its story about a banished nobleman with whom a gentle shepherdess unhappily falls in love until she dies of disappointment when he is united with his long-lost love, and the villain, who turns out to be her natural father, collapses by her coffin. Burney's verse creates an idyll of rural beauty and simple emotions, which jars with the melodramatic scheming of the villain.

At the end of the century Kotzebue and German drama exerted a powerful influence on British playwrights, reflected in frequent translations and imitations. Inchbald adapted *Lovers' Vows* and *The Wise Man of the East*. Mariana Starke, author of *The Widow of Malabar*, purported to have translated Kotzebue's *Agnes Bernauer*, printed under the title of *The Tournament* (1800). However, despite the new milieu – the heroine comes from the lower-classes – and the German setting, the author, in fact, adapted her model to fit familiar English themes: the forbidden marriage, the villain threatening rape, rescue from death in the nick of time. In the end Agnes, like so many an English heroine, turns out to have an aristocratic father and to be fully eligible as the prince's bride, so that no social taboos are actually broken. And both hero and villain, blind to common-sensical considerations of political expediency, seem to count the world well lost for love.

Joanna Baillie's *Count Basil* is of a different order, and, in spite of its medieval setting, its love involvement and its Italian villain, points towards the future in its Byronic hero, a taciturn superman lured by a flirtatious woman into postponing his departure into battle until his honour is compromised and he has to shoot himself. The tragedy, part of a series of plays on the human passions, excited attention on publication and led to speculation as to the identity of the unknown author. It is much better than the run-of-the-mill tragedies of the time, less shrill in tone, with sound characterisation of both the hero and his female antagonist, discarding unrequited passion as the cause of tragic deaths, although Walter Scott's comparison of the author with Shakespeare seems ridiculous nowadays. Baillie essentially belongs to the nineteenth century and will only be treated *passim* in this book. Her tragedy about hatred, *De Montfort*, attracted the attention of Kemble and Mrs Siddons because of its attractive acting parts, and they performed it with moderate success at Drury Lane in 1800. However, it is a poor and melodramatic work, never giving convincing reason for the morbid protagonist's rabid hatred of his enemy, which leads him to murder and death. De Montfort seems a madman and cad rather than a romantic hero, and his sister – the part Mrs Siddons took – is merely one more noble, moralistic and entirely dull late-eighteenth-century heroine.

More than half the tragedies surveyed were not accepted for production, not out of prejudice against women, but because they are genuinely bad. For the period in question it would, in general, be unsafe to draw inferences about quality from such a rejection, since women may have lacked connections, incurred the managers' ire, or have had social inhibitions about associating themselves with the public stage. There can also be no doubt that managers were high-handed, partial and shunned risk and experiment. But to blame the failure of aspiring women dramatists solely on these circumstances would be ridiculous. Their tragedies were often still-born: trite, repetitive and stereotypical. What is surprising is not the great number of rejects, but the fact that several of these weak tragedies should actually have been given an airing. Among these, the majority are translations or adaptations, which recommended themselves to the managers because of prestigious originals and, in many cases, were commissioned by them. Griffith and Brand may have utilised their connections as actresses to get their maiden ventures performed; More had Garrick's support; Griffith painfully tried to secure it, pestering the actor manager for 12 years with applications for employment; Cowley and Inchbald by the time they wrote tragedy had a record of comic successes; Burney was a celebrity because of her novels. None of the late-eighteenth-century tragedies by women dramatists has stood the test of time, yet they are interesting indices how women responded to the social climate of their time. However, comedy, whose traditional province is social interaction, is an even more indicative gauge of this response.

Sentimental comedies

The later eighteenth century was the great age of sentimental comedy, but the number of sentimental comedies written even by women, who were said to be tender hearted by nature, never outnumbered the 'laughing comedies' (discussed below). However, the prevailing fashion for sentimentality affected even those plays which cannot be classed among this category in the strict sense. In other words, even the farces of the time tended to include maudlin scenes of heartbreak and reconciliation, and adopt a sanctimonious tone.

Goldsmith, who deplored this development,[67] gave a simple formula for sentimental comedy: take a hero with a riband, a heroine with a title, insipid dialogue, characters devoid of humour but with mighty good hearts and fine clothes, blend them into a few pathetic scenes, and the ladies in the audience will cry and the gentlemen applaud. However, as Sherbo has pointed out,[68] it is not the appeal to the emotions itself that constitutes a sentimental comedy, but artificiality, insincerity and excess of shallow emotions (revealed in trite and bombastic language), revelling in grief disproportionate in cause, repetition of heart-rending detail and pathetic exaggeration of the protagonist's distress. This conglomeration then evaporates in a facile and completely improbable happy ending.

Writers of laughing comedy in general aimed at a (mildly) humorous picture of classes or character types and witty exchanges in the dialogue. Because of the emotionalism prevalent in all the drama of the time, it is impossible to draw a strict line between laughing and sentimental comedy, nor do specific dramatists consistently adhere to one or the other genre. The presence of some

humour in a sub-plot or minor character may well go hand in hand
with a focus that is sentimental and, on the other hand, even a
predominantly comic play may conclude in a mawkish tableau of
family reunion, character reform and moralising last lines, though,
to be sure, bawdiness or an ironical treatment of emotional histrionics preclude sentimentality.

The absolute queen of sentimental comedy in the eighteenth
century was Elizabeth 'Frances' Griffith, an actress and woman of
letters shrewd enough to tune her works to the demands of the
market. Except for her translation of Beaumarchais's *The Barber of
Seville, or The Useless Precaution* (seemingly unperformed), in which a
marquis and his servant Figaro dupe the stereotypical quack and
carry off his beautiful ward, all her comedies belong to the sentimental genre. *The Platonic Wife* (Drury Lane, 1765) was published
anonymously as 'by a lady'. It is also modelled on a French play, with
new characters and an intrigue added as a sub-plot, and sets out to
portray the one folly 'which has never yet been exposed by a theatrical representation' (Advertisement prefaced to the printed edition),
namely excessive simplicity. The plot centres on the naive Lady
Falkland, separated from her husband, who has not satisfied her
craving for romance, and constantly disappointed in her hope of
establishing a platonic relationship with another man. Her reputation
is sullied by Lord Falkland's former mistress and a villainous poor
relation, but she is reunited with her husband when she repents and
timidly hints at her change of mind by having her portrait repainted
to reflect melancholy and remorse. The sub-plot concerns the
attempt of the villain to abduct an heiress, who is, however, rescued
by her lover (who was sighing at Lady Falkland's feet only hours
before). The moralising tone and value judgements are typical of
sentimental comedy. The wife must learn reason and return to her
husband and protector; excessive reading of romances turns a
woman's weak head (a motif frequently reiterated); as in Pix's *The
Innocent Mistress* and Centlivre's *The Platonick Lady*, platonic friendships between men and women are shown to be mere chimeras;
cast-off mistresses are jealous and treacherous:

> All women who have forfeited their own title to virtue, envy
> those who possess it; and would wish to sink them to their own
> base level.
>
> (IV/ii/60)

The dialogue can occasionally muster some wit:

> we widows may chuse what hobby-horse we please; some-
> times, for variety, perhaps an ass; but oh! defend be from a
> mule, 'tis so vastly like a husband!
>
> (I/i/2)

But in general the tone is didactic and sanctimonious:

> Beware of that spirit, sense, and gaiety, Emilia, which have no
> virtue for their base!
>
> (IV/ii/59)

The Double Mistake (a success at Covent Garden in 1766) is also
conservative in its outlook and melodramatic in its plot. The innocent heroine flees to her uncle with a seemingly cock-and-bull story
about a stranger hiding in her closet. This intruder, a lazy coxcomb,
is in fact about to elope with another girl, and, upon discovery,
compromises the heroine a second time by pretending to have come
by *her* appointment. However, the truth is revealed, the giddy girl
who planned to run away with him confesses her misdemeanour
and true virtue is vindicated. As sentimental comedy, however, requires everyone to be happy in the end, even the villain repents
and is forgiven. The characters are entirely stereotypical: the tyrannous father, the dilettante uncle, the pedantic aunt who prides
herself on her Latin and Greek (although the picture is humorous
rather than acerbic) and, of course, the heroine in distress, who
illustrates that 'our helpless sex's strength lies in dependance' (IV/iv/
59). It is suggested once more that impressionable girls fed on romances are likely to come to grief and that a virtuous woman can
only love once and for all.

The School for Rakes (a hit at Drury Lane in 1769), despite its title
and the satire on misogynist prejudice in the Prologue ('I own my
failings – I both write, and read') is equally maudlin and moralising.
It was dedicated to Garrick in gratitude for his help in adapting
Beaumarchais's *Eugenie*. Griffith, however, changed the original by
conniving Lord Eustace's reform, which 'will render him more
worthy the favour of a British audience, whose generous natures
cannot brook the representation of any vice, upon the stage, except

in order to have it punished, or reclaimed' (Advertisement prefaced to the printed edition). The play comes out of the mould of sentimental comedy by tearfully presenting the plight of the innocent heroine, betrayed into a fake marriage by an aristocrat, who, when ordered to wed an eligible bride, tries to keep the duped wife and her relatives in the dark, even stealing their letters. The truth is revealed through a brusque seaman (another stereotypical figure). The heroine's father thereupon challenges the seducer to a duel, which the repentant Lord Eustace will fight with unloaded pistols – a resolution he confides to a perfect stranger who has rescued him from highwaymen, and, of course, turns out to be the heroine's brother, thus conveniently made privy to Lord Eustace's remorse. Since, even more conveniently, this brother is also in love with Lord Eustace's intended bride, the scene is set for a simple denouement. To be sure, the heroine at first refuses to forgive the man who has wronged her, but on her father's bidding, she falls into Lord Eustace's arms – a coyness diametrically opposed to the unflinching resolution of the insulted woman in *The Faithful General* half a century earlier. The villain who reforms, virtue in distress, the plain-dealing captain and the foolish aunt dazzled by titles are all familiar clichés, and the action is foolish and melodramatic to excess – so much so that the predicament of the heroine is even derided in Pye's Epilogue to the play. This gentle ridicule, however, did not detract from the play's success on stage.

Griffith's next comedy, *A Wife in the Right*, was heckled by a clique at Covent Garden in 1772. The action is somewhat blurred and contradictory. Lady Seaton suspects her husband of having a love affair with her friend, who is, in reality, quite innocent, though compromised when the amorous Lord Seaton kneels in front of her – for which he is forgiven by his wife. The play's real interest, however, does not centre on these two immaculate women, but on Lord Seaton's former mistress, who hopes to hook a rich Indian governor – the old figure of the fool adapted to a new social environment – who is blind to her faults, but prevented from marrying her just in time. The disreputable intriguing woman is duly punished and the passive virtues of the other two women are extolled. The play is full of pathos and didacticism. Thus an austerely virtuous 18-year-old sententiously censures her immoral school friend, expressing her 'hope that indiscretions rather than vice misled her steps from the sole paths of happiness and peace' (II/37).

The Times (Drury Lane, 1780), derived from Goldoni on Garrick's suggestion, exposes the national vice of gambling, like Centlivre's *The Gamester* and *The Basset Table*. The comparison, however, shows how sentimentalised the subject has become. Delicacy of feeling is substituted for wit, emotion for satirical exposure, and the gaming scenes have lost the flair and excitement of the earlier plays. The gambling couple, ruined by money lenders, are saved by the sister's high-minded suitor, reform and retire to the country.

Griffith was, of course, by no means the only woman to try her hand at sentimental comedy. Frances Sheridan, mother of the famous playwright and theatre manager, staged *The Discovery* at Drury Lane in 1763 with great success, a maudlin comedy, despite its confident jibes at the discrimination of women in the Prologue: 'For women, like state criminals, they think, / Should be debarr'd the use of pen and ink'. The plot focuses on an aristocrat who, having squandered his estates, tries to force his children into marrying money, but the widow he has selected for his son turns out to be his own illegitimate daughter, whereupon he leaves his children free to follow their own inclinations. He also plans an intrigue with an unhappily married young woman, until his wife warns the girl and counsels her to try to please her *own* spouse, whereupon the floundering marriage immediately improves. To top it all, the aristocrat is also reconciled to his wife. While not unamusing in the first half, the play turns cloyingly sentimental in the last two acts. Sheridan's wit, on the whole, consists in having the characters utter impertinences in a deadpan manner, with the result that the most unpleasant characters get the most effective lines. Thus the tyrannical father taunts his love-sick daughter in the following way:

> And now, miss, you may, if you please, retire to your chamber, and, in plaintive strains, either in verse or prose, bemoan your hard fate.

> (I/iv/20)

The quarrelling young couple merely seems childish by Restoration standards, and their easy reconciliation is entirely unconvincing. Indeed, Frances Sheridan judges by a double moral standard throughout: the immature husband torments his wife as he did his pets, yet it is she who must reform to make the marriage work and it is she who is blamed for milord's seduction attempt, since her complaints were an unwarranted provocation to a philandering male. Milord is, in fact, an irresponsible blackguard and sadist, who tyrannises the women in the family, but lacks courage to exert pressure on this son. Yet he is revered by all as the best of fathers and in the end returns to the happiness of the domestic hearth.

Sheridan's *The Dupe* (Drury Lane, 1764) is equally predictable in its moral judgements and comes down with unremitting severity on the mistress who persuades her old lover to marry her, but in fact constantly cheats on him, until he finds out that her son is not his at all, and pays her off to be rid of her. Atoning for the sins of one's youth by marrying one's mistress is portrayed as downright folly:

> a woman who has been used to consider a man as a kind of property, of whom she is to make the most, while his inclinations to her last, will not easily be brought to think, that there is but a common interest between them, as man and wife.
>
> (III/iii/39)

After the sentimentality and didacticism of these two comedies, Frances Sheridan's cynical third, *A Journey to Bath* (1764), comes as a complete surprise and timely reminder that sentiments expressed on stage often depended on commercial considerations and cannot be taken as personal convictions. Hardly unsurprisingly, the play was rejected by Garrick and remained unperformed. In the attitude it takes towards an immoral woman, it is the very reverse of the previous portrait. Featuring an amoral, down-and-out aristocratic pair of rogues who set out to catch two naive young nouveaux riches by playing on the snobbery of their relatives, it is unique among women's plays of this period in completely dispensing with moral judgements and, like a true Restoration comedy, directing our sympathy toward the witty rather than the good-hearted characters. No outrage is expressed at the woman's previous sexual licence; indeed, she prides herself on her emotional indifference to the young man she is trying to lure:

> LADY FILMONT: ... I have made a Coxcomb of him; any woman ... can make a fool of any man (as far I mean as it regards herself) but to make a Coxcomb pro bono publico, requires parts.
>
> (III/xiv/317)

It is interesting to juxtapose Frances Sheridan's treatment of a kept woman with the attitude Sophia Lee[69] takes to the same type of figure in one of the most successful sentimental comedies of the time, *The Chapter of Accidents*. The Lee sisters came from a family of actors and thus had more than ordinary familiarity with the theatre. When Sophia approached Harris, the manager of Covent Garden, he suggested that she cut out the serious sections and reduce her play to an afterpiece, which the strong-minded author refused to do, turning instead to the elder Coleman, who brought the comedy out at the Haymarket in 1780. It turned out to be one of the most spectacular hits of the era, revived with great applause at the two major theatres through many a season, and gaining its author the money to open a school in Bath. Unlike Frances Sheridan, Lee casts the 'fallen' woman as the noble heroine in distress, and commends her keeper for wishing to make up to her by marriage, in spite of the scandal this causes to respectable society: 'virtue never looks so lovely as when she stretches out her hand to the fallen!' (II/v/113). The young man's father, however, has the objectionable girl abducted and married to his valet – only the ruffians mistake the maid for her mistress. The latter, racked by remorse, has already fled the house, wins milord's love and admiration, and is finally discovered to be his own niece. The dishonest valet, who suspected this family relationship all along, finds himself saddled with the maid. But characterisation and motivation are quite secondary to the didactic purpose on the one hand, and the sustaining of mistaken identities on the other. The issue at stake initially looks like a contest over education, in the manner of Shadwell's *The Squire of Alsatia*: liberal town upbringing versus strict country life. The balance first tips in favour of the country (the young man about town has a mistress) and then against it (the country girl has fallen), so the two educational systems seem equally inadequate. In the end, however, Lee fails to make a judgement, but concludes with a hymn to universal goodness. Most of the minor characters are run of the mill, but the fallen woman metamorphosed into the distressed heroine is certainly exceptional. We have seen that even in the Restoration few playwrights sympathised with sexual offenders, and lack of virginity precluded a girl from qualifying as an admirable figure in the eighteenth century. Lee, however, calls her 'a daughter monarchs might contend for' (III/iii/133). To be sure, in the play the character is presented *post festum*, as it were, at a point when she already pines with remorse and shame and parts from the man she loves lest she ruin his career. In Lee's rather eccentric view, she is therefore 'most truly entitled to esteem; since it requires a far greater exertion to stop your course down the hill of vice, than to toil slowly up towards virtue' (V/ii/164). Sophia Lee must have sounded a chord in the sensibility of a time in which philanthropic energy was beginning to be spent on the reclaiming of prostitutes. The author plays on the heartstrings of the audience by wallowing in the girl's despair and misery. The vogue was all for self-sacrificing female paragons, who disarm men with their sublime virtue, instead of fighting them on the same ground, as Restoration heroines would have done.

If *The Chapter of Accidents* is unusual in its charitable attitude towards a sexual offender, it is quite conservative socially, since the girl turns out to be her seducer's cousin and hence an eligible bride. Although theatre audiences had long since become predominantly middle class, most dramatists continued to set their comedies in the town houses and country mansions of the aristocracy and to respect social decorum in their matching of couples. Seemingly low-born heroines frequently discover genteel forbears, thus proving their social as well as moral superiority. Hence Charlotte Smith, in *What Is She?* (Covent Garden, 1799), makes sure that the mysterious heroine is a gentleman's widow and can marry her aristocratic suitor, and that his giddy sister appropriately repents of her vanities before she weds her honest admirer. All this is served up with little wit but indigestible moralising. Mrs West, in the equally didactic *How Will It End?* (1799, unperformed), promotes an orphaned girl into an aristocrat's long-lost daughter, apart from redeeming the heroine's would-be seducer, exposing the villains, reforming the coquette and heaping ridicule on the amorous old woman.

However, there were also a few women playwrights who now and then presented more egalitarian views. In Anne Penny's didactic 'entertainment' *The Birthday* (unperformed, but published 1771), a rich and a poor family, absurdly, exchange their children at birth, and are rewarded with the satisfaction that the youngsters marry, thus presenting a son and daughter to each family. In a more substantial play, Charlotte Lennox's *The Sister* (hissed by a hostile crowd at Covent Garden in 1769), a young aristocrat falls in love with his tutor's sister, which the tutor, as a man of honour, tries to prevent, even at the expense of fighting a duel. Luckily, in sentimental comedy snobbish earls invariably relent. Milord allows a poor but virtuous English girl to be a worthy pursuit for his son, because she would 'sacrifice her fortune to her conscience, and subject her inclination to her duty' (V/72). The tutor, in turn, marries a charming young lady, much to the distress of her stepmother, the usual butt of ridicule, who believed herself beloved by the hero ever since he rescued her from a snake, which, however, turned out to be a caterpillar. Plot and characterisation are typical of sentimental comedy, but talking at cross-purposes is cleverly sustained, and the comedy has more wit and vivacity than is the wont in sentimental plays of the time.

Mrs Lennox also adapted Jonson's *Eastward Ho* in a play called *Old City Manners* (Drury Lane, 1775), which clearly illustrates that the differentiation between laughing and sentimental comedy depends not on subject matter but its treatment. The play didactically juxtaposes two daughters and two apprentices, a hard-working one, who marries the goldsmith's meek daughter, and a good-for-nothing, who ends up in prison. The vain daughter marries a fake knight, who cheats her out of her estate, but is shipwrecked and taken to prison with his cronies, from whence they are all released by the charitable goldsmith, on condition that the apprentice reforms and marries his humiliated daughter, and the knight returns her estate. The play ends with much moralising and praise of the middle class as the fountain of mercy and common sense.

'Laughing' Comedies

Although Goldsmith complained about the decline of 'laughing' comedy, the genre was, in fact, quite able to hold its own; indeed, some of the greatest theatrical successes of the late eighteenth century eschewed excessive emotionalism, namely R. B. Sheridan's *The School for Scandal* and Mrs Cowley's *The Belle's Stratagem*. It would be quite erroneous to assume that all women writers opted for sentiment. Indeed, the old Restoration plots, albeit chastened and sanitised, were still widely popular, and some of the minor writers went in for farce.

In *The Magnet*, a mock-heroic pastoral entertainment sung at Marylebone Gardens in 1771, the anonymous female author shows the power of the magnet, love, to convert a would-be seducer into an honest husband, and a jealous girl who pursued her rival with a large pin, of all things, into a good friend.

Mrs Parsons' farce *The Intrigues of a Morning* (Covent Garden, 1792), a translation from Molière, has two ingenious servants prevent the marriage of their young mistress to a boorish suitor by various tricks and disguises and bring about a more desirable match. While these lower-class characters are busy scheming, the girl throws herself into melodramatic poses ill fitted to the farcical context, and abjures the temptation to be an undutiful daughter 'who flies from the parental roof, to kneel at the altar with her lover, whilst her disobedience is plunging a dagger into her father's heart' (II/23).

Elizabeth Ryves' comic opera *The Prude* (accepted for performance but never staged, and finally published in 1777) illustrates that not only tragedy but also farcical comedy could be set at a historical remove and abused for rabid political propaganda. Ryves, an Irishwoman supposedly cheated out of her property, in her play presents all Catholics as cruel, hypocritical and lecherous. The upright Protestant hero even remonstrates with Queen Mary for her cruel treatment of Elizabeth! He is therefore proscribed, but still manages to rescue the heroine from the hands of her bigoted aunt and a villainous priest, her lover, and in the end is rewarded when Good Queen Bess ascends the throne.

At the harmless end of the scale, Anna Maria Edwards' musical entertainment *The Enchantress, or The Happy Island* (Chapel Street, Dublin, 1783) is an apolitical fairytale faintly reminiscent of *The Tempest*, in which the lovers on an enchanted island are protected by a benevolent fairy, who glues the pursuing uncle and the old suitor to a rock to be parched until they relent. Most comic operas are equally innocuous in subject matter and, like *The Lucky Escape* (Drury Lane, 1778)[70] by Mary Robinson (this author is not 'Perdita' of the same name), or Burke's *The Ward of the Castle*, deal with lovers torn apart and reunited.

Despite the competition from such low-brow entertainment, various more traditional comedies were also written. *The Oaks, or The Beauties of Canterbury* by Mrs Burgess, a pastry cook, follows a 'reformed' Restoration typecast. The comedy was performed in Canterbury in 1780, its title referring to a fashionable promenade in the town, where the hero meets an heiress, whom he wins by courting her maiden aunt and, in the guise of a fortune teller, persuading the old woman to obtain her brother's permission to marry. Since the names of the young and the old woman are the same, this serves to ensure the girl's fortune and freedom. Two further plot lines concern the fates of two other couples, and a low-life sub-plot is devoted to the antics and quarrels of the servants. Although the play is too crowded and the action stereotyped enough, complete with the usual ridicule of an amorous old woman, it is not unamusing and musters some liveliness and humour. So does Elizabeth Craven's *The Miniature Picture*, which revives the vivacious, active heroine of earlier periods. She blames women's 'errors' on the 'unjust usurpation of all their natural rights and liberties' (I/28) and, to win back her faithless lover, disguises herself as a man, courts a flirt and is given her own miniature portrait as a love token. A broadly farcical sub-plot makes fun of a stingy Scottish suitor who is doused with water and thrashed by the servants. The author, the Baroness Craven, later Margravine of Anspach, was a highly unconventional woman, not only because she was separated from her husband and children and took up abode with the Margrave of Brandenburg and Anspach, but also because she wrote not only for private theatricals in her own house (composing even the music for her comic operas herself and taking part in the performances), but also for the professional stage. She was displeased with the production of *The Miniature Picture* at Drury Lane in 1780. Nevertheless, she had her musical farce *The Silver Tankard, or the Point at Portsmouth* performed at the Haymarket in 1781 and *The Princess of Georgia* at Covent Garden in 1799 (not in print), both for an actor's benefit.

Mrs Cullum's *Charlotte, or One Thousand Seven Hundred and Seventy Three* (published anonymously in 1775) is a rather inept attempt to teach the economics of farming and the importance of an improvement in female education within a conventional comic plot concerning a strong-minded girl who gives her beloved £5000 to save him from ruin. A better-drawn lively heroine appears in *The Cottagers* (1788, unperformed) by Anna Ross, the 15-year-old daughter of a Covent Garden actress. Unfortunately, this hoyden heroine, who fights a duel in male disguise and fools both her foppish stepbrother and her old father, plays only a minor role in the plot, which centres on a young man bent on marrying a peasant girl, since:

> a fine person – a graceful carriage – and an amiable disposition, are all the titles of wealth I should look for in a woman.
>
> (I/v/25)

But, of course, the girl turns out to be of genteel descent and, as such plays go, her father conveniently inherits a title and fortune at just the right moment, just as in Frances Brooke's sentimental comic opera *Rosina* (Covent Garden, 1782) the noble squire falls in love with a gentlewoman brought up by peasants, with the reform of the rakish brother who meant to seduce the girl added as a moralistic icing. In Brooke's *Marian* (Covent Garden, 1788) the refined cottager, in similar vein, is transformed into a gentleman and heir to a fortune, so that nothing can impede his marriage to the charming heroine. The problem of class barriers and social hierarchies surfaces in laughing comedies just as it does in sentimental plays. Few dramatists tore down social barriers in their plays, though some did – in both genres.

Indeed, in subject matter Harriet Lee's[71] *The New Peerage, or Our Eyes May Deceive Us* (Drury Lane, 1787) is somewhat reminiscent of Lennox's dramas, but the treatment is predominantly satirical and farcical. Lee makes use of the well worn motif of two young men exchanging identities, the merchant's son courting a coquette in his aristocratic friend's guise, and the earl's son disturbing the sobriety of the merchant household. Things turn melodramatic when the merchant's daughter is abducted to the house of a lecherous antiquary. However, he is lured away from his intended rape by the lucrative offer of a picture of Venus, so that the girl can escape and her ridiculous old aunt, who is game for cruel fun, is found in the cabinet in her stead. The couples marry despite social ineligibility – which seems to present no problem at all – and the play ends with a praise of the sturdy qualities of English merchants. Nonetheless, the comedy largely skirts sentimentality and is vivacious and witty in some scenes, as, for instance, when the coquette mocks her pining suitor:

> Oh, [the secret] must be told on your knees, must it? Nay, then, I would not give a bouquet for it. For I have had so many important secrets told me by gentlemen upon their knees; and all of them lamentably alike.

> (IV/ii/57)

Hannah Brand's *Adelina* (1798, unperformed) is much more conservative socially, although, at first, it would seem to subvert hierarchical structures. The obstinate daughter of a marquis secretly marries the steward, who pretends to woo a beautiful peasant, whom the marquis saves from this enforced marriage. Of course, this gentle, refined creature turns out to be his true daughter who was swapped by a scheming nurse, and Adelina is a cuckoo in the nest. The play lacks direction, oscillating between a surprisingly feminist stance and complete conventionality. Adelina's intelligence, critical attitude and self-assurance initially seem very attractive amid the artificiality and flattery of the aristocratic world. She accuses her father and her bridegroom of over-ruling women's inclinations:

> The girl has *nothing* to think about: for she is precluded from the privilege of thinking to any purpose – and I assure you, that I think nothing about marrying you, my Lord!
>
> (I/xi/268)

However, such bluntness turns out to be a sign of low birth (modern readers may well suspect that Adelina's intractability is due to love-less treatment rather than genetics), whereas the absurdly refined bearing of the peasant immediately suggests her aristocratic descent. Thus the author ensures that social decorum is observed, no ineligible partners matched and no ingrained prejudices hurt.

Brand's 'heroick comedy' *The Conflict, or Love, Honour and Pride* (1798, unperformed) is an even more conventional return to heroic drama, with two princesses vying for the love of a shepherd who turns out to be heir to the throne of Arragon and brother to one of the heroines.

Joanna Baillie's *The Trial* (published in 1798) is much better than the run-of-the mill comedies of the time, and though hardly original is pleasant and good humoured, with effective comic scenes and witty verbal exchanges. An heiress and her portionless friend exchange places, the latter humbling various stereotypical suitors, such as a boor, a foppish aristocrat and his hanger-on, who is, literally, made to eat his promise of marriage when he learns the girl is without money. The frolicksome heiress has her eyes on an altruistic young lawyer, who falls in love with her though she alternately plays the scold and spendthrift. Interestingly enough, however, he proves his true worth by deciding to break off the engagement when he (falsely) suspects her of being a coward and liar. While, from Ariadne's *She Ventures and He Wins* onwards, women dramatists had expected an ideal mate to love the heroine unflinchingly, despite believing her a jilt or even a whore, the sensibilities of the age now regarded such infatuation as immoral and unmanly, and the heiress in the play is fully convinced of her suitor's admirable character only once he has proved himself master of his passions.

Mrs Holford's *Neither's the Man* (Theatre-Royal in Chester, 1799) reverses these gender roles of examiner and examinee which had become usual since the 1690s, by having the *man* test his bride's character, lest he should forever feel 'jealousy of [his] rent roll' (V/ 70). The girl is expected to decide between two despicable suitors recommended by her guardian, but, after some pranks at their expense, opts for a simple soldier, who, almost to her disappointment, turns out to be a rich aristocrat. The play is hardly remarkable except for its tasteless anti-Semitism, heaping abuse on the Jewish suitor's language, appearance and servile willingness to give up his customs in order to become socially acceptable.

More interesting and original is Mariana Starke's *The Sword of Peace, or A Voyage of Love* (Haymarket, 1788).[72] Set in India, it weaves a fairly traditional love story of high-minded protagonists into a devastating satire on the colonial upper crust, subject matter which was taken up by Elizabeth Inchbald in *Such Things Are*. Despite such variations of motif, most laughing comedies of the period are derivative, clichéd and even more predictable in plot and denouement than sentimental plays, with their penchant for far-fetched situations and highly strung figures.

Amid the host of tediously similar plays, some of the comedies of Fanny Burney stand out for their pointed satire and unusual milieu. Like her tragedies, they were written in the nineties, but the author refrained from having any of them performed or even printed. *The Witlings* contains some splendid lower-life scenes in a milliner's shop and in a vulgar boarding house, novel settings presented with sparkling humour, but the satirical brunt is born by a cruel caricature of Lady Mary Montagu in the character of the vain, semi-educated Lady Smatter, who gives herself airs as a literary critic and surrounds herself with flattering 'witlings'. It is easy to understand why Burney's family should have counselled her against having this insult to so prestigious a lady publicly staged and, indeed, the picture, one of the most devastating of a learned woman in the whole century, is cruel and drawn with malice. Lady Smatter constantly misquotes, misunderstands and confuses the famous authors she prides herself on knowing, and the true arbiter of taste in the play is an old misanthrope with a heart of gold, who befriends the bankrupt heroine and frightens Lady Smatter into consenting to her nephew's marriage. It is surprising that a woman dramatist should put forward two men – the old cynic and the young lover – as ideals and mouthpieces, and present all the female characters as either ludicrous or utterly helpless. In spite of starting out with an all-woman scene at the milliner's and giving most lines to women characters, *The Witlings* ridicules rather than endorses their flippant perspective and is anything but a feminist play.[73]

So obsessed was Burney with the character of Lady Smatter that she renewed her attack in *The Woman Hater*, which merely reiterates the old criticism. Other butts of satire are Smatter's jilted old suitor-turned-woman-hater, his mild-mannered friend, who mistakes a virtuous maiden for a prostitute and is himself suspected of libertinism, and an unlady-like hoyden with a liking for low company, who – as is the wont in a class-conscious age – turns out merely to be a nurse's daughter. However, the prominence given by the plot to the sufferings of a virtuous wife, separated from her husband by a series of misunderstandings, wallowing in self-pity, wringing her hands and dabbing her tear-stained face, before she is finally reconciled to him in the last act, proves that even an acerbic satirist like Burney was not immune to the virus of sentimentality.

Love and Fashion suffers from a similar excess of moralising. The pathetic sufferings of virtuous innocence (here embodied by a kindly father who has gone bankrupt) are grafted on to a satirical exposure of the vanities of fashion and worldly wisdom. Thus a foolish girl, mistaking a young man's indifference for inhibited passion, anxiously anticipates:

> so I suppose I shall have to go to Gretna Green! – and I have no tolerable travelling dress ready! – How tormenting! – nothing in the least becoming! – And Sir Archy is so elegant! – he'll hate any thing not pretty.
>
> (I/ii/119)

The witty caricature of fashionable inanities contrasts sharply with the hackneyed praise of the rural idyll and the charms of a simple domestic life. In the end the heroine breaks off the mercenary match she has been contemplating and marries her impecunious true love. The foppish brother repents and the debts are settled by the former villain. All this is wrapped up in a naive ghost story about a haunted house, where people coming and going through hidden doors keep the inhabitants constantly on their toes, and served with a good dose of moral seasoning.

A Busy Day, or An Arrival from India (unperformed in the eighteenth century, but given a modern production in Bristol in 1993 and London in 1994), on the other hand, goes in for broad social satire and, though featuring an impeccable heroine and a noble suitor, avoids sentimentality by refusing to turn the accomplished middle-class beauty into a princess in disguise, or to alleviate the terrible vulgarity of her parvenu relatives. Burney savours their tastelessness and ignorance, just as she relishes the caricature of aristocratic snobbishness, egotism and foppish superficiality. The news that the spendthrift younger son means to marry a nouveau riche's daughter puts the aristocratic family into a state of panic and his serious elder brother into a frenzy of jealousy. Burney tries to spin out the misunderstandings and mistaken identities for too long, making the hero look a fool, but the scenes in which the plebeians confront the insolent aristocrats make good farcical comedy.

Fanny Burney may also have had a hand in the writing of *The Triumphant Toadeater*, a musical entertainment which, however, is more often credited to Ralph Broome and his wife Charlotte Burney. The rather crude farce describes how a flatterer wins an inheritance and a foolish knight, and pokes fun at romantic girls, cowardly men and amorous old women.

All Burney's plays would have been improved by editing and advice on effective dramatic timing. Her range varies from broad farce and social satire to pathos and sentimentality (not to mention tragedy), a confusing polyphony blended by many playwrights of the age into the sentimental symphony of eighteenth-century comedy.

8
Hannah Cowley and Elizabeth Inchbald

Two women dramatists of the late eighteenth century deserve special attention: Hannah Cowley and Elizabeth Inchbald. They were different in temperament, background and style, but they were both highly professional and very successful. Both were mainly writers of comedy and, in many ways, exemplified the tastes and fashions of their period. But they were more adroit than their rivals in shaping effective plots, and they were also shrewder in their dealings with the male theatrical establishment.

Hannah Cowley
Although Hannah Cowley had no backstage experience, she was the most important female dramatist of the period. Unlike most other women playwrights, she did not try her hand at genres other than drama, but wrote 12 plays, two of which, *The School for Eloquence* (Drury Lane, 1780) and *The World As It Goes* (Covent Garden, 1781), were not printed. It is said that she started her successful theatrical career when, to disparage a performance she had seen, she bet her husband that she could do better, and within a fortnight she wrote *The Runaway*, which Garrick, one of whose protégées she was to become, with great success put on at Drury

Lane in 1776. The young writer humbly thanked the actor-manager in her Dedication, and depreciated her maiden work as 'a folly from a woman's pen', uninstructed in the classical rules. However, the play is well constructed and full of effective scenes of comic mis-understanding. In the play a young man falls in love with an incognita, the runaway of the title, who is to be forced into a loveless marriage. The young man's father, however, wants him to marry a rich and learned old woman, while everyone believes the old man himself is courting her. Disappointed by the young man's coldness and jealous of the unknown girl he is wooing, she has the stranger arrested as a common strolling player, but the girl is rescued from prison by the arrival of her guardian. She refuses to elope without his blessing and in the end is united with her lover, while the old woman leaves in a fury. In the sub-plot the hero's romantic sister and his equally romantic friend are, like Beatrice and Benedick in *Much Ado About Nothing*, tricked into believing the other one madly in love, at which point they drop the mask of shyness and confess their passions. The comedy is lively and largely free of maudlin sentiment. The sighing lovers are gently mocked, but, as is so often the case in eighteenth-century comedy, scorn is heaped on the learned woman, who is nothing but an old fool.

The short farce *Who's the Dupe* (Drury Lane, 1779) borrows from the sub-plot of Centlivre's *The Stolen Heiress, or The Salamanca Doctor Outplotted* and shows how a pedant is talked into playing a man of fashion, while the true lover plays the part of the classical scholar the uneducated father favours, actually winning the bride in a con-test of Latin and Greek quotations, in which he declaims in bogus language. The play became a favourite with the public and was performed 126 times in the eighteenth century. It introduces the first of Cowley's witty, resourceful heroines, who are so rare in the dramas of her female contemporaries.

The Belle's Stratagem (Covent Garden, 1780) is an even better play. Indeed, it was a sweeping success, one of the most often revived new plays of the period, second only to Sheridan's *School for Scandal*, and, in the figure of Doricourt, provided a vehicle for some of the best actors of the time. The title refers to the intrigue by which the heroine, Letitia, scorned for her English modesty by her Frenchified fiancé, wins his heart in the guise of a witty woman of doubtful morality, until, contrite, Doricourt acknowledges the superiority of English women: 'cursed be the hour ... in which *British* Ladies shall sacrifice to *foreign Graces* the Grace of Modesty' (V/v/82). In the sub-plot a naive young wife, angry at her husband's jealousy, becomes enmeshed in fashionable society and is in danger of being compromised by a rake. In a rare instance of a successful platonic relationship, she is saved by a sober male friend, who always mouths the correct moral precepts and patriotic sentiments (in favour of *English* servants and wholesome *English* manners), and who substitutes a whore for the lady, thereby exposing the rake to ridicule. The wife repentantly accepts her husband's protection, as she ought to have done in the first place. Despite this didactic sub-plot, with its criticism of 'the sullying breath' (III/iii/48) of fashionable society, the play is more vivacious than most comedies of the time. It revives, albeit in chastened form, the Restoration motif of the resourceful, active heroine, who disguises herself as a loose woman to attract the rake, and is in control of all the intrigues – a motif not only popular with women dramatists but used, for instance, to great effect in Goldsmith's *She Stoops to Conquer*. Yet behind this facade, Cowley's view of women is basically conservative. For all her accomplished wit, Letitia plays her different roles not in order to test her suitor's character, but only to comply to the tastes of the man she loves to distraction; chameleon-like, she throws off the 'bonds of Nature and Education' (V/v/81), transforming herself into whatever might please him best. Of course, in the end the hero opts for the patriotic English ideal of female modesty and submission. In her blatant chauvinism, as in her plots, Cowley is reminiscent of Centlivre.

Which is the Man? (Covent Garden, 1782) is the question a merry widow is to answer at a public gathering, when, of course, she chooses the poor but honest soldier instead of the vain and vicious aristocrat, who has just tried to seduce a naive young wife rescued in the nick of time and reunited with her husband. This weaker play again paints town life as immoral and superficial, yet the two country bumpkins who appear are hardly more attractive. Again, Cowley rings a note of high patriotism, sounding the praises of the English soldier, 'the first character in Europe', who makes Britain triumphant 'in every quarter of the globe' (V/i/53). The hero vows to 'divide [his] heart' (V/i/54) between his wife and his country, a split loyalty which his bride approves of, unlike the heroine in Cooper's *The Rival Widows* half a century earlier. The view of women's proper place is again conservative. Even the heroine's admiration for the salons of French women rings false, since she satirises a similar gathering of English literati as consisting of 'Masters of Art and Misses of Science' (III/iii/31). It is considered natural that a young widow should remarry and submit to a sensible husband, and nobody contradicts the male dictum that:

> the marriage-state is that in which your sex evinces its importance; and where, in the interesting circle of domestic duties, a woman has room to exercise every virtue that constitutes the Great and the Amiable.
>
> (II/i/14)

And yet the tradition of assertive, self-determined heroines was not completely extinct. Cowley borrowed from her predecessors not only an attractive motif, but some of the wit and feminist subversion of the earlier periods in one of her best plays, *A Bold Stroke for a Husband* (Covent Garden, 1783). The title acknowledges the influence of Centlivre's *A Bold Stroke for a Wife*, and Cowley indeed borrowed the central idea of play-acting to win a spouse, only with reversed gender roles. She also adopted the concept of the autonomous, self-willed heroine who moulds her own fate and the idea of female solidarity so conspicuous in Centlivre's works, giving her own comedy a tone and spirit absent in most late-eighteenth-century women's plays, with the exception, perhaps, of her own *The Belle's Stratagem*. Like her Restoration and turn-of-the-century precursors, Cowley contrasts a witty and a tragi-comic couple. The latter consists of a philandering husband, who has ruined his family by making over his estate to a whore, and his long-suffering wife, who courts this whore in male disguise and induces her to tear up the deed as invalid and worthless. Overcome by her goodness, the husband remorsefully returns to her. Although this self-sacrificing, all-forgiving paragon of a wife is occasionally given to moralising, she is, in fact, more sprightly than a bare outline of the plot might suggest and, unlike her hypocritical husband, remarkably friendly towards the whore, though the latter refuses her outstretched hand.

CARLOS: The fragments of the deed! the deed which that base
    woman –
VICTORIA: Speak not so harshly. – To you, Madam, I fear, I seem

reprehensible; yet when you consider my duties as wife
and mother, you will forgive me. – Be not afraid of poverty –
a woman has deceiv'd, but she will not desert you!

(V/i/71)

Sympathy for a hardened prostitute was rare in the eighteenth century, and the fact that Cowley lets her off so leniently, to seek new
prey elsewhere, is surprising.

The more attractive plot line involves the witty Olivia, who sets
her fancy on a rake and cleverly scares off all other suitors through
her feigned shrewishness, contradictoriness and extravagance.
When her father pretends to look for a bride himself in order to
frighten his daughter into marriage, the girl cooperates with the
daughter and the ruse misfires – one of the few examples of female
solidarity in women's drama of the time. In a revival of the popular
old motif, in the guise of a coquette Olivia hooks the rake, a genuine
Rover instead of the usual eighteenth-century milksop, though less
outspoken and full-blooded than his Restoration antecedent, who
also appreciates wit in a woman and scorns the meek feminine ideal
of the time. The maid, hoping to entice the libertine herself, secretly
brings him into the house, where, after a melee of mistaken identities, all misunderstandings are cleared up. All this is dished up with
wit and pleasant humour, and even the inevitable patriotic garnish-
ing is alleviated by satire.

More Ways Than One (Covent Garden, 1783), an adaptation from
Molière, is much more conventional. The title refers to the variety of
ways in which women are won by their ingenious suitors. The hero
introduces himself to a doctor as a dying patient to win the pity and
love of his naive niece, whom the doctor has promised in marriage
to the hero's superannuated uncle. In the end, the doctor switches
his allegiance, since the old miser has dared to question his professional competence. The second protagonist, on the other hand,
wins a coquette by pretending to be the author of an ill-natured
satire against her, in order to arouse her curiosity. The comedy
mostly relies on farcical situations and broad jibes against doctors,
senile old suitors and vulgar parvenus. The view of women is again
anything but subversive. The naive girl is so blissfully ignorant that
she cannot even read, which is exactly the female tabula rasa the
hero dreams of moulding to his liking. His friend may disdain the
role of a schoolmaster, yet is charmed by the belle's 'sensibility', the

indispensable quality of any nubile eighteenth-century maid, and paradoxically wins her affection by abusing her.

The main incidents of *A School for Greybeards, or The Mourning Bride* (Drury Lane, 1786) are lifted straight from Behn's *The Lucky Chance*, which again proves the influence of Restoration models on Cowley's writing, though in this case the changes are both marked and instructive. Cowley was vague in acknowledging the source, speaking only of 'an obsolete Comedy; the work of a poet of the drama, once highly celebrated' (Address to the reader), without mentioning the name, probably fearing Behn's unsavoury reputation. Although she was careful to purge the plot of looseness, leaving it rather insipid, this adaptation was decried for indecency, as *The Lucky Chance* itself had been, so that the author had to rely on publication to vindicate herself. In both cases the scandal hinged upon the fact that a woman should dare to write what was considered bawdy and sexually suggestive. Behn had indignantly defended the right of a woman to write like a man, and Cowley, too, in the unusually aggressive Dedication, protests against the misogynist confusion of art and life in the case of female dramatists, and defends the use of realistic dialogue appropriate to the characters and setting:

> Yet in my case it seems resolved that the point to be considered, is not whether that *dotard*, or that *pretender*, or that *coquet*, would so have given their feelings, but whether Mrs. *Cowley* ought so to have expressed herself.... I ... feel encompassed with chains when I write, which check me in my happiest flights, and force me continually to reflect, not, whether *this is just*, but, whether *this is safe*.

While Behn, however, had been somewhat disingenuous in claiming that there are no juicy passages in the play, the expression that caused most scandal in *A School for Greybeards* seems ridiculously harmless compared with the sexual innuendo of the original. When an angry father sentences his disobedient daughter to bread and water in a dark chamber, her newly wed husband replies with a smile: 'I confirm half your punishment; and a dark chamber she shall certainly have' (V/iv/72). This was enough to offend eighteenth-century ears. The anxiety to remove 'indecency', namely sexuality, from public life had resulted in a retreat from *coarseness* in language.

Tact in the presence of ladies demanded 'salutary restraints' in conversation, books, pictures, gesture and pronunciation. In an age when 'Codpiece Row' had to be renamed 'Coppice Row', and in which a 'bitch' became a 'mother mastiff', any sexual reference was considered anathema.[74]

It is indeed fascinating to gauge the distance comedy had travelled within the precisely 100 years that had intervened between the premieres of the two plays. Cowley bowdlerised her source in every respect, though she retained many of its incidents, such as the lie about the death of the first lover; the fact that the lover gains entrance to the house in disguise and lures the groom out of the house on the wedding night on pretence of a riot in the city; and the scene when the two old men gape at each other without comprehension. Instead of setting her comedy among traders 'of the lowest and most detestable manners' (Dedication), Cowley transferred it to the Portuguese nobility, a serious mistake, since the intrigue needs despicable people to function properly. The old husband is not painted as a figure of contempt, as Behn made him out to be, yet the plot requires a foolish old lover for its comic effects.

Most revealing, however, are the changes as far as the women characters are concerned. The Leticia character has not been forced into marriage to the old man by financial necessity, but has sought refuge with a 'guardian' of 'venerable age' (III/ii//40) from the sexual advances of her young admirers. As his bride, 'her duties to him will be of the most sacred sort, and she must fulfil them scrupulously' (I/ii/17), despite the fact that he lied to her about her lover's death! Her predecessor in Behn's play had vigorously negated such an obligation.[75] Indeed, throughout the play Cowley's bride never fails in her duties towards her husband, although, just to be on the safe side, the author has the marriage thwarted before the actual ceremony takes place. When Behn's heroine was caught making off with the jewels, she had no qualms about allaying her husband's suspicions. In the eighteenth century, lying to a lawful spouse would have been unseemly for a virtuous heroine and the necessary subterfuges are left to the maid.

The Julia character underwent an even more radical change. As the most active and vocal figure she still attracts the audience's sympathies, but from being a desiring subject she is reduced to a witty but superficial coquette. Neither as the flirtatious beauty of the beginning nor as the moralist at the end does she have a touch of the self-possession and self-knowledge Behn's Julia could boast of. She willingly accepts the amorous advances of a rake who takes her for her own stepdaughter, and seems to be heading towards adultery, when it transpires that she merely meant to aid her stepdaughter in gaining her lover and never thought of cuckolding her old husband, whom she assures of her fidelity: 'whilst you repose a generous confidence in me, and allow me to be the guardian of my own honour' (V/iv/71). The issue at stake is belittled to one of a wife's elbowroom, not the fundamental question of female desire. In view of her flirtatious behaviour, her chastity comes as a surprise, but countenancing adultery would have been unthinkable in late-eighteenth-century drama. Compared with many sentimental comedies of the time, *The School for Greybeards* is still entertaining, but a transgressor of sexual and social norms was no longer possible as a heroine.

With *A Day in Turkey, or The Russian Slaves* (Covent Garden, 1791), Cowley ran into another difficulty, namely the charge that her comedy was 'tainted with Politics' (as Cowley complained in the Advertisement prefaced to the printed edition), an indictment that, at a time when the French Revolution was throwing England into panic, deprived her of the honour of a command performance at Court, and was doubly wounding to a writer who was more than willing to leave such '*unfeminine*' (Advertisement) interests to Mary Wollstonecraft. The accusation is, indeed, ridiculous in so slight a farce. As Cowley herself argued, it was only natural to make a French character refer to the recent events in his country. The scene is set in a seraglio, where the heroine is protected by a kindly eunuch (although this offensive designation is scrupulously avoided). When the 'bassa' is fired by reports of her obstinacy, the eunuch substitutes a peasant girl in her stead, with whom the monarch indeed falls in love. He releases the heroine and her husband and is so impressed by her Christian charity that he promises to study the doctrines of her religion. The characters' motives are often unclear and the moral principles rather questionable. A relationship with a Turk would be a disgrace for the aristocratic heroine, but acceptable enough for a peasant, who considers even rape meet for a joke: 'Well, I may out-live such a misfortune as that; but I never heard of out-living a throat cut' (I/2). In fact, however, the bassa is a perfect gentleman, who marries the girl instead of enslaving her. The offensive politics is introduced by a French valet, who meant to give the

Russians 'some idea of the general equality of man; but ... they still continue to believe a prince is more than a porter, and that a lord is a better gentleman than his slave' (II/i/18), an obstinate belief the author evidently approves, for all her Whig convictions. And when one of the women hopes that 'the spirit [the French] have raised may reach even to a Turkish harem, and the rights of women be declared, as well as those of men' (V/i/69), this is to be taken as a joke. Cowley was not sympathetic towards female emancipation. In the play the eunuch teaches the girl that modesty is much more alluring than forwardness:

> if the sweet rogues knew what they lost by substituting rouge for blushing, and an undaunted look for modest timidity, we should soon see all their affectations swallow'd by one, and that would be the affectation of modesty.
>
> (V/ii/74)

Politics in comedy, of course, was perfectly acceptable as long as it consisted of patriotic hymns, not subversive French propaganda. Cowley's next play, *The Town Before You* (Covent Garden, 1794), is shriller in both its chauvinistic fervour and anti-feminism than her previous works. In the play two good-for-nothings impose on a nouveau riche and plan to abduct his daughter to force her into marriage. The girl is warned in time and they are arrested before they can do harm. In a second plot line the hero believes himself ruined, tears himself away from his aristocratic beloved, a sculptress, and enlists as a common sailor. After some misunderstandings involving the hero's rich uncle, who disapproves of the lady's art, the uncle and the fiancée acknowledge each other's merit and the hero is restored to wealth and felicity. The play is weak and pathetic, one of the few pieces in which Cowley clearly opted for sentimental rather than laughing comedy. She prided herself on the farcical scenes, some of which were added at the actors' suggestion during rehearsals, but the figures she intends as comic good-for-nothings are in fact melodramatic scoundrels. The hero, on the other hand, has the goodness of heart that makes a genuine sentimental paragon:

> birth, and beauty, and riches are all fine things; but when put into the scale against such innate goodness; such an upright

mind; such rectitude of character, it is weighing jewels against dross!

(II/v/38)

Women are unequivocally relegated to their proper place. The giddy girl runs herself into serious trouble, is shocked to her senses, and in the Epilogue vows to devote herself to her husband and HOME (with capital letters). The sculptress, of course, fashions only delicately veiled subjects of her own sex and yet still the play seems to endorse the philistine sentiments of her fiancé's uncle, who commands respect as a successful merchant and counsels her:

> Come, come, Madam, throw away your chisel and your marble blocks, and set about making a good wife. That ART is the noblest pride of an Englishwoman.

(V/vii/102)

All the virtuous characters are fired with patriotic fervour.

> Mention *parties* at an hour like this! O! let such distinctions melt into air, and be obliterated for ever! Let every party join hand and heart to save this country, and to cherish its BLESSED CONSTITUTION!

(V/vii/100)

If such unity prevails, the play resoundingly assures us at the end, 'ENGLAND MUST BE THE MISTRESS OF THE GLOBE' (V/vii/103).

Cowley also wrote two tragedies. *Albina, Countess of Raimond* involved her in an ugly controversy with Hannah More, whom she publicly accused of plagiarising the characters and incidents of this tragedy in her *Fatal Falsehood*. As has been discussed in the previous chapter, however, the plot elements are much too commonplace to allow any such speculation, and the public quarrel was humiliating for both competitors. *Albina* was finally produced at the Haymarket in 1779, but was not a financial success for the author. If it had not been for the debate, the play would hardly deserve so much attention. A villainous man and woman, in love with the hero and heroine, try to prevent their marriage; that failing, the man plans to murder the heroine, but stabs his accomplice by mistake. The role of women is once again defined as that of angels of the house:

A sweeter province Nature gave to us ...
For woman she reserv'd her choicest gift,
And call'd the blessing – Love.

(I/16)

The Fate of Sparta, or The Rival Kings (Drury Lane, 1788), a much
better play though no great success on the contemporary stage,
takes its story from Plutarch and puts a woman at the centre of the
traditional love–duty conflict. Chelonice is torn between her husband and her father, yet refuses to make a choice, since she can
combine two loves and two duties, that of a wife *and* of a child. She
persuades her husband to grant a truce to her father in besieged
Sparta, yet also protects him when he falls into her father's hands.
In the end, the possessive father is conveniently murdered by a
villain and his son-in-law generously avenges the deed, winning
the crown and the blessing of his dying erstwhile enemy. Despite
the shrill rhetoric about parricide, filicide (Chelonice could not live
with a man who has killed his father-in-law, or vice versa) and fratri-
cide (the villain also murders his own brother), the plot, because of
the classical model, is more acceptable and convincing than usual in
the age, and the heroine's moral dilemma seems genuine. Considering that virtue in distress was all the rage, Chelonice is an unusually
active tragic heroine, who proves that heroism is not 'only made for
man' (I/14), goes on a secret mission to the military camp, threatens
suicide if her husband does not grant the truce, calmly accepts im-
prisonment for her supposed treason, and courageously confronts
her father.

Cowley was the best woman dramatist of her time and the one
whose plays most obviously take up the patterns of her female fore-
bears. There are strong similarities to Susanna Centlivre. Like her
comedies, Cowley's are full of effective scenes and lively dialogue,
though marred sometimes by the shrill fervour of her patriotism
and – a typical late-eighteenth-century failing – at times by a chord
of sentimentality. Though basically conservative in her political attitude and view of women, in her plays Cowley nonetheless also
created strong and active female characters whose self-assertion and
independence of mind give the lie to the ideology of innate female
dependence and submissiveness propagated in her other works.
Her prefaces, too, allow some glimpses of the unresolved tensions
between the conservative ethos she seems to endorse in many of

her plays and her clear perception of the prejudices and disabilities hedging in her own position as a woman playwright.

Elizabeth Inchbald

Elizabeth Inchbald's work is more difficult to categorise. Throughout her career, she regularly alternated in her output between straight farce, sentimental comedy, problem plays and vestiges of Restoration drama, occasionally welding all four genres together. In all cases, however, she was unequivocally conservative in her picture of women and their place in society, censuring sexual transgressors and propagating the felicities of domesticity and motherhood.

Inchbald was a woman of unusual willpower. She came from farming stock, without extensive education, and was inhibited by a speech defect, yet became an actress and one of the most prolific playwrights of the century. After touring the provinces, she moved to London, where Harris, the manager of Covent Garden, tried to rape the beautiful young actress, but got nothing but his hair pulled. Inchbald was shrewd enough not to let this experience hinder her professional career, since she continued to act in Covent Garden and had plays produced there. In her dealings with managers she was an adroit negotiator and she was also a thrifty manager, who supported her destitute sisters with her income. At the end of her life she had, indeed, achieved a position of eminence not only as a dramatist, but also as a drama critic and anthologist, and earned more on one benefit night than in a whole year as an actress.

Her first efforts were rejected by the theatres and remained unpublished, but *The Mogul Tale* was performed at the Haymarket in 1784. This mixture of low farce, harlequinade and masquerade, which transports low-life English characters into a seraglio, matched the taste of the audience, made her a name, and remained popular for many years. Throughout her career Inchbald frequently returned to the genre of crude farce for many a hit comedy, although she refined her method considerably.

Her next play, *I'll Tell You What* (Haymarket, 1785), with its tumbling in and out of closets, has unmistakable echoes of Restoration comedy, yet the author is not really interested in social mores but rather in effectively timed horseplay. The plot hinges upon a divorcee, separated from her first husband because he found a man hidden in her closet and, by the end of the play, also divorced from this second husband because he, conversely, discovered the first spouse in the same closet. The numerous comic misunderstandings, especially about the woman's 'first' husband, presumed dead by all who hear about him, make for hilarious entertainment. However, the jokes levelled at the divorcee are always acerbic, and all men, including her present marriage partner, agree that she cannot be trusted. This dislike of 'emancipated' and assertive women links the farcical strand of action with the pathetic sub-plot about a father who has broken off contact with his son because of a misalliance, but saves his unknown, destitute daughter-in-law from prostitution, tearfully forgiving and reclaiming the (almost) fallen woman:

> I can excuse the feelings of a mother – the sudden starts, or rather madness of resolution, formed by the excessive anguish of the soul.... You are my daughter – and let the infamy you have escaped serve only to make you more amiable – make you more compassionate – compassionate to your own weak sex, in whatsoever suffering state you see them – They all were virtuous once, as well as you – and, had they met a father, might have been saved like you.
>
> (IV/i/64, 67f.)

Appearance Is Against Them (Covent Garden, 1785) repeats the set formula. With its rakes, women fishing for men and people hiding in bedrooms, it has the veneer of Restoration comedy, but the focus is again on knock-about farce. The title refers to a series of misunderstandings. In order to avoid a disagreeable meeting, a hapless moralist hides in the same bed as a woman of doubtful reputation and is henceforth taken for a libertine. A woman steals her friend's shawl to renew her acquaintance with an erstwhile admirer, but he fails to catch the hint and passes the gift on to his new flame. The original owner of the shawl gets back the valuable present in the end, but her betrothed uses her negligence as a pretext to break off the union. The play introduces a whole gallery of such despicable characters, all viewed with sharp derision and cold detachment.

The Widow's Vow (Haymarket, 1786), adapted from a French farce, features a widow who falls in love with a man disguised as a woman and who reneges on her stupid vow never to see a man again, since, as her uncle preaches, the only vow 'a woman is authorised to take' (II/ii/35) is the marriage vow. *The Midnight Hour*

(Covent Garden, 1787) is a Spanish intrigue farce, again taken from the French, involving a melee of disguises, mistaken identities and narrow escapes. The initiative rests in the hands of a young man and his wily servant, who outwit a watchful guardian, with the girl the passive prize to be gained. *Animal Magnetism* (Covent Garden, 1788), also adapted from a French play, is a mixture of Spanish intrigue comedy and harlequinade, completely belying the title. The usual dupe, the doctor, is persuaded to believe in the power of a wand to make all women fall in love with its owner, and is thereby tricked into consenting to his ward's marriage.

The Married Man (Haymarket, 1789), loosely derived from a French source as well, makes fun of the protagonist's qualms about confessing his marriage to his cronies and especially to his rich uncle. His indulgent wife meekly bears her burden, but her catty sister takes on the rich old man like a termagant, until he is glad to accept the meeker sister into the family. Inchbald again presents an assortment of despicable characters, whose misogyny, however, is sure to draw the laughter of the house: 'It is impossible for a married man to be a philosopher – and yet it is a state that requires more philosophy than any other' (I/i/17). She also includes a good dose of sentimentality in the portrayal of the long-suffering, self-sacrificing wife, who even offers to separate from her husband should he wish it.

The Hue and Cry (Drury Lane, 1791), also derived from a French play, is a farce about a nobleman and his servant, who believe they have killed a Spaniard, and hide in a chest, wherein they are mistakenly transported to the gaol, where the police also imprison the alleged victim and his servant on a false murder charge. The fact that there are now four men in prison, two of whom do not know where they are when they emerge from their hiding place, gives rise to hilarious misunderstandings and good situation comedy, until the mystery is unravelled. In *Young Men and Old Women* (Haymarket, 1792), one of the few plays which did not prove successful on stage, a young man is tricked into believing his betrothed unchaste and thereupon plays the fop to induce her proud father to dissolve the marriage contract. On being enlightened as to his mistake, he painstakingly has to undo the impression he has created and has to promise that he will change nothing in the estate except the old man's daughter – for 'in Women there is no Perfection, till they are made Wives and Mothers' (III/25). The other butt of humour referred to in the title is the destitute aunt, constantly scared into assenting to everything under the sun and then taunted by her brother for lying. Another short farce, *The Wedding Day* (Drury Lane, 1794) exploits the motif of an old man married to a young girl, whom he has to relinquish unwillingly when his first wife, long believed dead, suddenly reappears. Much of the humour of the play rests on the unflattering candour with which the naive bride answers her ageing husband's questions:

> SIR ADAM: ... Answer me this – would you change husbands with any one of your acquaintance?
>
> LADY CONTEST: ... I am sure, not one of my acquaintance would change with me....
>
> LADY CONTEST: ... I will always be obedient to you.... I will never be angry with you if you should go out and stay for a month – nay, for a year – or for as long as ever you like.
>
> (I/8, 9)

Wives As They Were, and Maids As They Are (Covent Garden, 1797) is as close as Inchbald got to social satire, but again with many farcical ingredients, an uneasy admixture of sentimentality and a heavy dose of misogyny. The wife of the title meekly welcomes her husband's tyranny and refuses to cuckold him even when he himself colludes in providing the opportunity for her. She justifies her tenacious obedience by the fact that all men are despotic: 'I was born to be the slave of some of you – I make the choice to obey my husband' (IV/2/59). Her fidelity only serves to confirm her husband's dictum that wives ought to be ill-treated and suppressed instead of spoiled. She is held up as a model to the frivolous young heroine, whose cantankerous father returns in disguise and, scandalised at her fashionable way of life, means to let her languish in a debtors' prison, yet is mollified by her generous offer to sell all she has left to relieve her father, whom she believes to be penniless. The return of a parent in disguise and the voice of nature summoning a child to its unknown father are well worn paraphernalia of sentimental comedy, but here the focus is more on the follies of fashionable society and on mistaken identities, and the sentimental aspects surface fully only in the last act.

In her last play, *To Marry or Not To Marry* (Covent Garden, 1805), the conversion of a confirmed bachelor into an ardent lover is treated comically rather than romantically, as is his friend's desperate attempt to induce *any* woman to accept his proposal of marriage. It is characteristic of the age that the bachelor is bewitched by the girl's supposed simplicity, only in this case, quite unsentimentally, she turns out to be quite artful.

While Inchbald was making a steady career in writing farcical comedy leavened with sentiment, she regularly turned out fully fledged sentimental plays in between, often switching between the two genres within one and the same year or, as we have already seen in some instances, mixing them within one and the same play. *Such Things Are* (Covent Garden, 1787) is a case in point, combining humanitarian fervour and maudlin moralisation with a satirical exposure of English colonial society. The hero, modelled on a real-life philanthropist, works charitable wonders in Indian prisons, gaining pardons for a variety of convicts, who thereupon reform melodramatically. This affords occasion for plenty of pathos, at odds with the acid satire on the selfish and cowardly English colonial officers and their hangers-on, portrayed in Inchbald's typically detached manner.

All On A Summer's Day (Covent Garden, 1787) is prepared according to the same recipe, but much more overtly misogynist. Long ago a rake seduced a supposedly poor orphan and jilted her. She now returns with her father, rich and engaged to a lord. When she treats him with contempt, he tells the story to her father to enforce his old rights and, indeed, it turns out that the girl is still in love with him. In the second plot a flirtatious wife tries to dupe her old husband and passes off her sister as her daughter to hide her intrigue. In the end all the women have to return to the patriarchal fold. Marriage to her erstwhile seducer is the only reparation the girl craves; the errant wife has to beg her husband on bended knees to forgive her; and the sister must confess that she has no claim on the rake, even though we have seen him vowing love to her. The voice of moral censure is put into the mouth of a celibate monk, who refuses to let women even touch him, as if they were infected or poisonous.

The Child of Nature (Covent Garden, 1788), based on a French source, shows Inchbald at her sentimental worst. The mawkish plot, with its typical motifs of resurrected parents and rags to riches, is unrelieved by humour. It caters to fantasies of male autogamy and of woman as a tabula rasa, which we have already encountered in Cowley's *More Ways Than One*. An aristocrat brings up a motherless girl in complete seclusion, forbidding her all society and books except those he himself selects, until, a second Frankenstein, he has completely formed the girl in his own image and falls in love with his own creation. She reciprocates this affection, and when her proscribed father returns to ask her to share his exile, she is faced with a pitiable dilemma, but, of course, he merely wants to test her filial dutifulness, and she can have both her father and her beloved mentor, combining the ideal female roles of daughter and wife to everybody's complete satisfaction.

Next Door Neighbours (Haymarket, 1791) continues in the same mawkish strain and again borrows from French sources. This time, the plot features a virtuous poor girl, whom a rake tries to seduce with the bribe of obtaining her father's release from the debtors' prison. Luckily, she indignantly rejects the proposal, because she turns out to be the rake's long-lost sister, who has inherited a fortune and can now marry her foster brother. The rake, for his part, has lost all his money at cards, but it is restored to him by his loyal fiancée, so that there can be general reconciliation and forgiveness in the denouement. There is no attempt at logical motivation; sentimentality and melodrama are given full swing, and the poor family is portrayed as the epitome of honour, virtue and magnanimity.

The Massacre (1792) is Inchbald's only attempt at high tragedy, inspired by reports of the Terror in France and by a French play about the St Bartholomew's Day Massacre of 1572, but, as the author realised, was too grisly to be suitable for performance. The melodrama describes the horrible fate of a nobleman, who miraculously escapes the massacre of Paris (described by quoting verbatim from newspaper reports), only to find that the revolution has spread to his home town and that his whole family has been arrested. He and his father are saved by an upright judge, but his wife and children are butchered by the mob. The aristocrats are presented as true humanitarians, charitable, benevolent and so angelic that they will not even kill their enemies to defend themselves. There is no reference whatsoever to social injustice and political corruption, only a sentimental picture of family affection set off against the inhuman cruelty of the revolutionaries.

Every One Has His Faults (Covent Garden, 1793) is gruelling melodrama cum farce. A divorced husband, on hearing a rumour that his wife is to remarry, is consumed with jealousy and entreats her to come back, a motif taken from Edward Howard's Restoration comedy *Women's Conquest*. A bachelor is alternately attracted to matrimony by the divorced man's passion and put off by the fate of his hen-pecked second friend. An aristocrat has disowned his daughter for marrying a penniless soldier, refuses to relieve her poverty (painted with the usual pathos), but secretly adopts his grandson. In a frenzy of despair, the impoverished soldier robs his father-in-law, but the boy, instinctively attracted to his unknown parents as fictional children are wont to be, steals the evidence and decides to share his parents' fate. However, everything is brought to a happy ending by the genuinely comic figure of an inveterate peace-maker, who has a knack for reconciling people by claiming that their enemies have spoken well of them behind their backs. In the end the divorced couple remarries, the bachelor weds an old spinster, and the robber is forgiven on pleading temporary insanity induced by despair.

For *Lovers' Vows* (Covent Garden, 1798), Inchbald used a literal translation of Kotzebue's drama, since she herself did not know German, but introduced some changes, since the original, she felt, was too indelicate and candid for an English palate. However, her play retained enough objectionable passion and sympathy for the baron's poor deserted mistress to shock a conservative audience, since in Austen's *Mansfield Park* an amateur private performance of *Lovers' Vows* awakens fears that the actresses involved may thereby have prejudiced their chances of advantageous marriage. The sentimental plot revolves around a lower-class woman jilted by an aristocrat, whose son, on seeing her starving, tries to rob his unknown father. Much is made of their poverty and their having bread and water as their only food – stock exaggerations by which dramatists could be sure of drawing tears from the audience, as Trotter had done in *Fatal Friendship* a century earlier. The aristocrat, who has long rued his youthful sin, forgives his son, marries his ex-mistress and allows his daughter to marry her tutor. The play ends with a grotesque version of the indispensable sentimental family tableau, the baron on his knees before his former mistress, framed by their children, and the priest raising his hands in benediction.

The Wise Man of the East (Covent Garden, 1799) considerably alters Kotzebue's original plot and once more proves Inchbald's predilection, in later years, for unmitigated sentimentality. The plot bears some resemblance to *Next Door Neighbours* in that a sup-posedly kind-hearted rake tries to seduce an impoverished girl, but the distress of virtue is considerably exacerbated by dismissal from service, slander, exposure to inclement weather and starvation. She is rescued by an Indian magician, who is, in fact, the rake's father in disguise, believed to have perished in a fire. This 'wise man from the East' finally affects the rake's reform and restores the preternaturally virtuous poor family to wealth. Inchbald tacks on to this maudlin tale a satire on the mercenary nature and cold-heartedness of Quakers, who were popular targets of ridicule in comedy, for instance in Centlivre's *A Bold Stroke for a Wife*.

The Case of Conscience (1800) failed to be staged owing to quarrels extraneous to the play between the Drury Lane management and its star actors, Kemble and Mrs Siddons. It is sentimental and hypocritical, presenting the sadistic protagonist as a victim rather than a heartless villain and making his masochistic wife comfort rather than censure him. Poisoned by suspicion that she has foisted an illegitimate son on him, he treats her with cruelty and even hands his son over to the Inquisition. But this suspicion was nourished by his own rival, disguised as a hermit and Macchiavellian after 20 years of unrequited passion. The news of the son's execution, however, turns out to be false and a happy ending can be engineered.

Unlike Hannah Cowley, Inchbald fused a variety of seemingly incompatible genres in an attempt to cater to the tastes of the audience. Her range varies from detached ridicule and satirical exposure of folly and vice to cloying sentimentality and spurious emotionalism. Despite occasional Restoration echoes, her plays never give moral offence, but reinforce a conservative and patriarchal viewpoint. Indeed, Elizabeth Inchbald was one of the few women playwrights who largely escaped censure, and who could, in her prologues, proudly refer to the applause with which the public had deigned to greet many of her previous ventures. Her continued popularity for more than 25 years was possible only because she spoke in the approved discourse. She was severely critical of the immorality of her Restoration and early-eighteenth-century female predecessors. One wonders whether this strong-minded woman truly believed that a woman's appropriate place was that of dependency, domesticity and meek subordination, yet her plays give no indication of inconsistency on this point, diffuse as they may be in style and diverse in subject matter.

Part IV
Performance and Tradition

9
Contemporary and Modern Performances of the Plays

Contemporary Staging

In the Restoration period, a number of superb actors walked the stage, but it was felt that, in acting, nature must be augmented by dignity and beauty. Accordingly, acting was stylised, delivery was declamatory, and set gestures and facial expressions were used to convey specific emotions: a stamp of the foot implied anger, guilt was expressed by eyes cast to one side and head bent low, bashfulness by a hand placed over the mouth.[76] Most performers did not stay in character when it was their colleagues' turn to speak and up to Garrick in the middle of the eighteenth century there was little sense of ensemble acting. Garrick also introduced a more natural style of acting and delivery. However, when the two legitimate theatres were rebuilt at the end of the eighteenth century to seat more than 3000 spectators each, performers were dwarfed by these dimensions and returned to a more artificial and melodramatic acting style to make themselves understood in the gallery.

Garrick also used costumes appropriate to the time in which a play was set. In the Restoration period and the early eighteenth century, contemporary dress had invariably been worn. So Philip's Roman Pompey, Manley's first Christian British King Lucius and

Wiseman's Syrian King Antiochus would have appeared in Restoration wig, feathered hat and embroidered coat, just as Pix's medieval Queen Catherine, the Faithful General's Byzantine daughter and Robe's Greek Jocasta would have entered in hooped skirts and fashionable hairdo. For seraglio settings, vaguely orientalised costumes with turbans and feathers were used, but there was no attempt at historical verisimilitude.

Plays were written for amusement and geared to please the audience. Scenes of horseplay (as in Polwhele's *Frolicks* or Pix's *Spanish Wives*), which may seem dead on the printed page, could be very effective on stage and were widely popular. Spectators were also fascinated by sophisticated sets (Manley's *The Royal Mischief*, for instance, in the fourth act features a lavish scene with illuminated boats on a river) and enjoyed the use of theatrical machinery for dazzling spectacle (employed effectively, for instance, in Behn's *The Emperor of the Moon* and satirised in *The Female Wits*). The success of a play could well depend on a spectacular tableau or one moving encounter between characters just as on good acting. The realistic gambling scenes in Centlivre's *The Gamester* enthralled contemporaneous audiences. Spectators were always moved to tears when in *Ibrahim* Morena vainly slits her arm to prevent the sultan from raping her.

On the other hand, even a well acted play failed if it was politically suspect. Thus Centlivre's *Perplexed Lovers* got into trouble because of its purportedly Whiggish Epilogue, and references to the French Revolution cost Cowley a royal command performance of *A Day in Turkey*. From the 1680s onwards, the charge of indecency could also cause damage, however good the actors. Both Behn and Cowley, for instance, complain about unjust objections on the part of the audience to the bawdiness and indecent language in *The Lucky Chance* and *The School for Greybeards*, respectively. In the eighteenth century, criticism focused on moral issues and plays were recommended for the moral edification they afforded, rather than for their wit or theatricality; performers were praised for moving the audience to tears, though comic talent was equally appreciated.

As a rule, we know the names of the cast of a particular play. However, apart from some vague contemporary comments on a performance or a writer's grateful acknowledgement of the actors' excellence or complaints about their failure, we know very little about the actual staging of the plays. There is one picture extant showing Anne Bracegirdle as the Indian Queen Semernia in Behn's *The Widow Ranter*, which gives some impression of the splendour of staging and costume common in Restoration theatres. Semernia is clad in what is basically a lavish contemporary dress, embellished with feathers on the head, a jewel necklace, bracelet and headband, and she is accompanied by two black children with feather skirts and head-dresses, carrying her train and shading her from the sun with a parasol. No realistic representation of an Indian woman is attempted. Indeed, the Indian queen, unlike her black attendants, is quite obviously white. A black queen would have been considered sexually unattractive and, furthermore, unacceptable as a heroine. A century earlier, Queen Anne and her maids of honour had not felt any scruples about appearing as 'blackamoors' in Jonson's *Masque of Blackness*, scandalising the more Puritanical courtiers. In the Restoration period, however, no actress would have disfigured herself by blackening her face, nor would such 'realism' have been expected or appreciated. This is also evinced by the fact that Southerne, in his adaptation for the stage of Behn's narrative *Oroonoko*, quite explicitly turned her African princess Imoinda into a *white* woman, although her husband, the title hero, remained an enslaved *black* prince.

The splendour of Restoration costume and scenery can also be estimated by the fact that Lady Castlemaine was decked out in the crown jewels for her performance in Philips' *Horace* at Court, and that Aphra Behn in *Oroonoko* claims to have donated to Drury Lane an authentic Indian feather costume brought back from Surinam, which was used for a performance of Dryden's *The Indian Queen*. Rich costumes and expensive dresses were used to dazzle the audience, and some actresses secretly borrowed the splendid gowns from the theatre for private purposes, though this was strictly forbidden. In *The Rover* Behn employed lavish garments, making the characters change in and out of different masques, gowns and disguises. Hellena appears in various colourful carnival costumes, including that of a gypsy and a boy; because of Angelica's sponsorship Willmore can shed his old buff clothes for an elegant new outfit, while Blunt is robbed of his clothes and exposed to ridicule in his long johns, before he dons an absurd Spanish habit.

As far as the acting in specific plays is concerned, we have little to go on. Mountfort must have given a charismatically sensuous appeal to his impersonation of the Rover, otherwise Queen Anne could hardly have found the rake's vice alluring. Other actors were less successful or conscientious and drunkenness and imperfect memorising of lines were not uncommon. Young Thomas Otway, whom Behn had given the small role of the king in *The Forc'd Marriage*, had such stage fright that he could not deliver the text and gave up acting altogether, turning playwright instead. Behn blamed the failure of *The Dutch Lover* on the incompetence of the cast, especially the actor of the title figure, who forgot his lines and made up his own text, and on the sloppy costumes, which rendered the complicated intrigue plot incomprehensible. A century later, Fanny Burney's *Edwy and Elgiva* was also ruined by incompetent staging. Elgiva, murdered in the thick woods, was discovered reclining on a couch in the middle of the forest, on which she was dumped again after she had expired – an absurdity which aroused hissing laughter instead of the tears of sympathy Burney had hoped for in this scene.

Centlivre's *The Wonder!*, on the other hand, moderately popular during her lifetime, owed its lasting popularity to Garrick's masterful representation of the jealous Don Felix, whom he showed fidgeting in his chair, slowly moving it closer and closer to Violante, and reflecting in his expression all the conflicting emotions of pride, remorse, jealousy and love.

Many of the women's plays surveyed never made it to the repertory after their initial run, or were discarded after a few years. Behn's plays were still revived in the early decades of the eighteenth century, but were later regarded as being too disreputable for the 'reformed' stage. Centlivre's hit comedies went through hundreds of performances throughout the eighteenth century and continued to be popular in the Victorian period. Then, however, they, too, fell into oblivion, and it was not until the 1980s that interest in early women dramatists was revived.

Modern Performances in London and Abroad
Behn's plays had been out of repertory for more than two centuries when Peter Stevenson revived *The Rover* at the small Upstream Theatre, London, in 1984, with Willmore as a jolly Don Juan. However, the real breakthrough in a renewed appreciation of the author came not from this fringe production, but from Jules Wright's revival of *The Lucky Chance* at the Royal Court in the same year. The visually opulent production, with its studied

artificiality of acting, and sexually suggestive company dance, interpreted the comedy as a hymn to the phallus rather than a feminist statement, and Gayman was played as a sensuous *homme fatale*. The unrealistic happy ending converting Julia's husband's miserliness into avuncular benevolence was cut, and in a fine directorial gag all 11 minor roles, male and female, were played by one actress.

John Barton's acclaimed adaptation of *The Rover* for the Royal Shakespeare Company in 1986 cut some 500 lines from the original, adding some 350 new ones from Killigrew's *Thomaso* and his own pen, and transferred the action from Naples to the West Indies, giving it the flair of a colourful Mardi Gras. The comedy was played as a boisterous romp, with Willmore as a dashing romantic swashbuckler. Barton tidied character relationships by turning the three girls in search of husbands into three sisters, and added an aspect of racial exploitation to the sexual one by making Lucetta a former slave, who avenges herself by fleecing her clients. This racial antagonism, however, was not maintained consistently, because the part of Belville was taken by a black actor as well, which imbued the otherwise insipid Florinda character with greater courage and independence of mind by marrying out of her race.

The New Cross Theatre performance of 1991, on the other hand, examined the darker sides of the play, revealing a sense of urgency in all the characters' pursuits realistic enough in view of the violence of the time portrayed and the average life expectancy, and giving the men's libertinism a genuinely threatening quality. Jules Wright's production of *The Rover* for Women's Playhouse Trust at Jacob Street Studios in 1994 also stressed the potential of violence in the play, the double sexual standard and the attempted rapes, downplaying the farcical side and making little of the spirit of fiesta celebrated by the Royal Shakespeare Company. Again, the setting was changed, this time to colonial India, complete with rickshaws, exotic incense and alluring Kathakali movements (on the part of Angelica), which introduced the element of a clash of cultures as well as sexes derived from works like *Oroonoko* rather than from the comedy itself.

The 1996 revival of *The Rover* at Salisbury Playhouse for the first time included *The Rover, Part II* as well, staged under the title of *The Banished Cavaliers*. Without completely disregarding the sexual violence in the play, director Jonathan Church gave the production a frolicking rather than a sensuous flair, somewhat dampened by the sombre all-black sets.

In 1991 Women in the Moon staged *The False Count*, making do with a minimal set creatively and wittily used. Director Vivienne Cottress stressed the play's unconventional sexual mores and enlightened comments on social status, without exploring the darker implications of the theme, although the miserly old husband was depicted as something of an East End Shylock.

After Behn, Centlivre came in for reappreciation, though productions at first failed to enthuse the reviewers. As early as 1983, before the Behn fashion started, Fidelis Morgan staged at the King's Head, under the title of *Wedlock/Deadlock*, an adaptation of Centlivre's *A Bickerstaff's Burying*. Morgan expanded the original plot by scenes from other plays by Centlivre and from her own pen, and also added a musical score. The production, set in a colourful Rousseau-esque jungle, came in for criticism because of its forced feminist tones and the xenophobia of exploiting foreign cultures for a laugh. Caroline Lynch's revival of *The Wonder! A Woman Keeps a Secret* at the Gate in 1989 also stressed Centlivre's feminist concerns, but reviewers felt that Isabella's egotism of endangering her friend's happiness to ensure her own rendered claims of the author's feminism unconvincing.

The exuberant and deliberately stylised production of *The Artifice* at the Orange Tree Theatre in 1992 used costumes spanning several centuries, from eighteenth-century gowns and nineteenth-century police uniforms to 1960s glitter trouser suits. The stunning set, symbolising the world of trickery portrayed, reproduced sections from a manual for card sharpers, and a snakes-and-ladders board, with the serpents sporting human heads. Peter Barlow's 1993 Bridge Lane production of *The Busybody* transferred the action into the swinging twenties and roaring forties, clad the actors in consciously tacky costumes and used tangos, foxtrots and boogies as metaphors of sexual passion. *The Basset Table*, adapted by Rosa McRae and directed by Guy K. Retallack for the New End in the same year, used specially designed period costumes and sumptuous sets, culminating in a magnificent scene at the basset table. All critics agreed that the mock rape through which Lady Reveller is brought to heel looked authentic, yet its misogynic threat was downplayed in the light-hearted atmosphere of the production.

The year 1992 saw a spurt of revivals of other early women dramatists as well. In the Sound and Fury Theatre Company's production of Pix's *The Beau Defeated* at the White Bear, Catherine Donnelly combined period manners and pastiche, using lavishly gross costumes and accoutrements and going in for broad caricature. The swindler Sir John appeared with a rose between his teeth and wig powder spraying in his wake, and the cast included two dogs. Trotter's *Love at a Loss*, directed by Helen Fry at the Link, dispensed with such burlesque and used period dress but modern make-up, stunning hairdos and other modern paraphernalia. The production emphasised the feminist aspects of reversed gender roles and of female solidarity and tried to recapture a Restoration theatre atmosphere by introducing strong interaction between the actors and the audience. Vivienne Cottrell's and Women in the Moon's *She Ventures and He Wins* also emphasised the active role women take in the plot, yet seemed to ignore what critics regarded as unwarranted cruelty in the heroine's generic revenge on men, meted out in advance. Instead, the production made much of the farcical plot elements, especially the Falstaffian chastening of Squire Wouldbe.

The few out-of-London productions mentioned in the following happened to come to the present author's notice. As early as 1982 (a year before the first London revival of an early woman playwright) Beverly Blankenship had staged Centlivre's *The Wonder! A Woman Keeps a Secret* in Sydney, Australia. Inspired by historical eighteenth-century female transvestites, some of whom had indeed been soldiers or even pirates, Blankenship had an actress take the role of the English colonel, giving a lesbian undertone to the play's celebration of female friendship. She repeated this cross-gender casting in her new German production of the play at Vienna's fringe theatre in the Drachengasse in 1995, which made do with a cast of six, zanily doubling and even tripling roles, thereby illuminating satirically the generic patterns in the behaviour of the male and female characters. Role doubling and cross-gender casting had also been used in Blankenship's riotously funny German production of Behn's *Feigned Courtesans* at the same Austrian theatre in 1993, which featured an all-male, an all-female and a mixed pair of lovers, effectively undermining stereotype gender roles.

The spate of revivals in the mid-1980s and again in the early nineties had no doubt been inspired by a new interest in Behn and her female successors in academe and had, above all, been sparked off by the new editions of seventeenth- and eighteenth-century women's dramas, making these long-lost texts once again available. On the other hand, however, the acclaimed and highly successful productions also had their influence on scholars, who concerned themselves with renewed vigour with plays whose attractiveness and continued appeal to modern audiences had been amply demonstrated. Such an interaction is a rare and fruitful impetus for reappreciation. Indeed, Fidelis Morgan was a pioneer both in the editing of forgotten plays and in producing them on stage, and the actress Felicity Kendal, for her part, turned editor and brought out a collection of little-known early women playwrights.

Significantly, only comedies were rediscovered by the theatres, as, truly, they are much better and more stageworthy than all the maudlin Restoration or eighteenth-century tragedies, which would hardly bear revival. Most modern productions were interested in the feminist potential of the texts, which throw new light on the established canon of Restoration drama and resurrect a tradition long lost and buried and, indeed, until recently never even acknowledged either by scholars or in the theatre. So directors (many of them women themselves) made much of reversed gender roles, female solidarity and the deconstruction of patriarchal norms. What really made these productions successful, however, was the splendid theatricality of the plays themselves; they come alive comically on stage and make for hilarious entertainment. Many productions were deliberately stylised, satirising the facade of social decorum and role play screening the predatory nature of individuals and social structures.

Beyond their perennial amusement value, however, the plays are also complex and allow for completely different interpretations. Their stereotypes can be recast in accordance with modern thinking and they can accommodate topical references, such as a culture or racial clash on top of a sexual and economic one, because their authors had been keenly aware of the existence of a double standard and of the strategies to which suppressed minorities resort in order to get their own back. It is this innate potential for affording unexpected new insights and original reinterpretation which constitutes the plays' major attraction for the modern stage.

10
Towards a Female Tradition in the Theatre

Is there a distinctive female tone in women's drama between 1550 and 1800? Or did female playwrights completely internalise the male norms of their eras, and are their works hence indistinguishable from those of men? The question is complicated not only by the diverse and contradictory nature of the material surveyed, but also by fundamental disagreement, even among critics of modern drama, where feminist stances are much more pronounced, as to what, in fact, constitutes women's theatre. Any drama written by a woman? Or only theatre made and done by feminists? All plays concentrating on the quotidian concerns of women, no matter whether written by women or men? Or only political theatre revealing the dynamics of power and gender, and deconstructing traditional forms of presentation?[77]

A survey of plays based solely on the author's gender yields a completely diffuse mass of inhomogenous works. Criteria for establishing a female tradition based on a presentation of women's problems, or on passages complaining about the prevailing double standard, would leave us with a lot of plays by male authors which would fit the definition, yet, in their fundamental attitude, are far removed from true sympathy with women's lot and in reality view the female figures entirely against the background of patriarchal sexual morality.

There are no consistently *feminist* women playwrights in the period under consideration, and even very few unequivocally feminist plays. Drama was commercial, not a forum for sexual politics, and, not surprisingly, class membership and social decorum were, in most cases, more formative in a writer's attitudes than gender.

As we have seen, the sense of a female tradition among women playwrights themselves was only tenuous. In their dedications, addresses to the reader or congratulatory verses, the Female Wits frequently commended each other's works and consciously competed for the female poetic throne vacant after Behn's death. Towards the end of the eighteenth century, Cowley in the title of her *Bold Stroke for a Husband* affectionately deferred to her forerunner Centlivre and her famous *Bold Stroke for a Wife*, and Mrs Holford in *Neither's the Man* in turn did homage to Cowley's successful comedy *Which is the Man?*. As a rule, however, eighteenth-century female dramatists, grateful to be admitted to a closed shop, were careful not to stress a separate tradition going back to the 'rakish' Restoration women playwrights, lest they encourage moral censure, patronising criticism or downright rejection. To be sure, among women dramatists of the period there was widespread awareness of male prejudices against their species and of the different reception and evaluation accorded to women's works. But whereas writers like Behn, Manley, Centlivre and Cowley confronted these biases head on, sometimes satirically, sometimes bitterly, late-eighteenth-century playwrights tended to conceal their anger behind defensive postures of humility and self-justification. Such verbal gestures themselves, however, indicate the knowledge that women dramatists were defending an embattled position in hostile territory, as does the common appeal to the ladies in the audience to support a woman's work out of female solidarity.

Any such group awareness of shared professional difficulties caused by male animosity was confined to prefatory material and rarely found direct reflection in the plays themselves, whose tenor occasionally even contradicted these introductory complaints about discrimination against women. Even dramatists who sounded a feminist tone in some of their plays were equivocal in their outlook, and often quite conservative in other works. Indeed, even within one and the same play we have encountered misogyny side by side with feminist subversion.

Nonetheless, in the course of this analysis some common factors have emerged. Women playwrights, as a rule, take a greater interest in female characters, investing them with more importance in the plot and, as Pearson has pointed out,[78] giving them more lines to speak, though such prominence need not necessarily entail a more liberal attitude or sympathy with a female viewpoint.

Plot adaptation must be discarded as a useful category for tracing a sense of common tradition, because all writers of the period, both male and female, borrowed freely from their predecessors and from foreign sources. Certain motifs, however, such as female figures subjecting their suitors to a number of ordeals to test their integrity, or heroines assuming the disguise of harlots or shrews, were particularly popular among female dramatists and were taken up by one woman playwright after the other. Female friendship and solidarity are also described more frequently by women writers than by men, from Cavendish, Behn, Trotter, Pix, Centlivre and Davys to Cowley and Baillie. On the other hand, the converse motif, namely female jealousy, so popular among male dramatists, is not as common with female playwrights, though it does feature prominently in such plays as *The False Friend*, *The Rival Widows* or *Albina*. *Agnes de Castro*, for instance, portrays both an unconventional friendship (despite both women loving the same man) and a stereotypical jealous villainess. Most women dramatists, however, tended to evade conflicts of jealousy between their female protagonists by making them fall in love with different men and allowing them to coexist peacefully. What is conspicuously absent in women's drama is the sense of male bonding and an all-male struggle for power so frequently palpable in Restoration and eighteenth-century male playwrights.

The reinterpretation of specific female stereotypes, particularly the whore and the adulteress, in the works of Behn, Centlivre, Frances Sheridan and Sophia Lee is a remarkable but not a regular characteristic of women's writing. More often we encounter a failure to deconstruct misogynist stereotypes, such as the learned woman, the amorous old hag, or the middle-class social climber. Far more conspicuous in women's plays is the presentation of strong-minded and intellectually autonomous heroines, who initiate action, determine the course of events and shape their own destinies. To be sure, intelligent and witty heroines frequently appear in the Restoration comedies of male dramatists as well. Yet for all her sparkle, Congreve's Millamant is dependent on Mirabell's superior stratagem for her economic survival (as are all the other women characters in *The Way of the World*), whereas the indebted protagonist in Polwhele's *The Frolicks*, for instance, depends on the resourceful heroine for *his* rescue from prison and for the suggestion as to how to outwit his creditor. From Cavendish and Brackley to Centlivre, from Davys to Cowley, these women of action lead men by the nose and by their wit, inventiveness, clever role play and sheer force of will orchestrate the final surrender of the elusive male. Farquhar and Southerne, also praised for creating such active heroines, may well have learned from Behn, so they may represent a case of men adopting a female tradition, rather than vice versa, just as Goldsmith was later to borrow this female stereotype and the popular motif of cross-class disguise in *She Stoops to Conquer*. Indeed, Southerne even adapted Behn's *Oroonoko* for the stage. Yet in Southerne's supposedly feminist *The Wives' Excuse* the heroine's accomplishment again consists of her staunch chastity and sexual constancy in adversity, whereas in *She Ventures and He Wins* and its many successors it is *male* chastity and constancy that count. Here the traditional pattern of (male) narrative is reversed, with a female protagonist on the quest to find a perfect mate, whose devotion to her in turn proves her own immaculate character.

Restoration and turn-of-the-century women dramatists, in particular, often turned their heroines into desiring subjects instead of mere objects, and even the more prudish eighteenth-century writers, skirting overt eroticism, frequently focused on a woman's pursuit of a male object of desire. On an even more fundamental level, female dramatists completely reversed the notorious binary gender opposition of (male) subject and *other* by putting women into the subject position, and casting men as the *other*, unreasonable, obsessive or at best unknown, in need of careful vetting against the standards established by the dominant woman character. Female figures, not men, constitute the norm of reason and normality, the moral consciousness striving for autonomy from outside influence. This reversal does not necessarily entail a feminist re-evaluation of prevalent standards, nor, obviously, does it hold true of every female writer, or of each and every play. There is no biological necessity enforcing such a perspective, though this realignment of subject and *other* seems to have come naturally to many a woman playwright.

From *The Concealed Fancies* and *Marcelia* sub-plot, right to *The Rival Widows* and *A Bold Stroke for a Husband*, women fight for their independence and escape their preordained roles, whereas the men want to suppress and enslave them, or to turn them into objects for barter. Even the intriguing female figures in *Love at a Loss* are always a step ahead of the conceited men, whom they outwit and manipulate. Charke's tragedy queen, for all her histrionics, has a raison d'être which the stupid managers who dismiss her have not. Clive's female Bays, weak though her play may be, has the same justification, unlike her narrow-minded detractors (and, significantly, unlike the ridiculous female playwright in *The Female Wits*, which was written by a man).

This female perspective can be traced not only in comedy, but also in tragedy. It is not sufficient, however, that a woman character be given the main part, if she is assessed entirely according to her chastity and submissiveness to male guidance. The learned heroine of *The Faithful General* defends her individual conscience and female dignity against both sexual harassment and patriarchal indoctrination. The intelligent and courageous Almyna cures the paranoid sultan of his murderous misogyny. In Robe's *Fatal Legacy*, Jocasta and Antigona constitute the voices of common sense and moderation, whereas the fratricidal brothers and the villain Creon are unamenable to reason or even common humanity. Pix's *Queen Catherine* focuses on two noble heroines destroyed by male treachery and treason. Trotter, on the other hand, in *The Unhappy Penitent*, punishes her heroine for relinquishing the passivity and tutelage appropriate to women – an example of how male viewpoints may surface in a woman's play as well. *Mary, Queen of Scots* casts the two rival queens as central political actors. In *The Fate of Sparta* Chelonice defends her right to autonomous moral decision against the possessive love of both her father and her husband. The yardstick set up by women characters need not necessarily be a moral one. Homais is simply more alive and erotic than her effeminate male counterparts, whom she despises. Antiochus' mistress Leonice is an unchaste woman, but she has an emotional life independent of the normative censure of a repressive patriarchal ideology which expects a woman to rue her voluntary surrender as an unforgivable sin. Mariam, though reproached for not being submissive to her husband, is an autonomous human being torn between love and hatred, whereas Herod is viewed as an unreasonably jealous and suspicious force which annihilates her. Even More's *Percy* can be fitted into this scheme, since the figure of the married woman, not the nominal hero, is the true moral consciousness of the play, wavering between exalted virtue and adulterous passion, whereas the rivalling male characters are merely objects of her desire, revulsion or anger.

Which plays do not fit in? Notably, there is, for instance, Behn's *Abdelazar*, or the main plot of *The Town Fop*, though written by a woman whom we credit with much more feminist sympathy than More. But in some of her works Behn simply takes over the stereotype dichotomy of a woman as lustful villainess or virtue in distress, as does her weak anonymous imitator in *The Unnatural Mother*. Most eighteenth-century tragedies operate with the same contrast between chastity and promiscuity and cast the virtuous heroine merely as the prize to be won by the hero. Comedies embody the female viewpoint more often, but Centlivre's *A Bold Stroke for a Wife*, for instance, focuses entirely on the ingenious role playing of the hero to hoodwink an heiress's guardians and, in its perspective, is indistinguishable from plays written by men. Pix, though not unsympathetic towards married women's lot, in several comedies also retains this masculine stance, juxtaposing romantic dreamers and viragos (*The Innocent Mistress*), hypocrites and virtuous paragons (*The Different Widows*) or faithful wives (if treated liberally) and oppressed cuckold-makers (*The Spanish Wives*). Fanny Burney, too, usually portrays male characters as epitomes of common sense, while female figures are often painted as being flippant, conceited or unbelievably good. Indeed, most sentimental comedies cannot be fitted into the pattern, since, like affective tragedies, they capitalise on female passivity and victimisation as the easiest way of eliciting sympathy for women characters and, in order to turn them into deserving objects of pity, tend to endow them with ethereal virtue, elevating them above the common norm of humanity. Thereby they transform women back into the *other*, albeit idealised in this case. Hence constraints of genre, quite clearly, take precedence over any female perspective. The preponderance of sentiment in all eighteenth-century drama may also be the reason why the female tradition, distinct enough in the earlier centuries, sounds so muted at the end of our period.

Notes

Part I

1. Jean Elizabeth Gagen, *The New Woman. Her Emergence in English Drama 1600–1730* (New York: Twayne, 1954), p. 16.

2. Hilda L. Smith, *Reason's Disciples. Seventeenth-Century English Feminists* (Urbana: University of Illinois Press, 1982), p. 59. A trust is an agreement under which property or legal rights are vested by the owner of the property or rights in persons who then hold or exercise them on behalf of the truster. Husbands could make their wives trustees of their property and rights during their absence.

3. Mary Astell, *Some Reflections Upon Marriage, Occasion'd by the Duke & Duchess of Mazarine's Case; Which is also Consider'd* (London, 1700), p. 29.

4. Vincent to Benson, *Calendar of State Papers, Domestic Series* (Public Record Office, SP14/12/14, 10 January 1605); and letter of Sir Dudley Carleton to Ralph Winwood, 6 January 1605 (Boughton House, Winwood Papers III, Northamptonshire Record Office). Both printed in S. P. Cerasano and Marion Wynne-Davies, eds, *Renaissance Drama by Women: Texts and Documents* (London: Routledge, 1996), pp. 168ff.

5. Nancy Cotton, *Women Playwrights in England c. 1363–1750* (Lewisberg: Bucknell University Press, 1980), p. 38.

1 Women Dramatists of the Sixteenth and Early Seventeenth Centuries

6. Germaine Greer, ed., *Kissing the Rod* (London: Virago, 1988), pp. 5, 7.

7. Cerasano and Wynne-Davies, eds, *Renaissance Drama*, p. 8. I am indebted to these editors and their introductory essays throughout this chapter.

8. Alice Luce, ed., *The Countess of Pembroke's 'Antonie'* (Weimar: Schluck and Waldberg, 1897), p. 39, claims that the higher literary circles objected to English romantic drama, a fact disputed by Cerasano and Wynne-Davies, eds, *Renaissance Drama*, p. 16.

9. Cotton, *Women Playwrights*, p. 36.

10. Cerasano and Wynne-Davies, eds, *Renaissance Drama*, p. 93.

11. Cerasano and Wynne-Davies, eds, *Renaissance Drama*, p. 92. They also point out the various loves and their significance (p. 94).

12. Elizabeth Brackley had married the Viscount Brackley at the age of 15, but was allowed to remain with her family for some time because she was so young.

Part II

13. Katherine Eisaman Maus, '"Playhouse Flesh and Blood": Sexual Ideology and the Restoration Actress', *English Literary History* 46 (1979), p. 603.

2 Women Dramatists of the Early Restoration Period

14. Greer, *Kissing the Rod*, p. 6.

15. Samuel Pepys, *The Diary of Samuel Pepys*, eds Robert Latham and William Matthews, Vol. 9 (London: G. Bell & Sons, 1976), p. 420.

16. Jacqueline Pearson, *The Prostituted Muse. Images of Women & Women Dramatists 1642–1737* (New York: Harvester-Wheatsheaf, 1988), p. 134.

17. Robert D. Hume and Judith Milhous, eds, *The Frolicks, or The Lawyer Cheated* (Elizabeth Polwhele) (Ithaca: Cornell University Press, 1977), pp. 44–6. The editors of *The Frolicks* describe *The Faithful Virgins* as a Jacobean horror tragedy about three faithful virgins and an unchaste fourth involved in a tangle of hopeless love and unrequited passion which finally ends in a blood bath – material reminiscent of Tourneur or Webster, which Polwhele was unable to infuse with life (pp. 39–44). The Reverend Jeremy Collier in 1698 published his controversial *Short View of the Immorality and Profaneness of the English Stage*, a pamphlet attacking the leading playwrights of the day. However, he is only the best-known among several moralists who castigated the supposed lewdness of the theatre. Another aspiring playwright was the unknown 'Ephlia', whose play *The Pair of Royal Coxcombs* was performed in a dancing school in 1678. Except for some songs and the Prologue and Epilogue, the text is lost.

3 Aphra Behn

18. Virginia Woolf, *A Room of One's Own and Three Guineas* (London: Chatto & Windus, 1984), p. 61.

19. Germaine Greer, *Slip-Shod Sybils. Recognition, Rejection and the Woman Poet* (London: Viking, 1995), p. 196.

20. Quoted by Gerard Langbaine, *An Account of the English Dramatick Poets. Or, Some Observations and Remarks On the Lives and Writings, of all those that have Publish'd either Comedies, Tragedies, Tragi-Comedies, Pastorals, Masques, Interludes, Farces, or Opera's in the English Tongue* (Oxford, 1691), p. 24. Dryden admired her style (see below) and in the Epilogue to Charles Saunders' *Tamerlane the Great* (1681) says 'a woman wit has often graced the stage'.

21. Anonymous, *Epistle to Julian*, c. 1687, quoted in Fidelis Morgan, *The Female Wits. Women Playwrights on the London Stage 166–1720* (London: Virago, 1981), p. 22.

22. Aaron R. Walden, ed., *The Widow Ranter; or The History of Bacon in Virginia. A Critical Edition based on the Huntington Library Copy of the 1690 Edition, With a Full Complement of Contemporary Documents and Records of Bacon's 1676 Virginia Rebellion* (Aphra Behn) (New York: Garland, 1993), p. xxiv.

23. Maureen Duffy, *The Passionate Shepherdess. Aphra Behn 1640–89* (London: Jonathan Cape, 1977), p. 27.

24. Janet Todd, *The Sign of Angellica. Women, Writing and Fiction 1660–1800* (London: Virago, 1989), p. 41; Duffy, *The Passionate Shepherdess*, p. 27 and 145; Heidi Hutner, ed., *Rereading Aphra Behn: History, Theory and Criticism* (Charlottesville: University Press of Virginia, 1993), p. 102; Greer, *Slip-Shod Sibyls*, p. 204; as opposed, for instance, to Jones De Ritter, 'The Gypsy, *The Rover*, and the Wanderer: Aphra Behn's Revision of Thomas Killigrew', *Restoration* 10 (1986), pp. 86f.; or Arthur Gewitz, *Restoration Adaptations of Early Seventeenth Century Comedies* (Washington: University Press of America, 1982), p. 96.

25. De Ritter, 'The Gypsy, *The Rover*, and the Wanderer', p. 87.

26. Pearson, *The Prostituted Muse*, p. 146.

27. Catherine Gallagher, 'Who Was That Masked Woman? The Prostitute and the Playwright in the Comedies of Aphra Behn', in *Rereading Aphra Behn. History, Theory and Criticism*, ed. Heidi Hutner (Charlottesville: University Press of Virginia, 1993), p. 66.

28. Nancy Copeland, '"Once a Whore and Ever?" Whore and Virgin in *The Rover* and Its Antecedents', *Restoration* 16 (1992), pp. 25f.

29. Gewitz, *Restoration Adaptations*, p. 105.

30. Jane Spencer, '"Deceit, Dissembling, all that's Woman": Comic Plot and Female Action in *The Feigned Courtesans*', in *Rereading Aphra Behn. History, Theory and Criticism*, ed. Heidi Hutner (Charlottesville: University Press of Virginia, 1993), pp. 98f.

31. Gallagher, 'Who Was That Masked Woman?, p. 66: 'the doing of the deed would be the undoing of her power'.

32. Jane Spencer, ed., *Aphra Behn: The Rover. The Feigned Courtesans. The Lucky Chance. The Emperor of the Moon* (Oxford: Clarendon, 1995), p. xvii.

33. Duffy, *The Passionate Shepherdess*, p. 161.

34. Quoted in Cotton, *Women Playwrights*, p. 76.

4 Women Dramatists at the Turn of the Century

35. Cf. David Roberts, *The Ladies. Female Patronage of Drama 1660–1700* (Oxford: Clarendon, 1989).

36. Gwendolyn B. Needham, 'Mary de la Riviere Manley, Tory Defender', *The Huntington Library Quarterly* 12 (1949), p. 256.

37. Cotton, *Women Playwrights*, p. 87.

38. Robert Markley speaks of Behn in these terms in '"Be Impudent, Be Saucy, Forward, Bold, Touzing, and Leud": The Politics of Masculine Sexuality and Feminine Desire in Behn's Tory Comedies', in *Cultural Readings of Restoration and Eighteenth-Century English Theater*, eds J. Douglas Canfield and Deborah C. Payne (Athens: University of Georgia Press, 1995), p. 116.

39. Cynthia S. Matlack, '"Spectatress of the Mischief Which She Made": Tragic Woman Perceived and Perceiver', *Studies in Eighteenth Century Culture*, 6 (1977), 317–30.

40. Apart from the reversal of gender roles, it is also undeniable that Levan wants to execute his wife for her supposed adultery, yet blithely commits incest with his aunt himself. This double think was attacked in *The Female Wits*, yet is, in fact, not uncommon in the drama of the time.

41. Cotton, *Women Playwrights*, p. 102

42. Constance Clark, *Three Augustan Women Playwrights* (New York: Peter Lang, 1986), p. 77.

43. Laura Brown, *English Dramatic Form, 1660–1760. An Essay in Generic History* (New Haven: Yale University Press, 1981).

44. Catherine Trotter, *The Works of Mrs. Catherine Cockburn [Trotter], Theological, Moral, Dramatic and Poetical, with an Account of the Life of the Author by Thomas Birch*, vol. 1 (London, 1751), pp. xxii–xxiii. Quoted in Constance Clark, *Three Augustan Women Playwrights* (New York: Peter Lang, 1986), p. 90.

45. *Spectator*, 28 April 1711, p. 51.

46. Juliet McLaren, 'Presumptuous Poetess, Pen-Feathered Muse: The Comedies of Mary Pix', in *Gender at Work. Four Women Writers of the Eighteenth Century*, ed. Ann Messenger (Detroit: Wayne State University Press, 1990), pp. 82ff.

47. McLaren, 'Presumptuous Poetess', p. 90.

48. This is a misprint in the modern edition: the original edition reads 'citizens', which is metrically more appropriate.

49. Douglas J. Canfield, 'Royalism's Last Dramatic Stand: English Political Tragedy, 1679–89', *Studies in Philology* 82 (1985), pp. 234–63.

50. Felicity Kendal, ed., *Love and Thunder. Plays by Women in the Age of Queen Anne* (London: Methuen, 1988), p. 114. On the other hand, Milhous and Hume, *Roscius Anglicanus*, suggest that she may have been an actress (p. 58).

51. Kendal, *Love and Thunder*, p. 117.

52. Matlack points out the patriarchal viewpoint assumed in she tragedies written by men in '"Spectatress of the Mischief Which She Made"'.

5 Susanna Centlivre

53. In modern terms, 475 performances in 90 years may well seem unspectacular. However, plays on eighteenth-century stages generally had

extremely short runs, and even six performances were considered a success. Only two to four per cent of the London population regularly went to the theatre and constant variety was required. When one considers, furthermore, that the comedy became genuinely popular only after Centlivre's death, around the middle of the century, it must then have been revived almost every year and had uncommonly long runs.

54. Richard C. Frushell, 'Marriage and Marrying in Susanna Centlivre's Plays', *Papers on Language and Literature* 22 (1986), pp. 36f.

Part III

55. Moira Ferguson, *First Feminists. British Women Writers 1578–1799* (Bloomington: Indiana University Press, 1985), p. 3.

56. Duncombe, *The Femiad* (1754), quoted by Pearson, *The Prostituted Muse*, p. 8.

57. Roy Porter, *English Society in the Eighteenth Century* (Harmondsworth: Penguin, 1990), p. 100.

6 Women Dramatists of the Early Eighteenth Century

58. Allardyce Nicholl, *A History of Early Eighteenth Century Drama 1700–1750* (Cambridge: Cambridge University Press, 1925). On the other hand, David Erskine Baker, *The Companion to the Play-house: or, an Historical account of all the dramatic writers – and their works – that have appeared in Great Britain and Ireland, from the commencement of our theatrical exhibition, down to the present year 1764* (London, 1764), identifies Weddell as 'a journeyman printer in the service of Mr. Richardson'.

59. Her first comedy, *The Carnival; or, Harlequin Blunderer*, had been performed at Lincoln's Inn Fields in 1735, but was not printed.

60. Alexander Pope, *The Dunciad*, ed. James Sutherland, 3rd edn (London: Methuen, 1963), p. 120.

61. The play traces the touching story of the African princess Yarico, who rescues the shipwrecked white Incle, but is treacherously sold into slavery by her lover, who will not 'demean' himself to marry a heathen, and dies in childbirth, whereas Incle is killed by an Englishman in retribution for another seduction at home. The play takes up the antislavery campaign Behn had first sounded with her story *Oroonoko*, painting in very black colours the treachery and ingratitude of the white philanderer and dwelling extensively on the pathos of poor Yarico's distress.

62. Valerie C. Rudolph, ed., *The Plays of Eliza Haywood* (New York: Garland, 1983), pp. xi ff., claims that most of Haywood's plays contain a political message, and that she shared Fielding's anti-Walpole sentiments.

63. Samuel Johnson, 'Prologue At the Opening of the Theatre in Drury Lane 1747', *The Poems of Samuel Johnson*, eds David Nichol Smith and Edward L. McAdam (Oxford: Clarendon, 1941), p. 54.

7 Women Dramatists of the Late Eighteenth Century

64. Ellen Donkin, *Getting into the Act. Women Playwrights in London 1776–1829* (London: Routledge, 1995), 186–8.

65. Letitia Pilkington, in 1748, had also started a Virginia tragedy, called *The Roman Father*.

66. A notable exception would be *The Group* by the American writer Mercy Otis Warren, a rather crude piece of political propaganda, which presents the loyalists as rapacious turncoats, cynics, fools and wife-beaters, who, as in a morality play, comment on their own despicability, and in fact admire the bravery of the patriotic Americans and admit the justice of their cause. Although the sentiments are absurdly overwrought and the political zeal heated, the play is a rarity in the eighteenth century in centring exclusively on a contemporary political problem and excluding all love interest, and doubly interesting in coming from a woman, who normally was not expected to interest herself in political matters.

67. Oliver Goldsmith, 'A Comparison Between Sentimental and Laughing Comedy', *Westminster Magazine*, January 1773.

68. Arthur Sherbo, *English Sentimental Drama* (East Lansing: Michigan State University Press, 1957).

69. A comic opera by Sophia Lee, *The Assignation* (Drury Lane, 1807), was not printed.

70. A second play, *Nobody* (Drury Lane, 1794), was not printed.

71. Another play by Harriet Lee, *The Three Strangers*, was staged at Covent Garden in 1825. The subject was also treated by Byron in his tragedy *Werner*.

72. Another comedy by Starke, *The British Orphan*, was performed at Mrs Crespigny's private theatre in Camberwell in 1790.

73. In fact, it exemplifies the danger of attaching too much importance to Pearson's statistical approach of counting the number of lines and scenes involving women – Pearson, *The Prostituted Muse*.

8 Hannah Cowley and Elizabeth Inchbald

74. Porter, *English Society in the Eighteenth Century*, p. 307.

75. LETICIA: ... Old man, forgive me, thou the aggressor art,
   Who rudely forced the hand without the heart.
   She cannot from the paths of honour rove,
   Whose guide's religion, and whose end is love.
   (*The Lucky Chance*, III/ii/106)

9 Contemporary and Modern Performances of the Plays

76. Peter Arnott, *The Theatre In Its Time* (Boston: Little Brown, 1981), p. 293.

10 Towards a Female Tradition in the Theatre

77. Sue Ellen Case, *Feminism and Theatre* (Basingstoke: Macmillan, 1988); Lizbeth Goodman, *Contemporary Feminist Theatres. To Each Her Own* (London: Routledge 1993); Helene Keyssar, *Feminist Theatre* (Basingstoke: Macmillan, 1984); and Michelene Wandor, *Carry On, Understudies. Theatre and Sexual Politics*, 2nd edn (London: Routledge, 1986).

78. Pearson, *The Prostituted Muse*.

Bibliography

Primary Sources

Anon. *The Argument of the Pastorall of Florimene. With the Depiction of the Scenes and Intermedij*. London, 1635.

Anon. *The Unnatural Mother, The Scene in the Kingdom of Siam*. London, 1698.

Anon. *The Faithful General*. London, 1706.

Anon. *A Dramatick Pastoral. Occasioned by the Collection at Glocester on the Coronation Day for Portioning Young Women of Virtuous Character*. Gloucester, 1762.

Anon. *The Magnet*, London 1771.

Anon. *The Little French Lawyer*. London, 1778.

Anon. *The Female Wits, or The Triumvirate of Poets at Rehearsal*. Ed. Fidelis Morgan. London: Virago, 1981, 390–433.

'Ariadne'. *She Ventures and He Wins*. In *Female Playwrights of the Restoration. Five Comedies*. Eds Paddy Lyons and Fidelis Morgan. London: Dent, 1991, 103–59.

Astell, Mary. *Some Reflections Upon Marriage, Occasion'd by the Duke & Duchess of Mazarine's Case; Which is also Consider'd*. London, 1700.

Aubert, Mrs. *Harlequin Hydaspes, or The Greshamite*. London, 1719.

Aubin, Penelope. *The Humours of the Masqueraders*. London, 1733.

Baillie, Joanna. *Plays on the Passions*. Vol. 1. London, 1798.

Barrell, Maria. *The Captive*. London 1790.

Behn, Aphra. *Feigned Courtesans*. In *Female Playwrights of the Restoration. Five Comedies*. Eds Paddy Lyons and Fidelis Morgan. London: Dent, 1991, 1–101.

Behn, Aphra. *Sir Patient Fancy*. In *The Meridian Anthology of Restoration and Eighteenth Century Plays by Women*. Ed. Katherine Rogers. New York: Meridian, 1994, 21–124.

Behn, Aphra. *The Lucky Chance, or An Alderman's Bargain*. In *The Female Wits*. Ed. Fidelis Morgan. London: Virago, 1981, 73–143.

Behn, Aphra. *The Rover*. Ed. Bill Naismith. London: Methuen, 1993.

Behn, Aphra. *The Rover. The Feigned Courtesans. The Lucky Chance. The Emperor of the Moon*. Ed. Jane Spencer. Oxford: Clarendon, 1995.

Behn, Aphra. *The Widow Ranter; or The History of Bacon in Virginia. A Critical Edition based on the Huntington Library Copy of the 1690 Edition, With a Full Complement of Contemporary Documents and Records of Bacon's 1676 Virginia Rebellion*. Ed. Aaron R. Walden. New York: Garland, 1993.

Behn, Aphra. *The Works of Aphra Behn*. Ed. Montague Summers. 4 vols. London: Heinemann, 1915.

Behn, Aphra. *The Works of Aphra Behn*. Ed. Janet Todd. Vols 5–7. London: Pickering, 1996.

Boothby, Frances. *Marcelia, or The Treacherous Friend*. London, 1670.

Bowes, Mary. *The Siege of Jerusalem*. London, 1774.

Boyd, Elizabeth. *Don Sancho, or The Students Whim. A Ballad Opera, With Minerva's Triumph. A Masque*. London, 1739.

Brand, Hannah. *Plays and Poems*. Norwich, 1798.

Brooke, Frances. *Marian*. London, 1800.

Brooke, Frances. *Rosina*. 2nd edn. London, 1783.

Brooke, Frances. *The Siege of Sinope*. London, 1781.

Brooke, Frances. *Virginia, A Tragedy with Odes, Pastorals and Translations*. Dublin, 1754.

Burgess, Mrs. *The Oaks, or The Beauties of Canterbury*. Canterbury, 1780.

Burney, Frances. *The Complete Plays of Frances Burney*. Ed. Peter Sabor. 2 vols. London: Pickering, 1995.

Burney, Frances. *The Witlings*. In *The Meridian Anthology of Restoration and Eighteenth Century Plays by Women*. Ed. Katherine Rogers. New York: Meridian, 1994, 293–405.

Cary, Elizabeth, Viscountess Falkland. *The Tragedy of Mariam, the Fair*

Queen of Jewry. In *Renaissance Drama by Women: Texts and Documents*. Eds S. P. Cerasano and Marion Wynne-Davies. London: Routledge, 1996, 49–75.

Cavendish, Jane and Elizabeth Brackley. *The Concealed Fancies*. In *Renaissance Drama by Women: Texts and Documents*. Eds S. P. Cerasano and Marion Wynne-Davies. London: Routledge, 1996, 132–60.

Cavendish, Margaret. *Playes*. London, 1662.

Cavendish, Margaret. *Plays Never Before Printed*. London, 1668.

Celesia, Dorothea. *Almida*. London, 1771.

Centlivre, Susanna. *A Bold Stroke for a Wife*. In *The Meridian Anthology of Restoration and Eighteenth Century Plays by Women*. Ed. Katherine Rogers. New York: Meridian, 1994, 187–256.

Centlivre, Susanna. *The Adventures of Venice*. In *Love and Thunder. Plays by Women in the Age of Queen Anne*. Ed. Felicity Kendal. London: Methuen, 1988, 18–28.

Centlivre, Susanna. *The Basset Table*. In *Female Playwrights of the Restoration. Five Comedies*. Eds Paddy Lyons and Fidelis Morgan. London: Dent, 1991, 235–91.

Centlivre, Susanna. *The Busybody*. In *Female Playwrights of the Restoration. Five Comedies*. Eds Paddy Lyons and Fidelis Morgan. London: Dent, 1991, 293–363.

Centlivre, Susanna. *The Plays of Susanna Centlivre*. Ed. Richard C. Frushell. 3 vols. New York: Garland, 1982.

Centlivre, Susanna. *The Wonder! A Woman Keeps a Secret*. In *The Female Wits*. Ed. Fidelis Morgan. London: Virago, 1981, 329–87.

Charke, Charlotte. *The Art of Management, or Tragedy Expell'd*. London, 1735.

Cibber, Susanna. *The Oracle*. London, 1741.

Clive, Catherine. *The Rehearsal, or Bays in Petticoats*. London, 1753.

Cooper, Elizabeth. *The Rival Widows, or The Fair Libertine*. London, 1735.

Cowley, Hannah. *The Belle's Stratagem*. In *The Meridian Anthology of Restoration and Eighteenth Century Plays by Women*. Ed. Katherine Rogers. New York: Meridian, 409–86.

Cowley, Hannah. *The Plays of Hannah Cowley*. Ed. Frederick Link. 3 vols. New York: Garland, 1979.

Craven, Elizabeth. *The Miniature Picture*. London, 1781.

Cullum, Mrs. *Charlotte, or One Thousand Seven Hundred and Seventy Three*. London, 1775.

Davys, Mary. *The Northern Heiress, or The Humours of York*. London, 1716.

Davys, Mary. *Works*. Vol. 1. London, 1725.

Deverell, Mary. *Mary, Queen of Scots*. London, 1792.

Downes, John. *Roscius Anglicanus, or An Historical Review of the Stage from 1660 to 1706*. London: J. W. Jarvis, 1886.

Edwards, Anna Maria. *Poems on Various Subjects*. Dublin, 1787.

Elizabeth I. *Hercules Oetaeus*. In *Renaissance Drama by Women: Texts and Documents*. Eds S. P. Cerasano and Marion Wynne-Davies. London: Routledge, 1996, 10–12.

Finch, Anne, Countess of Winchilsea. *The Poems of Anne Countess of Winchilsea*. Ed. Myra Reynolds. Chicago: Chicago University Press, 1903.

Goldsmith, Oliver. 'A Comparison Between Sentimental and Laughing Comedy'. *Westminster Magazine*, January 1773.

Griffith, Elizabeth. *A Wife in the Right*. London, 1772.

Griffith, Elizabeth. *Amana*. London, 1764.

Griffith, Elizabeth. *The Barber of Seville, or The Useless Precaution*. London, 1776.

Griffith, Elizabeth. *The Double Mistake*. London, 1766.

Griffith, Elizabeth. *The Platonic Wife*. London, 1765.

Griffith, Elizabeth. *The School for Rakes*. London, 1769.

Griffith, Elizabeth. *The Times*. London, 1780.

Haywood, Eliza. *The Plays of Eliza Haywood*. Ed. Valerie C. Rudolph. New York: Garland, 1983.

Holford, Margaret. *Neither's the Man*. London, 1799.

Hoper, Mrs. *Queen Tragedy Restor'd*. London, 1749.

Hughes, Anne. *Moral Drama's. Intended for Private Presentation*. London, 1790.

Huxley, Aldous. *F. Sheridan's 'Discovery' Adapted for the Modern Stage*. London: Chatto & Windus, 1924.

Inchbald, Elizabeth. *The Plays of Elizabeth Inchbald*. Ed. Paula R. Backscheider. 2 vols. New York: Garland, 1980.

Inchbald, Elizabeth. *Such Things Are*. In *The Meridian Anthology of Restoration and Eighteenth Century Plays by Women*. Ed. Katherine Rogers. New York: Meridian, 1994, 491–556.

Johnson, Samuel. *The Poems of Samuel Johnson*. Eds David Nichol Smith and Edward L. McAdam. Oxford: Clarendon, 1941.

Langbaine, Gerard. *An Account of the English Dramatick Poets. Or, Some Observations and Remarks On the Lives and Writings, of all those that have Publish'd either Comedies, Tragedies, Tragi-Comedies, Pastorals, Masques, Interludes, Farces, or Opera's in the English Tongue.* Oxford, 1691.

Leapor, Mary. *Poems Upon Several Occasions.* Vol. 2. London, 1751.

Lee, Harriet. *The Mysterious Marriage, or The Heirship of Roselva.* London, 1798.

Lee, Harriet. *The New Peerage, or Our Eyes May Deceive Us.* London, 1787.

Lee, Sophia. *Almeyda, Queen of Grenada.* Dublin, 1796.

Lee, Sophia. *The Chapter of Accidents. The Modern Theatre.* Ed. Elizabeth Inchbald. Vol. 8. London, 1811.

Lennox, Charlotte. *Old City Manners.* London, 1775.

Lennox, Charlotte. *Philander. A Dramatic Pastoral.* London, 1758.

Lennox, Charlotte. *The Sister.* London, 1769.

Lumley, Jane. *Iphigenia at Aulis.* Translated by Lady Lumney. Ed. Harold Child. London: Chiswick, 1909.

Manley, Delarivier. *Almyna, or The Arabian Vow.* London, 1707.

Manley, Delarivier. *Lucius, the First Christian King of Britain.* London, 1717.

Manley, Delarivier. *The Lost Lover, or The Jealous Husband.* London, 1696.

Manley, Delarivier. *The Royal Mischief.* London, 1696.

Manley, Delarivier. *The Royal Mischief. In The Female Wits.* Ed. Fidelis Morgan. London: Virago, 1981, 209–61.

Montagu, Mary Wortley. *Essays and Poems and Simplicity, A Comedy.* Eds Robert Halsband and Isobel Grundy. Oxford: Clarendon, 1977.

More, Hannah. *Percy. The British Theatre, or A Collection of Plays Acted at the Theatre Royal.* Ed. Elizabeth Inchbald. Vol. 7. London, 1808.

More, Hannah. *The Fatal Falsehood.* London, 1779.

More, Hannah. *The Inflexible Captive.* Bristol, 1774.

More, Hannah. *The Search After Happiness; and other Poems: Sacred Dramas; and Essays on Various Subjects.* London, 1845.

Parsons, Eliza. *The Intrigues of a Morning.* London, 1792.

Penny, Anne. *Poems With a Dramatic Entertainment.* London, 1771.

Pepys, Samuel. *The Diary of Samuel Pepys.* Eds Robert Latham and William Matthews. Vol. 9. London: G. Bell & Sons, 1976.

Philips, Katherine. *Poems, to Which Is Added Monsieur Corneilles Pompey & Horace.* London, 1678.

Pix, Mary. *The Beau Defeated.* In *Female Playwrights of the Restoration. Five Comedies.* Eds Paddy Lyons and Fidelis Morgan. London: Dent, 1991, 161–233.

Pix, Mary, *The Innocent Mistress.* In *The Female Wits.* Ed. Fidelis Morgan. London: Virago, 1981, 263–327.

Pix, Mary. *The Plays of Mary Pix and Catharine Trotter.* Ed. Edna Steeves. Vol. 1. New York: Garland, 1982.

Pix, Mary. *The Spanish Wives.* In *Love and Thunder. Plays by Women in the Age of Queen Anne.* Ed. Felicity Kendal. London: Methuen, 1988, 35–62.

Pix, Mary. *The Spanish Wives.* In *The Meridian Anthology of Restoration and Eighteenth Century Plays by Women.* Ed. Katherine Rogers. New York: Meridian, 1994, 131–84.

Polwhele, Elizabeth. *The Frolicks, or The Lawyer Cheated.* Ed. Robert D. Hume and Judith Milhous. Ithaca: Cornell University Press, 1977.

Pope, Alexander, *The Dunciad.* Ed. James Sutherland. 3rd edn. London: Methuen, 1963.

Robe, Jane. *The Fatal Legacy.* London, 1723.

Roberts, R. *Malcolm.* London, 1779.

Robinson, Mary. *The Lucky Escape.* London, n.d.

Robinson, Mary. *The Sicilian Lover.* London, 1796.

Ross, Anna. *The Cottagers.* London, 1788.

Rowe, Nicholas. *The Works of Nicholas Rowe.* Vol. 2. London, 1766.

Ryves, Elizabeth. *Poems on Several Occasions.* London, 1777.

Sheridan, Frances. 'A Journey to Bath'. *Sheridan's Plays now printed as he wrote them, and his Mother's unpublished comedy "A Journey to Bath".* Ed. W. Fraser Rae. London: David Null, 1902.

Sheridan, Frances. *The Discovery.* London, 1763.

Sheridan, Frances. *The Dupe.* London, 1764.

Sidney, Mary. *The Tragedy of Antonie.* In *Renaissance Drama by Women: Texts and Documents.* Eds S. P. Cerasano and Marion Wynne-Davies. London: Routledge, 1996, 19–42.

Sidney, Mary. *The Triumph of Death and Other Unpublished and Uncollected Poems by Mary Sidney.* Ed. Gary F. Waller. Salzburg: Salzburg University Press, 1977.

Smith, Charlotte. *What Is She?* Dublin, 1799.

Starke, Mariana. *The Sword of Peace, or A Voyage of Love.* London, 1789.

Starke, Mariana. *The Tournament. A Tragedy Imitated from the Celebrated German Drama Agnes Bernauer.* London, 1800.

Starke, Mariana. *The Widow of Malabar*. London, 1791.

Thomas, Elizabeth. *A Dramatick Pastoral. Occasioned by the Collection at Glocester on the Coronation Day for Portioning Young Women of Virtuous Character*. Gloucester, 1762.

Tollet, Elizabeth. *Poems on Several Occasions*. London, 1755.

Trotter, Catherine. *Love at a Loss*. In *Love and Thunder. Plays by Women in the Age of Queen Anne*. Ed. Felicity Kendal. London: Methuen, 1988, 69–112.

Trotter, Catherine. *Plays. The Plays of Mary Pix and Catharine Trotter*. Ed. Edna Steeves. Vol. 2. New York: Garland, 1982.

Trotter, Catherine. *The Fatal Friendship*. In *The Female Wits*. Ed. Fidelis Morgan. London: Virago, 1981, 145–207.

Warren, Mercy Otis. *The Group*. In *The Meridian Anthology of Restoration and Eighteenth Century Plays by Women*. Ed. Katherine Rogers. New York: Meridian, 1994, 263–87.

Weddell, Mrs. *Incle and Yarico*. London, 1742.

Weddell, Mrs. *The City Farce*. London, 1737.

West, Jane. *Poems and Plays*. 4 vols. London, 1799–1805.

Whincop, Thomas. *Scanderberg*. London, 1747.

Wiseman, Jane. *Antiochus the Great*. In *Love and Thunder. Plays by Women in the Age of Queen Anne*. Ed. Felicity Kendal. London: Methuen, 1988, 118–53.

Woolf Virginia. *A Room of One's Own and Three Guineas*. London: Chatto & Windus, 1984.

Wroth, Mary. *Love's Victory*. In *Renaissance Drama by Women: Texts and Documents*. Eds. S. P. Cerasano and Marion Wynne-Davies. London: Routledge, 1996, 97–126.

Secondary Works

Arnott, Peter. *The Theatre In Its Time*. Boston: Little Brown, 1981.

Backscheider, Paula R. Ed. *The Plays of Elizabeth Inchbald*. 2 vols. New York: Garland, 1980.

Baker, David Erskine. *The Companion to the Play-house: or, an Historical account of all the dramatic writers – and their works – that have appeared in Great Britain and Ireland, from the commencement of our theatrical exhibition, down to the present year 1764*. London, 1764.

Bevis, Richard. *English Drama: Restoration and Eighteenth Century, 1660–1789*. London: Longman, 1988.

Bowyer, John Wilson. *The Celebrated Mrs Centlivre*. New York: Greenwood, 1968 (reprint).

Brown, Laura. *English Dramatic Form, 1660–1760. An Essay in Generic History*. New Haven: Yale University Press, 1981.

Canfield, J. Douglas. 'Royalism's Last Dramatic Stand: English Political Tragedy, 1679–89'. *Studies in Philology* 82 (1985), 234–63.

Carver, Larry. 'Aphra Behn: The Poet's Heart in a Woman's Body'. *Papers on Language and Literature* 14 (1978), 414–24.

Case, Sue Ellen. *Feminism and Theatre*. Basingstoke: Macmillan, 1988.

Cerasano, S. P. and Marion Wynne-Davies. Eds. *Renaissance Drama by Women: Texts and Documents*. London: Routledge, 1996.

Clark, Constance. *Three Augustan Women Playwrights*. New York: Peter Lang, 1986.

Copeland, Nancy. '"Once a Whore and Ever?" Whore and Virgin in *The Rover* and Its Antecedents'. *Restoration* 16 (1992), 20–7.

Cotton, Nancy. *Women Playwrights in England c. 1363–1750*. Lewisberg: Bucknell University Press, 1980.

De Ritter, Jones. 'The Gypsy, *The Rover*, and the Wanderer: Aphra Behn's Revision of Thomas Killigrew'. *Restoration* 10 (1986), 82–92.

Diamond, Elin. '*Gestus* and Signature in Aphra Behn's *The Rover*'. *English Literary History* 56 (1989), 519–41.

Donkin, Ellen. *Getting into the Act. Women Playwrights in London 1776–1829*. London: Routledge, 1995.

Downes, John. *Roscius Anglicanus*. Eds Judith Milhous and Robert D. Hume. London: Society for Theatre Research, 1987.

Duffy, Maureen, *The Passionate Shepherdess. Aphra Behn 1640–89*. London: Jonathan Cape, 1977.

Ferguson, Moira. *First Feminists. British Women Writers 1578–1799*. Bloomington: Indiana University Press, 1985.

Fitzgerald, Percy. *The Life of Mrs Catherine Clive. With an Account of her Adventures On and Off the Stage. A Round of her Characters together with her Correspondence*. London: Reader, 1888.

Foss, Michael. *Man of Wit to Man of Business. The Arts and Changing Patronage 1660–1750*. Bristol: Bristol Classical Press, 1988.

Frushell, Richard C. 'Marriage and Marrying in Susanna Centlivre's Plays'. *Papers on Language and Literature* 22 (1986), 16–38.

Frushell, Richard C. Ed. *The Plays of Susanna Centlivre*. 2 vols. New York: Garland, 1982.

Gagen, Jean Elizabeth. *The New Woman. Her Emergence in English Drama 1600–1730*. New York: Twayne, 1954.

Gallagher, Catherine. 'Who Was That Masked Woman? The

Prostitute and the Playwright in the Comedies of Aphra Behn'. In *Rereading Aphra Behn. History, Theory and Criticism.* Ed. Heidi Hutner. Charlottesville: University Press of Virginia, 1993, 65–85.

Gewitz, Arthur. *Restoration Adaptations of Early Seventeenth Century Comedies.* Washington: University Press of America, 1982.

Goodman, Lizbeth. *Contemporary Feminist Theatres. To Each Her Own.* London: Routledge, 1993.

Goreau, Angeline. *Reconstructing Aphra: A Social Biography of Aphra Behn.* New York: Dial Press, 1980.

Gosse, Edmund. 'Catherine Trotter, the Precursor of the Blue-Stockings'. *Transactions of the Royal Society of Literature* (2nd series) 34 (1916), 87–118.

Greer, Germaine. Ed. *Kissing the Rod.* London: Virago, 1988.

Greer, Germaine. *Slip-Shod Sibyls. Recognition, Rejection and the Woman Poet.* London: Viking, 1995.

Holland, Peter. *The Ornament of Action. Text and Performance in Restoration Comedy.* Cambridge: Cambridge University Press, 1979.

Howe, Elizabeth. *The First English Actresses. Women and Drama 1660–1700.* Cambridge: Cambridge University Press, 1992.

Hume, Robert D. and Judith Milhous. Eds. *Elizabeth Polwhele. The Frolicks, or The Lawyer Cheated.* Ithaca: Cornell University Press, 1977.

Hume, Robert D. *The Development of English Drama in the Late Seventeenth Century.* Oxford: Oxford University Press, 1976.

Hume, Robert D. *The Rakish Stage: Studies in English Drama 1660–1800.* Carbondale: Southern Illinois University Press, 1983.

Hume, Robert D. Ed. *The London Theatre World, 1660–1800.* Carbondale: Southern Illinois University Press, 1980.

Hutner, Heidi. Ed. *Rereading Aphra Behn: History, Theory and Criticism.* Charlottesville: University Press of Virginia, 1993.

Hutner, Heidi. 'Rereading Aphra Behn. An Introduction'. In *Rereading Aphra Behn. History, Theory and Criticism.* Ed. Heidi Hutner. Charlottesville: University Press of Virginia, 1993, 1–13.

Hutner, Heidi. 'Revisioning the Female Body. Aphra Behn's *The Rover*, Parts I and II'. In *Rereading Aphra Behn. History, Theory and Criticism.* Ed. Heidi Hutner. Charlottesville: University Press of Virginia, 1993, 102–20.

Kendal, Felicity. Ed. *Love and Thunder. Plays by Women in the Age of Queen Anne.* London: Methuen, 1988.

Keyssar, Helene. *Feminist Theatre*. Basingstoke: Macmillan, 1984.

Langdell, Cheri Davis. 'Aphra Behn and Sexual Politics: A Dramatist's Discourse with Her Audience'. In *Drama, Sex and Politics*. Ed. James Redmond. Cambridge: Cambridge University Press, 1985, 109–28.

Link, Frederick M. *Aphra Behn*. New York: Twaine, 1968.

Link, Frederick. *The Plays of Hannah Cowley*. 3 vols. New York. Garland, 1979.

Loftis, John, Richard Southern, Marion Jones and A. H. Scouten. *The Revels History of Drama in English. Vol. 6: 1660–1750*. London: Methuen, 1976

Luce, Alice. Ed. *The Countess of Pembroke's 'Antonie'*. Weimar: Schluck and Waldberg, 1897.

Lyons, Paddy and Fidelis Morgan. Eds. *Female Playwrights of the Restoration. Five Comedies*. London: Dent, 1991.

Markley, Robert. '"Be Impudent, Be Saucy, Forward, Bold, Touzing, and Leud": The Politics of Masculine Sexuality and Feminine Desire in Behn's Tory Comedies'. In *Cultural Readings of Restoration and Eighteenth-Century English Theater*. Eds J. Douglas Canfield and Deborah C. Payne. Athens: University of Georgia Press, 1995, 114–40.

Matlack, Cynthia S. '"Spectatress of the Mischief Which She Made": Tragic Woman Perceived and Perceiver'. *Studies in Eighteenth Century Culture* 6 (1977), 317–30.

Maus, Katherine Eisaman. '"Playhouse Flesh and Blood": Sexual Ideology and the Restoration Actress'. *English Literary History* 46 (1979), 595–617.

McLaren, Juliet. 'Presumptuous Poetess, Pen-Feathered Muse: The Comedies of Mary Pix'. In *Gender at Work. Four Women Writers of the Eighteenth Century*. Ed. Ann Messenger. Detroit: Wayne State University Press, 1990, 77–114.

Needham, Gwendolyn B. 'Mary de la Reviere Manley, Tory Defender'. *Huntington Library Quarterly* 12 (1949), 253–88.

Nicholl, Allardyce. *A History of Eighteenth Century Drama, 1700–1750*. Cambridge: Cambridge University Press, 1925.

Pearson, Jacqueline. *The Prostituted Muse. Images of Women & Women Dramatists 1642–1737*. New York: Harvester-Wheatsheaf, 1988.

Porter, Roy. *English Society in the Eighteenth Century*. Harmondsworth: Penguin, 1990.

Roberts, David. *The Ladies. Female Patronage of Restoration Drama 1660–1700*. Oxford: Clarendon, 1989.

Rogers, Katherine. Ed. *The Meridian Anthology of Restoration and Eighteenth Century Plays by Women*. New York: Meridian, 1994.

Schofield, Mary Anne and Cecilia Macheski. Eds. *Curtain Calls. British and American Women and the Theatre, 1660–1820*. Athens: Ohio University Press, 1991.

Sherbo, Arthur. *English Sentimental Drama*. East Lansing: Michigan State University Press, 1957.

Smith, Hilda L. *Reason's Disciples. Seventeenth-Century English Feminists*. Urbana: University of Illinois Press, 1982.

Spencer, Jane. '"Deceit, Dissembling, all that's Woman": Comic Plot and Female Action in *The Feigned Courtesans'*. In *Rereading Aphra Behn. History, Theory and Criticism*. Ed. Heidi Hutner. Charlottesville: University Press of Virginia, 1993, 86–101.

Spencer, Jane. Ed. *Aphra Behn: The Rover. The Feigned Courtesans. The Lucky Chance. The Emperor of the Moon*. Oxford: Clarendon, 1995.

Steeves, Edna. Ed. *The Plays of Mary Pix and Catharine Trotter*. 2 vols. New York: Garland, 1982.

Todd, Janet. *The Sign of Angellica. Women, Writing and Fiction 1660–1800*. London: Virago, 1989.

Valency, Maurice J. *The Tragedies of Herod & Mariam*. New York: Columbia University Press, 1940.

Wandor, Michelene. *Carry On, Understudies. Theatre and Sexual Politics*. 2nd edn. London: Routledge, 1986.

Ward, Adolphus W. *A History of English Dramatic Literature to the Death of Queen Anne*. London: Macmillan, 1875.

Wilson, Katherina M. and Frank J. Warnke. Eds. *Women Writers of the Seventeenth Century*. Athens: University of Georgia Press, 1989.

Index